W A T E R
Markets

W A T E R
Markets
PRIMING THE INVISIBLE PUMP

TERRY L. ANDERSON AND PAMELA SNYDER

INSTITUTE
Washington, D.C.

Library of Congress Cataloging-in-Publication Data

Anderson, Terry Lee, 1946–
    Water markets : priming the invisible pump / Terry L. Anderson &
Pamela Snyder.
        p.   cm.
    Includes bibliographical references and index.
    ISBN 1-882577-43-4. — ISBN 1-882577-44-2 (pbk.)
    1. Water-supply—Economic aspects—United States.   I. Snyder,
Pamela.   II. Title.
HD1694.A5A75   1997
333.91'16'0973—dc21   97-14369
                                                                                                         CIP

Printed in the United States of America.

CATO INSTITUTE
1000 Massachusetts Ave., N.W.
Washington, D.C. 20001

Contents

Acknowledgments

In the early 1980s, I began conducting research on the prospects for using markets to solve water problems. Since that time, giant strides forward have been made in water marketing. This book builds on the first edition of *Water Crisis: Ending the Policy Drought* and updates the progress that has been made. It also suggests where further advances are possible.

The project began as a minor revision of *Water Crisis: Ending the Policy Drought* but turned into a new book for two reasons. First, the changes that have occurred in water policy have been significant. What were calls for dramatic reforms to allow water marketing in 1983 have become commonplace approaches in 1996. Second, the contribution of my coauthor, Pam Snyder, clearly turned the revision into a new book. Comparing this book to the earlier one reveals her fresh insights and legal expertise.

We thank the Cato Institute for supporting this project. Jerry Taylor encouraged us to do it and shepherded it through the publication process, and Peter Van Doren provided useful editorial comments.

Fortunately a number of organizations have provided general support that made our research possible. Special thanks to the Sarah Scaife Foundation, Lilly Endowment, Inc., Procter & Gamble, the Liberty Fund, and the Roe Foundation.

Finally, we wish to acknowledge support and contributions from our colleagues at PERC (the Political Economy Research Center). Holly Lippke Fretwell provided research assistance on global water issues. We borrowed heavily from Don Leal's insights into the application of markets to instream flows. As usual, support from Monica Lane Guenther, Michelle Johnson, Pam Malyurek, and Dianna Rienhart was invaluable. The reader can thank all these people for making the book better and blame us for not taking their advice more often.

Terry L. Anderson

1. Why Water Crises?

Droughts epitomize water scarcity. But while droughts capture headlines and our attention, the far greater threat posed by escalating water consumption goes largely unnoticed—our water use is depleting and exceeding the limits of natural systems in many parts of the world. "Signs of water stress abound. Water tables are falling, lakes are shrinking, and wetlands are disappearing" (Postel 1992, 18–19). As population continues to increase, and water shortages become more common, we are forced to wonder: Are we running out of water?

The Evidence

With most natural resources, concern over future availability is based on an inventory view. This view compares existing or predicted quantities of resource availability with predicted consumption patterns. Whenever rising rates of consumption collide with declining availability, a crisis is predicted. Many general studies of resource use have concluded that both renewable and nonrenewable resources are being used at an alarming rate. *The Limits to Growth* study, originally published in the early 1970s, for example, was bold enough to pinpoint a year early in the next century when our growing consumption of resources will collide with our dwindling supplies (Meadows et al. 1972). *The Global 2000 Report*, a similar study commissioned by the Carter administration, concluded:

> If present trends continue, the world in 2000 will be more crowded, more polluted, less stable ecologically, and more vulnerable to disruption than the world we live in now. Serious stresses involving population, resources, and environment are clearly visible ahead. (Council on Environmental Quality [CEQ] 1980, 1)

These same conclusions also have been reached regarding the availability of water. The U.S. Water Resources Council (USWRC)

1

has estimated the availability of the nation's water resources and concluded that

> on the average, about 40,000 bgd (billion gallons per day) of water passes over the coterminous United States in the form of water vapor. Of this, approximately 10 per cent (about 4,200 bgd) is precipitated as rainfall, snow, sleet, or hail. The remainder continues in atmospheric suspension. Of the 4,200 bgd . . . about 2,750 bgd is evaporated immediately from the wet surfaces or transpired by vegetation. The remaining 1,450 bgd accumulates in ground or surface storage; flows to the oceans, the Gulf of Mexico or across the Nation's boundaries; is consumptively used; or is evaporated from reservoirs. (USWRC 1978, 12)[1]

Since the beginning of the 20th century, the U.S. population increased 200 percent while per capita water use shot up 500 to 800 percent (Kenski 1990, 5). Between 1960 and 1970, water use in the United States increased 37 percent (270 bgd to 370 bgd) and increased another 22 percent between 1970 and 1980 (370 bgd to 420 bgd) (Conservation Foundation 1987, 225).

Water consumption, like withdrawals, also has increased steadily for most water uses. On average, about one-fourth of the water withdrawn in the United States is consumed. The other three-fourths returns to surface-water or ground-water supplies. However, the growth in consumption appears to be slowing down. "Between 1970 and 1980, consumption increased by only 14 percent, compared with a 44 percent increase [during] the previous decade" (Conservation Foundation 1987, 226–227). See Figure 1.1.

The slowdown in the growth rate of consumption is generally attributed to a decline in industrial withdrawals resulting from improvements in production and technology and tougher laws on water pollution that encourage water conservation in production processes (U.S. Geological Survey [USGS] 1990, 81–83).

While the difference between withdrawal and consumption might indicate a plentiful water supply rather than a shortage, some of the water must be left to flow into Canada and Mexico. Furthermore, locational demands for water do not always coincide with supplies. For example, the western United States receives less rainfall than the East. Southern California receives less than 10 inches of rain each year, compared with 33 inches in Chicago and 44 in New York.

Figure 1.1
TRENDS IN U.S. WATER WITHDRAWALS AND CONSUMPTION
1960–1990

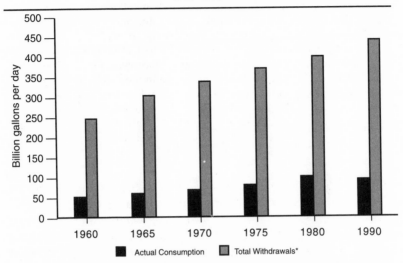

*Includes withdrawals for public and rural supplies, irrigation, and steam electric and other industries.

SOURCE: The Conservation Foundation (1987). Reprinted with permission of World Wildlife Fund. Data from U.S. Geological Survey.

Nevertheless, 80 percent of the nation's water is consumed in the West. With California's population mushrooming from 20 to 30 million in the last 20 years, the demand for water west of the 95th meridian is not likely to decrease (World Resources Institute 1993, 35; Conservation Foundation 1987, 229).

Between 1987 and 1993, California's growing population was accompanied by less than normal precipitation, resulting in a severe water shortage. The state's reservoirs fell to as low as one-third of capacity. In 1991, the State Water Project cut off supplies to farmers and the federal Bureau of Reclamation cut its supplies to farmers by 75 percent from its Central Valley Project, forcing the nation's largest supplier of produce to allow thousands of acres to lie fallow and pump what they could from already depleted ground-water supplies. Towns and cities rationed water under threat of similar cuts. The environmental toll was devastating. Although the return

3

of the rains in 1993 officially ended the drought, Californians still face future water shortages as population continues to increase in the arid southern part of the state, while 85 percent of the state's water is used in irrigation.

Globally, water use has increased even more dramatically, having tripled since 1950. Demand for water has outstripped population growth. Per capita water supplies are one-third lower than in 1970, due to the addition of 1.8 billion people to the planet since then. Almost a quarter of the world's nations lack sufficient fresh water to meet the needs of their burgeoning populations. Most of the water-scarce countries are located in the Middle East and Africa, and most are poor. The water shortages in these areas threaten the health of humans and riparian ecosystems and hamper economic development (*USA Today* 1993; *Economist* 1992a).

> Nearly one out of every three people in the developing world—some 1.2 billion people in all—do not have access to a safe and reliable [water] supply for their daily needs. Often they resort to shallow wells or stagnant pools that are easily contaminated with human and animal waste. As a result, waterborne diseases account for an estimated 80 percent of all illnesses in developing countries. And women and children walk several kilometers each day just to collect enough water for drinking, cooking, and cleaning, a drudgery that saps time and energy from more productive activities. (Postel 1992, 21; World Bank 1992, 48)

By the turn of the next century, water shortages are likely to become even more widespread. Although the U.S. Water Resources Council predicts that withdrawals from streams will decrease by 9 percent between 1975 and 2000, during the same period, consumption of fresh water is expected to increase by almost 27 percent.

Portions of this deficit between decreased surface-water withdrawals and increased overall consumption will be made up from ground-water sources and more efficient use resulting from conservation efforts and improved technology. Nevertheless, the Water Resources Council estimates that 17 subregions of the United States either have or will have by the year 2000 a serious problem of inadequate surface-water supply (USWRC 1978, 2; USGS 1991, 99).

The problem is even worse if ground water is considered separately. Ground-water use increased from 35 bgd in 1950 to 87 bgd in 1980. According to an estimate by the American Institute of Professional Geologists, Americans pumped 100 bgd of ground water in 1985, a 12 percent increase over 1980 figures (Kenski 1990, 5). Ground-water mining, or aquifer withdrawals in excess of natural recharge, is causing subsidence, salt water intrusion, higher pumping costs, and general alarm about the future of ground-water supplies. Ground-water levels are dropping at disturbing rates. In Texas, the water tables beneath Dallas-Fort Worth have dropped 492 feet since 1960. A similar situation exists in Arizona, where the water tables around Phoenix have dropped 400 feet in the last 50 years. In China, the water tables near two major manufacturing cities, Beijing and Tianjin, are decreasing by 3 to 12 feet per year (Fenichell 1986, 15; Conservation Foundation 1987, 231).

Ground-water depletion is not limited to urban areas, however. In southern India, water tables have dropped 80 to 96 feet in 10 years due to heavy pumping for irrigation. The water table beneath the San Luis Valley in Colorado has dropped 75 feet, and scientists estimate that by the year 2020, 25 percent of the original supply in the Ogallala Aquifer, underlying 170,000 square miles of the Great Plains, will be depleted (Fenichell 1986, 15; Steinhart 1990, 38; World Resources Institute 1992, 92).

Pollution of both surface and ground water also poses a serious threat to future water supplies. In 1975, the Water Resources Council was optimistic that "water-quality conditions will be improved substantially. With the emphasis on more intensive use and reuse of available supplies, improvement of quality should become an important facet of water management procedures" (USWRC 1978, 78). Unfortunately, the optimism of the Water Resources Council has not blossomed into reality. According to the World Resources Institute,

> The first global assessment of freshwater quality, recently carried out under the auspices of the [United Nations Environment Programme's] Global Environmental Monitoring System (GEMS), found that contamination of water resources continues to increase in much of the world. . . . Traditionally, effluents from human activities have been diluted by the volume of river flow and often eliminated by the self-cleansing action of streams. But as populations and economic activity increase, these effluents threaten the life of some river basins. (World Resources Institute 1990, 161)[2]

5

Poland is a prime example. There, the portion of river water suitable for drinking has dropped from 32 percent to less than 5 percent over the last 20 years. Three-quarters of Poland's river water is now too contaminated even for industrial use. Similar situations are increasing in developing countries, where unchecked pollution poses a mounting threat during industrialization (Postel 1992, 21 to 22).

In the United States, the Great Lakes are plagued by phosphates from household laundry detergent, toxic chemicals that have been discharged by industry, pesticides that have drifted on air currents and settled in the lakes, and fertilizer runoff. The Chesapeake Bay is the recipient of toxic industrial wastes, harmful substances from solid waste, and pesticides from farms and other nonpoint sources. Both public and private efforts have been undertaken to restore the quality of these water bodies, however, and some progress has been made (World Resources Institute 1992, 93–98).

The Global 2000 study concluded that "pollution, GNP, and resource projections all imply rapidly increasing demands for fresh water. Increases of at least 200 to 300 percent in world water withdrawals are expected over the 1975 to 2000 period." The estimated increased demand is based largely on population growth, which is expected to "cause demands for water to at least double relative to 1971 in nearly half of the countries of the world" (CEQ 1980, 26). In the western half of the United States as well as the area from Texas to Maryland, this would result in a decline of available water from the 1971 level of more than 10,000 cubic meters per person per year to between 5,000 and 10,000 per capita. The rest of the country would experience a decline from 5,000 to 10,000 cubic meters per capita down to 1,000 to 5,000 cubic meters. Increased food production, new energy production, conventional power generation, and other industrial needs were predicted to aggravate water shortages. The rising cost of energy was expected to affect adversely the economics of many water development projects and to reduce the amount of water available for a variety of uses. Irrigation, which usually requires large amounts of energy for pumping, would be particularly affected (CEQ 1980, 26–27).

As shown above, the Global 2000 estimates have proven reasonably accurate thus far. Both population and water demand have increased substantially since 1971. Water tables have dropped, resulting in increased energy consumption and food production costs. Urban areas are experiencing water shortages as their populations expand and are competing with irrigators for limited water supplies.

Unfortunately, increasing the water supply, at least in the United States, by building immense dams and aqueduct systems is no longer a realistic option. Few good reservoir sites remain; the federal government is moving away from dam building; and concern about the environmental impacts of such projects has increased (USGS 1990, 139). The bottom line is that unless we change our ways, future water crises are inevitable.

What Causes a Crisis?

It is true that "the energy crisis and the water shortage are inextricably linked" (*Newsweek* 1981, 27), but the connection is probably more subtle than most people understand. Rising energy prices have made supplying water more costly, but the general link between energy and water is more directly related to the extent to which prices are allowed to influence demand and supply. In economic terms, a crisis exists when the quantity demanded is greater than the quantity available and when there is little time to adjust either of them. This is exactly what the energy crisis was and what any water crisis is likely to be. The question is, why does quantity demanded not equal quantity supplied?

The 1970s taught us an important lesson: When government regulations keep fuel prices below market-clearing levels, shortages inevitably follow. Further, once shortages occur and as price controls block normal market mechanisms, government is forced into the business of allocating scarce supplies. Federal price controls for gasoline and the blundering attempts to allocate gasoline in 1974 and 1979 had social costs that far exceeded the limited relief provided to gasoline purchasers. Experience around the world has demonstrated over and over again that the only successful way to avoid fuel shortages is to rely on free-market pricing and allocation (Hall and Pindyck 1981, 68).

The same circumstances are causing problems with water. Water prices have been kept artificially low, and the inevitable shortages have followed. Governments have responded by attempting to restrain demand, ration water, and increase the available supply.

7

For example, in the face of the California drought in the late 1980s through early 1990s, municipalities implemented rationing, began constructing desalinization plants, paid thousands of dollars for cloud seeding, and in 1991, the state cut off supplies to farmers (Schaefer 1991; *Business Week* 1991). Nevertheless, except in isolated cases where shortages have been caused by drought and where a cooperative community spirit has developed, efforts to ration water have not been successful. Increased water supplies have only been made possible through the construction of massive water projects, which have dammed many of our free-flowing rivers. These projects have been extremely costly, and it is doubtful that Congress will continue to fund them. If not, water crises will continue to arise apart from a price mechanism operating on water supply and demand.

Could Markets Do Better?

In arguing that the price mechanism has not been allowed to work for allocating water, there is the implicit assumption that price rationing could help resolve water crises. At higher prices people tend to consume less of a commodity and search for alternative means of achieving their desired ends. Water is no exception. The data in Table 1.1 suggest that different technologies allow different patterns of water use depending on water availability.

The actual responsiveness of water consumption to price changes will vary among regions with the variations depending on such variables as income and precipitation. In their study of six subregions of the United States, Bruce Beattie and Henry Foster (1980) found that a 10 percent increase in the price of water would produce between a 3.75 and 12.63 percent decrease in urban residential water consumption. The Northern California and Pacific Northwest region, with its abundant rainfall, was the most responsive, and the arid Southwest region was the least responsive. While these estimates may suggest that higher water prices could reduce consumption, it must be noted that in 57 percent of the 23 cities studied real water prices declined between 1960 and 1976. Only three cities had real water rate increases of more than $1 per 1,000 cubic feet per year. Beattie and Foster (1980, 444–45) concluded that

> the water utility industry has done a good job for consumers. Unfortunately, because of this good job water users have adjusted their way of life so that needs for water are great. . . .

Table 1.1
WATER USE OF VARIOUS INDUSTRIES

Industry	Range of Flow (gal/ton product)
Cannery	
Green beans	12,000-17,000
Peaches and pears	3,600-4,800
Other fruits and vegetables	960-8,400
Chemical	
Ammonia	24,000-72,000
Carbon dioxide	14,400-21,600
Lactose	144,000-192,000
Sulfur	1,920-2,400
Food and beverage	
Beer	2,400-3,840
Bread	480-960
Meatpacking	3,600-4,800
Milk products	2,400-4,800[a]
Whiskey	14,400-19,200
Pulp and paper	
Pulp	60,000-190,000
Paper	29,000-38,000
Textile	
Bleaching	48,000-72,000[b]
Dyeing	7,200-14,400[b]

SOURCE: Rogers (1993). Reprinted with permission.
[a] Live weight.
[b] Cotton.

Thus, how much water consumers need depends not only on willingness and ability to pay, but most importantly on the real price charged. If it is a lot, only a modest amount of water is needed. If the charge is a little, a lot is needed. The choice is largely up to the water utility industry.

Similar data suggest that the agricultural sector demand for water is also price-responsive. Demand responsiveness varies by crops, of course, but some aggregate estimates for California show that a 10 percent increase in price would bring about a 6.5 percent decrease in water consumption. The same price increase would cause an overall average consumption decrease of 3.7 percent for the 17 Western states. Estimates for homogeneous production areas in California show that at a price of $17, a 10 percent increase in price would yield a 20 percent decrease in water use (Gardner 1983). These relatively large responses in quantity demanded to changes in price, known as elasticity of demand, indicate that farmers in homogeneous production areas

> would not be using all the water DWR (the California Department of Water Resources) was planning to send them—at the price DWR was planning to charge. . . . [T]he marginal cost of water to the farmer would have to be reduced between $4 and $6 per acre-foot (from a contractual price of $14.70 per acre-foot in one HPA [homogeneous production area] and $16.36 in the other) before DWR's projected 1 million acres would be brought into production. (Gardner 1983, 88)[3]

The implications are significant. If water prices are kept low, more demands will be placed on water resources. The additional water use will be subject to diminishing returns—the last units consumed will generate much less value than the first. What is seen as waste or inefficient water use in rural and urban areas is simply the users' rational response to low water prices. When water for lawns is left to run into storm gutters or when irrigation water erodes the field without reaching the roots of the plant, it is easy to say that users are being wasteful. But users can afford to be wasteful only when water is cheap. In agriculture, if water carried a higher price, it is likely that less water would be applied to any given crop, that different irrigation technology or water application practices would be used, and that different cropping patterns might appear.

Research conducted at the University of California suggests that reduced water application would decrease most crop yields but that at higher water prices such reduction would be economical. Flood irrigation techniques conserve labor but use large amounts of water. With high water prices, it makes sense to substitute labor and capital for water and to use drip irrigation or similar techniques. Trimble Hedges provided similar evidence in a simulation of a 640-acre farm in Yolo County, California (Hedges 1977). Hedges showed that the optimal cropping pattern at a zero water price would call for 150 acres each of tomatoes, sugar beets, and wheat; 47 acres of alfalfa; 65 acres of beans; and 38 acres of safflower. If the water price were increased to $13.50 per acre foot, alfalfa acreage would drop out and safflower acreage, a crop that uses less water, would expand. The point is that many choices are available to water consumers and they will respond rationally to water prices.

In motivating agricultural consumers to reduce consumption through improved irrigation techniques and modified cropping patterns, higher water prices would free up irrigation water for municipal and other uses. It is estimated that if 5 percent of agricultural water were transferred to municipal use, the needs of urban areas in the western United States would be met for the next 25 years (Spencer 1992, 70). Higher water prices would also reduce the need to build costly supply projects and delivery systems that dam and divert free-flowing streams. Higher prices would encourage private, profit-making firms to enter the water supply industry, taking the burden off the public treasury. If the price mechanism were allowed to operate, demand could be reduced, supply could be increased, water would be reallocated, and water crises could become obsolete.

Five years of drought moved Californians toward various pricing mechanisms to reduce demand for water and reallocate the scarce supplies. In 1991, when water supplies from the State Water Project and the federal Central Valley Project were cut, some cities, such as Santa Barbara, began using an escalating price scale for water to encourage conservation (Hayward 1991). Rather than regulating water consumption, or using the state's regulatory power to shift water from one use to another, California Governor Pete Wilson opted to facilitate water marketing by creating the California Drought Emergency Water Bank (Krautkraemer and Willey 1991). Under the Bank system, the Department of Water Resources bought water from farmers for $125 per acre-foot (most farmers pay less than $50 per acre-foot), and made the water available for other uses according to extreme critical needs. In so doing, the Department "guarantee[d] sellers that the transactions [would not] be regarded . . . as evidence of available surplus water or of wasteful or inefficient use on the part of the seller" (Hayward 1991, 46). Apart from this guarantee, sellers would risk losing their water rights under the "use-it-or-lose-it" rule of California water law. Water users jumped

11

at the opportunity afforded by the Bank, which quickly exceeded its goal of purchasing 500,000 acre-feet of water (Hayward 1991, 47).[4]

While the Water Bank was a step in the right direction, Governor Wilson stopped short of creating a true market, because only the Bank was authorized to buy water under the plan. In addition, limitations on the sale of federal water from the Bureau of Reclamation's Central Valley Project effectively prevented those water users from selling their water to the state.

Passage of the Central Valley Project Improvement Act[5] changed that by allowing water from the Central Valley Project to be traded outside the project area at fair market prices. The act, part of an omnibus water bill signed by President Bush on October 30, 1992,[6] also established a tiered pricing system for project water, a major change from the long-held policy of providing federal reclamation water to farmers at subsidized prices. Both the water trading and the tiered pricing system for project water provide market incentives to farmers for improved efficiency and conservation.

In addition to providing market incentives to conserve water, however, the Central Valley Project Improvement Act also set aside 800,000 acre-feet, or about 10 percent of project water, for environmental purposes, such as restoration and protection of fisheries, wetlands, and water quality. Exactly where this water will come from and how it will be used remains to be seen.

What Lies Ahead?

Overall, the institutions that currently govern water allocation do not promote market solutions to water problems. But for those institutions and policies to change, a new perspective on the role of information and incentives is necessary. Free-market environmentalism, described in Chapter 2, provides that perspective. Rather than following the traditional economic approach that calls for better cost-benefit analyses and better bureaucrats, the new resource economics calls for a closer look at the rules of the game that determine incentives.

An examination of the history of water institutions reveals that an efficient set of property rights evolved in the American West during the last half of the 19th century and that entrepreneurs set up projects for storing and delivering water. By early in the 20th century, however, the basis for a private, market solution to water allocation, for all practical purposes, had been eroded. Chapter 3 details the evolution from private to public water institutions. Chapter 4 discusses how court interpretations eroded the prior appropriation doctrine and how public reclamation projects discouraged private investment.

If we are to solve water crises, it is necessary to discover how existing institutions must change. Chapter 5 shows that by removing restrictions on the transfer of surface-water rights, markets could be used to a greater extent to promote efficient allocation. In Chapter 6 we see how instream uses can also be left more to market forces if restrictions on ownership of instream flow rights are eliminated.

Chapter 7 discusses how property rights to water and the common law may provide a better way to deal with water pollution than regulation under the Clean Water Act. Chapter 8 looks at how ground water, which has traditionally been considered a common pool resource, can be bought and sold in markets if rights to groundwater storage and recharge are established. And finally, chapter 9 details the establishment and success of water markets in the United States and around the world.

By considering isolated examples of market solutions to water allocation problems, perhaps the political institutions that presently dominate can be replaced with private institutions that promote efficiency and individual freedom. It is unlikely that the institutions necessary for a well-functioning market can be imposed through a central government. The history of water rights suggests that order, not lawlessness, was promoted by miners in the mining camps of the American West (Anderson and Hill 1979). To be sure, these camps were a form of government, but they were far more decentralized than the current legislative solutions. If a market solution to the water crisis is to be achieved, the current morass of legislative and administrative rules will have to be replaced. A way must be found to channel collective action into the definition and enforcement of private property rights that can be traded in a market.

Because the points emphasized in this book follow closely the work of Jack Hirshleifer, James DeHaven, and Jerome Milliman, it is appropriate to consider their view of decentralization:

> Other things being equal, we prefer local to state authority,
> state to federal—and private decision-making (the extreme

of decentralization) to any of these. Our fundamental reason for this preference is the belief that the cause of human liberty is best served by a minimum of government compulsion and that, if compulsion is necessary, local and decentralized authority is more acceptable than dictation from a remote centralized source of power. This is an "extra market value" for which we at least would be willing to make some sacrifices in terms of loss of economic efficiency. . . . Even on grounds of efficiency, however, we have some faith that, the more nearly the costs and benefits of water projects are brought home to those who make decisions, the more correct those decisions are likely to be—a consideration which argues for decentralization in practice. (Hirshleifer, DeHaven, and Milliman 1960, 361–62)

The lack of well-defined and enforced property rights in most aspects of water allocation has promoted centralized decision-making. All levels of government have become involved in water use and distribution, and the federal government particularly has seen its role expand since the turn of the century. To reverse this trend, private rights must be established to enable individuals acting in a market to determine water allocation. This book describes how such rights can be defined to encourage efficiency in a society of free and responsible individuals.

Notes

1. See also U.S. Geological Survey (1991, 99).

2. GEMS is the only global water monitoring entity. Unfortunately, its water quality data "are spotty, both spatially and temporally. Not all stations measure or report on all water quality parameters, or even the same water quality parameters from year to year" (World Resources Institute 1990, 329).

The sufficiency of water quality data in the United States is also questionable. While surface waters have been monitored for years for several conventional water quality parameters, only recently have toxic contaminants been included. Moreover, virtually no information on changes in ground-water quality exists. Even the data that are collected are insufficient. Many lack adequate quality control procedures. Many "come from widely separated fixed stations and do not adequately represent water quality in the intervening reaches. . . . Only a few conventional pollutants are commonly monitored, leaving substantial gaps in our knowledge of other contaminants that may present a greater risk. And the data are not processed or analyzed in a timely manner. . . . Conclusions regarding water quality are often based on subjective assessments by pollution control agency personnel and water quality experts" (Conservation Foundation 1987, 88).

3. While Gardner's study remains a definitive source of information concerning price elasticity of demand for irrigation water among California farmers; see Carlson,

Zilberman, and Miranowski (1993, 332–36, 357–58), for a more current discussion and case study, and Dinar and Zilberman (1991, 285–93), for a study involving farmers' response to a block-rate pricing structure to accomplish drainwater reduction.

4. In 1991, the Bank bought 820,000 acre-feet of water at $125 each and sold almost 400,000 acre-feet at $175. The State Water Project received the balance (*Economist* 1992b, 24).

5. Pub. L. 102–575, Title XXXIV, 106 Stat. 4706 et seq., 30 October 1992.

6. Reclamation Projects Authorization and Adjustment Act of 1992, Pub. L. No. 102–575, 106 Stat. 4600, 30 October 1992.

2. The Political Economy of Water Policy

Environmentalists and fiscal conservatives. Sound like strange bedfellows? Certainly most environmentalists and most agricultural and industrial water users would find the prospects of forming a coalition on water policy highly unlikely. Nonetheless, a growing number of people are beginning to understand that the potential for such coalitions lies in greater reliance on market forces. Applying the approach known as free market environmentalism to water policy was touted as early as 1982 by Thomas Graff, general counsel for the Environmental Defense Fund, following the defeat of Proposition 9, California's Peripheral Canal Bill. He asked, "What now? Will it be development without environmental protection as some have threatened? Or has all future water project development been choked off by the new conservationist-conservative alliance . . . ?" (Graff 1982, V-2). Graff's solution for making California water policy environmentally and economically sound called for three reforms: legal and institutional barriers to voluntary sale and purchase of water rights must be eliminated; public investment must be committed to lower-cost projects only; and water pricing must be reformed so consumers will face the true cost of the resources they use.

The reasons for the emergence of this alliance and its implications for solving water crises are questions addressed in this book. But before answering those questions, we must consider traditional approaches to the economics of water policy that have led to greater governmental involvement resulting in subsidies, price distortions, and environmental destruction. Against that traditional policy backdrop, free-market environmentalism provides an alternative that is sensitive to both fiscal and environmental constraints. That approach emphasizes the importance of getting the incentives right and questions whether that can be accomplished in the political sector. The basic conclusion is that, while markets may not work perfectly, they provide an improvement over existing policies—especially with regard to water use efficiency, environmental quality, and fiscal responsibility.

17

Rationalizing the State in Water Policy

Traditional economic policy analysis has emphasized efficiency without considering the institutions that foster it. In the traditional approach, good resource allocation is supposed to come from a careful weighing of the additional (marginal) benefits of employing a resource in one use relative to the additional (marginal) cost of not using it elsewhere. Accordingly, if an additional unit of water is worth $10 to industry and only $9 to agriculture, it will be efficient to continue reallocating units of water from the lower to the higher valued use as long as the differential value exists. That simple but high-powered principle not only explains how markets work but provides economists with a *raison d'etre* when it comes to governmental planning.

In explaining how markets work, the principle elucidates how people cope with scarcity. When scarcity drives up the price of a resource, users of the resource are motivated to find alternative sources of supply, new technologies, or substitute resources. Research by many economists (see Bailey 1995 and Simon 1995) shows that this response has allowed humankind to avoid constraints that would limit population and economic growth. In the case of water, such price signals are often lacking, but where they do exist, efficiency gains from marginal adjustments are significant.

For example, Tucson, Arizona, was able to reduce average peak daily water demand by 20 percent in the mid-1970s using a combination of price increases and other forms of rationing (Tucson Water Department 1996). Beattie and Foster found that a 10 percent increase in the price of water would reduce urban domestic water consumption between 4 and 13 percent. Similar data for the agricultural sector, which generally consumes 80 to 90 percent of all water withdrawn for human use, suggest that demand among those users is also price-responsive because of improved irrigation technology and modified cropping patterns. The dramatic voluntary response to California's Drought Water Bank that offered water users a chance to sell water at a profit is evidence of just how price-responsive users can be.[1]

These data on efficiency gains from market processes notwithstanding, some economists are skeptical about markets because individuals must act in a world of uncertainty without perfect information. In the traditional economics paradigm, uncertainty and information costs imply market failure that warrants government intervention. For example, in the presence of uncertainty about water availability, many states have drought plans ready to be implemented by "water experts" in state agencies. Economist Thomas Sowell (1987, 46) notes that "the conduct of social activities depends upon the special knowledge of the few being used to guide the actions of the many." Experts who know what water is available and what it is worth in various alternative uses are best capable of efficiently allocating the precious resource. In this view, where markets fail because of uncertainty and imperfect information, only government planning experts can improve resource use (see Simmons 1994).

Third-party effects are a second and more commonly cited example of market failure justifying government intervention. According to this rationale, individuals not party to a particular market transaction may be harmed; thus, there is no guarantee that exchange leads to efficiency. For example, suppose that one water user who values water at $20 per unit purchases water from another who values it at $15. The potential gain from trade appears to be $5. However, if a third party is harmed, say by pollution generated by the new user, in the amount of $10, there is actually a net loss when all water users are considered. Of course, if the harmed party has a property right to clean water and can make the others pay for the pollution, no exchange between the first two parties would take place because it would not be worth it for them to reallocate the water and pay the damages to the third party.

The problem of third-party effects also results when resources are held in common with access available to everyone. For example, pumping from a ground-water basin can result in the "tragedy of the commons" (Hardin 1968) if anyone can extract water without regard to the costs imposed on other users. When individual pumpers extract water, they do not take into account their impact on the pumping costs of other users or on the level of ground-water stocks remaining for future use. Hence, third-party effects arise that might justify governmental intervention to improve ground-water allocation.

Many water policy analysts have concluded that third-party effects are pervasive. Economist Robert Haveman (1973, 868) argued that the "use of natural and environmental resources is dominated by market failures." According to Howe, Alexander, and Moses

19

(1982, 383), "any [water] transaction between two users would ignore the return flow effects on the others." George A. Gould (1988, 22) stated that "[t]hird-party effects greatly impede the development of markets in appropriative [water] rights." Gould and others believe third-party effects justify substantial government intervention and regulation of water transfers and markets.[2]

Calling for government intervention to improve water allocation is one thing, but implementing effective intervention is another. In an attempt to make government decisions mimic ideal market conditions, economists have employed benefit-cost analysis. Volumes have been written on this subject and on its application to water resources, and all government agencies involved in water resource allocation have tried to employ the technique. Their efforts, of course, are complicated by two factors. First, the value derived from water and the opportunity costs associated with its use accrue over time. That fact necessitates discounting future values, thus raising the question of what is the appropriate discount rate. For the private sector entrepreneur, the answer to the question is dictated by capital markets, but in the political sector, debates rage over the appropriate "social discount rate" vis-à-vis the "private discount rate." Depending on the rate chosen, very different numbers can be generated from benefit-cost analysis.

To make matters worse, many of the values associated with government water projects do not have an accurate market analogue. For example, in estimating the benefits and costs of dams, economists have had to consider flood control and recreational values. Arriving at numbers for the benefits amounts to little more than guesswork. The debate in the Pacific Northwest over storing and diverting water for agricultural, industrial, and municipal uses as opposed to spilling the water over the dams to save salmon illustrates the limits of benefit-cost analysis.

In the end, if market failure exists, it means that there will be no market prices to use as proxies in benefit-cost analysis. Thus, government failure becomes just as likely.

The Myth of the Efficient State

Assuming that government intervention can improve resource allocation when market failure is present fails to recognize problems inherent in the political process. Government agencies, such as the

Bureau of Reclamation and the Army Corps of Engineers, are assumed to be professional agencies staffed by scientific managers who will apply benefit-cost analysis to obtain the optimal allocation of water. Assuming the scientific manager is *not* motivated by profit or self-interest, he or she is supposed to apply theory and methods impartially and efficiently to accomplish what is best for the public. But assuming managers should behave in the public interest will not necessarily produce a better result.

Those who call for command-and-control as an improvement over markets fail to recognize that incentives and information problems must be overcome in both the private and political arenas. Politicians and bureaucrats face incentives that are very different from those in the private sector, but those incentives are no less important to outcomes. It will not do to assume that because they are in the public sector they are working toward the public interest. Votes, campaign coffers, influence, and budgets are all factors that affect decisions in the political sector. Even where politicians want to do what is good for their constituents or for the country, they still face the problem of knowing what the people want. Suppliers in the private sector sell their products to individual consumers who vote with dollars, making the link between demand and supply quite clear. But suppliers in the political sector sell their products to the entire citizenry, which expresses its demand through special-interest groups as well as elections. In the latter setting, the link between demand and supply is much less clear.

Applying benefit-cost analysis to political decisions is an attempt to replicate the market forces of demand and supply, but the results of benefit-cost studies often go unheeded because of the incentives faced by politicians and bureaucrats. In the private sector, benefit-cost analysis is useful because decisionmakers have information in the form of market prices and profits as a reward for taking actions that improve efficiency. In the political sector, neither of these conditions holds. The outputs that are generated from publicly owned resources are, for the most part, zero-priced. Because there are no markets, the political resource manager is forced to make comparisons without the benefit of information contained in market prices. That lack of economic information forces the political manager to make tradeoffs between alternative resource uses in political currencies such as votes and campaign contributions. Those currencies, at best, provide distorted measures of value.

Analyzing water policy requires a healthy understanding of public choice economics, that branch of economics that incorporates economics and political science.[3] The public choice approach recognizes that the incentive structure in the public sector is quite different from that in the private sector. In the private sector, owners of firms receive the difference between revenues and costs, or profits. Given this claim on the residual, the owner has an incentive to find good information and use it to improve efficiency, which in turn enhances profits. In the political sector, however, there is no owner with a claim on the profit. The rewards for state water engineers do not depend on maximizing the net value of water resources. The salary of the manager of a Bureau of Reclamation project does not depend on whether recipients of the water pay off their loans. Though there is no consensus in the economics literature on what bureaucrats maximize, most economists agree that efficiency is not the decision-maker's main goal.

Free-Market Environmentalism

Free-market environmentalism is an alternative paradigm that emphasizes the importance of getting the incentives right in both the private and political sectors. It stands in sharp contrast to public interest theories of government by building on two important schools of economic thought: property rights and public choice. The property rights approach brings into focus the relationship between institutions and incentives, while the public choice approach draws attention to the incentives of bureaucrats and public officials and examines the likelihood that collective action will achieve efficiency or equity.

Property Rights, Incentives, and Information

Free-market environmentalism begins with the individual, especially the entrepreneur. Motivated by profits, entrepreneurs search for opportunities to move resources from lower valued to higher valued uses. As they respond to such opportunities, resource allocation is improved not because entrepreneurs care about efficiency but because they can profit by pursuing efficiency. The question is whether the opportunities they discover and the actions they take will increase wealth for society or simply redistribute existing wealth.

If entrepreneurs face the full costs of their actions, they will take only those actions that produce positive net benefits for themselves and for society. The entrepreneur who discovers a higher valued use for water, for example, stands to gain from transferring his water to the higher valued use. If allocation to that higher use requires the entrepreneur to bear the opportunity costs of current use, the reallocation will take place only if the net difference is positive. Responsibility for opportunity costs is crucial. If the change in water use generates pollution, the result will again be positive sum if responsibility for the pollution is placed on the entrepreneur. However, if the cost of pollution falls on others and the entrepreneur is not held accountable, all bets regarding net gains are off because there is no guarantee that the benefits captured by the entrepreneur will exceed the resulting costs including pollution.

The system of property rights to water determines the extent to which all the costs and benefits of water use are taken into account by decisionmakers. If water rights are well defined, enforced, and transferable, benefits and costs of reallocation will be taken into account by water owners and markets will allocate water efficiently. Well-defined water rights give individuals a clear idea of what it is they own and hence what actions they can take regarding the resource. For example, well-defined water rights might specify the amount of water that can be diverted from a stream and the quantity and quality that must be returned. Where water rights are not well defined, allocation becomes difficult because one person's diversions can affect another's rights. Without well-defined rights, conflicts become inevitable and market trades impossible.

Enforcement of property rights determines how likely it is that a water owner can enjoy the benefits of his or her ownership. Because rights cannot be perfectly enforced, ownership will always be probabilistic. But when the probability of capturing benefits from a use is low, it is less likely that the owner will husband the resource. For example, if a water user is able to install a more efficient irrigation system but is not sure that he can use or sell the conserved water, he will have little incentive to improve water-use efficiency. Or if a water owner wishes to leave water in the stream to improve fish habitat but is unable to exclude other diverters from withdrawing the water or to exclude fishermen who pay nothing from using the stream, he will be less likely to provide instream flows. In this sense, enforcement is the ability to exclude other users. As long as exclusion is possible, owners can capture the benefits from the uses of their resources.

Finally, water rights must be transferable if the owner is to be fully aware of the opportunity costs of his actions. A water owner who is not allowed to transfer resources to another use will not consider the full opportunity costs of that use. Even if the alternative use has a higher value, that value will be ignored if profitable transfers are prohibited. Laws forbidding the sale or lease of diverted water to environmental groups for enhancing environmental amenities, for example, tell irrigators to ignore environmental values.

It is important to emphasize that all decisions are made under conditions of uncertainty and mistakes will be made. An entrepreneur who moves water from one use to another does so with the expectation that the new use has a higher value. The expectation depends on the entrepreneur's subjective evaluation of the world. The basic economic problem, therefore, becomes one of using knowledge that is time- and place-specific. For example, a farmer may have a good idea how effective irrigation will be on a certain field without having studied soils or hydrology at a university. Because better knowledge can come from experience, it is difficult to specify what constitutes the best irrigation practice without time- and place-specific information. That fact makes the efficacy of centralized planning questionable and instead focuses attention on the importance of the individual resource owner. Conservationist Aldo Leopold recognized the importance of time- and place-specific information with his concept of the "land ethic." Leopold emphasized that people who know their land (and water) are in the best position to conserve it and use it wisely.

Gathering information with which to make decisions requires careful comparison of benefits and costs. Should a farmer install a new sprinkler irrigation system that reduces water use by 25 percent? What is the cost of the capital? What is the value of the water saved? How long will the system last? There is an endless list of questions that can be asked, but at some point the value of additional information compared to the cost of acquiring that information makes further study uneconomical. Reducing uncertainty is good but only if the expected benefits from the search activity exceed the expected costs. Of course, what may be the optimal amount of search for one person may not be optimal for another, so it is easy for observers to argue that better decisions could result if more information were collected. But perfect information is not the norm to which we should compare the real world.

Public Choice and Government Failure

A system of complete property rights will ensure that the entrepreneurial process will improve efficiency, producing the only free lunch available to society. But what happens if the entrepreneur can shift costs to others? After all, the entrepreneur seeking profit does not care whether she is creating a free lunch or dining at someone else's expense.

Suppose the entrepreneur perceives two opportunities, one in which profits can be created through improved allocation of privately owned resources and one in which profits are derived from exploiting resources held in common. First, consider the potential "tragedy of the commons" wherein an individual pumping from a ground-water basin observes others beginning to pump from the same source. He realizes that any water left in the ground will be taken by the other pumpers. Therefore, he has an incentive to pump water until the net value of additional water is zero. Exploiting the common pool resource benefits the individual but results in overpumping.

Instead of overinvesting in pumping, entrepreneurs may overinvest in political activities that capture subsidies. Economists call this rent seeking. Simply put, rent seeking occurs when decisionmakers use the powers of government to increase personal wealth at the expense of others. For example, when a special interest group convinces the Congress that it should receive subsidized water paid for by taxpayers, a transfer has occurred. As a result, the special interest group will invest its time and money in efforts to obtain the transfer while taxpayers, if well enough organized, will invest in trying to prevent it. When the Department of Interior decides whether water will be used for recreational or municipal uses, it affects the distribution of benefits and costs. The decision on whether to increase flows in the Columbia River to enhance the prospects of salmon survival or to continue diverting the water for agricultural production determines whether environmentalists will capture the value of water or whether farmers will continue to benefit. Interest groups spend large amounts of money and other resources trying to influence those decisions. When the entrepreneur discovers opportunities to use government to increase his wealth through subsidies, rent creation— a positive-sum game—is replaced with rent seeking—a negative-sum game.

Such entrepreneurial efforts explain the demand for rent seeking while the activities of politicians and bureaucrats explain the supply. Just as entrepreneurs in the marketplace recognize and fill demands for goods and services, politicians and bureaucrats discover opportunities to meet the demands of their constituencies. The constraints in the political sector, however, are very different from those in the private sector. Private entrepreneurs provide new goods and services only if the benefits from those goods and services exceed the costs of the resources used in production. And with well-specified property rights, the supplier will pay the costs and capture the profits. On the other hand, politicians or bureaucrats who provide goods and services to interest groups in the political sector do not directly face the costs of supply.

Property rights to resources that are "owned" by the government are only informally defined and can be disputed at every legislative session. For example, the Bureau of Reclamation "owns" vast amounts of water. Rights to use are held by the groups who derive benefits from the water. Because these rights are continually up for grabs, if agricultural interests want an increase in irrigation withdrawals, they can attempt to convince bureaucrats to take rights away from environmental interests. If the bureaucrats do so, they might be concerned with alienating the environmental groups, but they do not have to face the full opportunity costs of their actions.

In seeking to maximize budgetary discretion, each bureaucrat realizes that he has access to the common pool of the government treasury. He asks, "What is the gain to my agency (and hence to me) of capturing another dollar from the treasury?" The budgetary increase finances the agency's activities, and the costs of the capture are spread among all other bureaucracies in lost opportunities. To increase the agency's share, each bureaucrat must find ways to increase the magnitude and scope of the agency's activity. By pursuing programs that concentrate benefits on the agency and its constituents while diffusing the costs over the general population, it will be possible to maximize support and minimize opposition. In this way, agencies build a constituency for increased activity.

Opportunity costs are not internalized in the political allocation process, so there is no direct reality check on whether the benefits of spending more on one agency or project exceed the benefits of spending it on another or returning it to the taxpayers. Hence, enterprising politicians and bureaucrats can increase their domain regardless of whether it is efficient. The economics of public choice teaches us to view public sector activities like any other activity. Politicians and bureaucrats are trying to maximize certain objectives, such as votes, budgets, power, prestige, and discretion. As those goals are pursued through collective action, public decisionmakers face costs that differ substantially from those in the private sector because politics allows those who bear the costs to be separated from those who receive the benefits.

Building on the premise that actors in the political system are likely to be motivated by self-interest, the public choice paradigm has uncovered several reasons why governmental action has failed to meet efficiency criteria:

1. *Voter ignorance and imperfect information.* In a democratic society, where it is unlikely that any voter, even a well-informed one, can influence the outcome of the political process, the benefits of being well informed cannot be fully captured by the individual. At the same time, obtaining information about candidates and issues is costly for the voter. Thus, voters remain rationally ignorant; that is, they do not incur great costs to obtain information except on issues that are important to them personally.

2. *Special interest effects.* Those voters who do become well informed and politically active on any issue tend to be those who will benefit from a particular governmental action. With benefits concentrated on a few recipients, it is worth the recipient group's time to try to bring about specific governmental action. Because the costs of governmental action—subsidies, transfer payments, tariffs, regulations, and so forth—tend to be diffused over the entire population of taxpayers and consumers, any action costs each individual so little that it is not worth his time to organize in opposition. With the combination of concentrated benefits and diffused costs, well-informed and articulate interest groups (that contribute to campaigns) will dominate the political process and receive political favors.

3. *Shortsighted effects.* Politicians who must face the electorate every few years tend to be more concerned with the short run than with the long run. They will have little interest in policies that are efficient but that take time to produce results.

4. *Little incentive for candidates to account for individual preferences.* In the marketplace, consumers are generally able to tailor their purchases very closely to their own preferences, and each individual gets the particular kind of product he wants. In the political marketplace, however, voters must decide on alternative bundles of governmental expenditure and tax proposals offered by competing politicians. There is no opportunity for individuals to pick some of one candidate's positions and some of another's, and at the same time reject both candidates' positions on other issues. To capture as many votes as possible, the candidates' policy bundles tend to reflect a majority coalition, not the wishes of individual voters.

Given the incentive structures in the political sector, entrepreneurial talents are expended by interest groups trying to influence decisions and by politicians and bureaucrats trying to fill niches that satisfy constituents. Without the reality check of profits found in the private sector, the potential for negative-sum games is very real. The most obvious examples of governmental failure in water resource management include policies that promote subsidized water use in agriculture, construction of dams that cannot pass the benefit-cost test, and laws that allow polluters to avoid the full cost of their actions.

Conclusion

The lesson from economics that good decisions require a weighing of costs and benefits is critical to good resource allocation. It does not follow from this lesson, however, that good decisions will flow from all institutional settings as long as benefit-cost analysis is performed. Focusing totally on benefit-cost analysis makes it appear that the economic problem facing society is simply one of allocating resources among competing uses where the values are known or can be discovered by experts. This focus misses the real economic problem, which is how to generate information about values that are not known and how to structure incentives to reward good resource stewardship.[4]

Throughout the federal reclamation system are countless examples of projects that do not pass benefit-cost muster and that have significant adverse environmental consequences. In light of scientific management we might ask why these projects were built. Are they anomalies or do systematic biases in the water allocation process encourage inefficient resource use? The answer lies in the institutional structure that defines the incentives of decisionmakers.

In the chapters that follow we will explore the incentives faced by politicians, bureaucrats, and their constituents and ask how those incentives can be changed. Free-market environmentalism begins by examining individual behavior with the assumption that self-interest prevails. If authority can be linked to responsibility through private property rights, self-interest can be linked to efficiency. In the absence of such a link, nothing in the economic process will push the system toward efficiency.

How does free-market environmentalism fit into the mainstream of natural resource economics? Alan Randall (1981, 37), in a natural resource economics textbook, argued that to the right of mainstream economists "is a group of free-market zealots, who see the economic system in very simple terms, and who cannot understand why others fail to see what, to them, is obvious. They divide their time between proselytizing for free-market solutions among noneconomists and attempting to keep the other groups of mainstream economists on the straight-and-narrow."

Since then, the mainstream of environmental economics has moved toward free-market environmentalism. Belief in the ability of the market system to coordinate resource allocation is derived from a preponderance of evidence supporting the efficiency that results when market processes are applied to water problems. The approach taken in this book will not offer much hope to the central water planner who wants to supplant entrepreneurial decisions with bureaucratic ones. The emphasis on decentralized decision processes that offer the potential for generating positive-sum games will, however, offer hope and encouragement to those who value efficiency, productivity, and individual freedom.

Notes

1. For a discussion of price responsiveness see Anderson (1995b).
2. See Chapter 5.
3. For an excellent introduction to public choice see Mitchell and Simmons (1995).
4. See Hayek (1945).

3. The Evolution of Water Institutions

To understand the contemporary institutions that govern water allocation, we must begin with an understanding of how and why those institutions have changed over time. When English settlers arrived on the Atlantic seaboard, water was not scarce so there was little reason to worry about how it was used. However, conditions on the arid Great Plains were vastly different, which made it necessary to hammer out new water institutions.

When people face increasing scarcity of a resource such as water, they will put more effort into trying to establish and strengthen claims to that resource. For example, witness how individuals and groups have attempted to better define their claims to wildlife and wildlife habitat as those resources have become more scarce. Recognizing that hunters are willing to pay for access, farmers and ranchers have invested in habitat improvements that make the hunting better, and they have increased their enforcement against trespassing and poaching.[1] In Montana, for example, landowners have sought and obtained legislation allowing them to post land against trespassing by simply marking access points with orange paint.

Changes in the technology whereby property rights are defined and enforced also can alter institutions. A perfect example is the introduction of barbed wire in the 1870s. To the homesteader whose land was invaded by cowboys and their herds, barbed wire defined his private property. It also allowed stockmen to control grazing, to rotate cattle on pastures, to selectively breed their livestock, and to control water holes.

Establishment of property rights does not depend on formal government, as evidenced by the evolution of water institutions on the American frontier (Demsetz 1967, 354). As the early settlers arrived in the West ahead of the legal machinery of state and federal governments, they found it necessary to generate their own rules. Without the power of government, those rules depended on voluntary agreements among the settlers. Wagon trains, cattlemen's associations,

31

and mining camps all provide excellent examples of the evolution of social contracts (Anderson and Hill 1975; Umbeck 1977). To be sure, not all people had equal power in the bargaining process, and in some cases the six-gun introduced an element of coercion. But the image of the Wild West often ignores the role that contracts played in establishing property rights. The role of contracts is nowhere more evident than in the evolution of western water rights.

Riparian Rights vs. Prior Appropriation

To the frontiersmen entering the Great Plains, it was clear that access to water would be a prime factor in locating a suitable farm or ranch site. Hence initial settlement patterns can be traced to the river and stream bottoms. If an individual found that a stream location was already taken, he simply moved to another water supply. Under those circumstances, the right to use the water accrued to whoever owned the stream bank and had access to it by virtue of position.

It is not difficult to understand why such riparian water rights, whether implicit or explicit, were adopted by the frontiersmen. Those rights found historical precedent in eastern laws, which had been borrowed from English common law. Early judges and lawyers in the West were familiar only with eastern law and were inclined to transfer it to the western legal system (Webb 1931, 447). In addition, land with adjacent water was abundant relative to the number of settlers; that is, water was not a relatively scarce factor. As long as those conditions held, rights that granted all riparian owners equal use of the flowing stream sufficed for resource allocation. The benefits of changing the existing institutions governing water were not sufficient remuneration for the time and effort required to initiate the change.

Two factors worked to change the benefits and costs of altering property rights to water. First, mining technology required that water be taken from the stream and moved to nonriparian locations. Because the riparian rules gave all riparian owners the right to an undiminished quantity and quality of water, diversions for mining and irrigation were not feasible. Second, a great deal of nonriparian agricultural land could be made more productive if irrigation water could be moved to it.

32

Because the California mining camps were the first to feel major population pressure, it is not surprising that miners played an important role in the evolution of what became known as the prior appropriation doctrine.[2]

> Following a tradition of collective action on the mining frontiers of other continents, the miners formed districts, embracing from one to several of the existing "camps" or "diggings," and promulgated regulations for marking and recording claims. The miners universally adopted the priority principle, which simply recognized the superior claims of the first-arrival. . . . The miners' codes defined the maximum size of claims, set limits on the number of claims a single individual might work, and established regulations designating certain actions—long absence, long diligence, and the like—as equivalent to the forfeiture of rights. A similar body of district rules regulated the use of water flowing on the public domain. (McCurdy 1976, 236–37)

The miners quickly realized that gold was found not only along streambeds, where only a pan and shovel were needed to extract the precious mineral. When deposits were discovered several miles from water, it made economic sense to appropriate water from the streams. "It universally became one of the mining customs that the right to divert and use a specified quantity of water could be acquired by prior appropriation" (McCurdy 1976, 254). These customs had "one principle embodied in them all, and on which rests the 'Arid Region Doctrine' of the ownership and use of water, and that was the recognition of discovery, followed by prior appropriation, as the inception of the possessor's title, and development by working the claim as the condition of its retention" (Kinney 1912, 598).

While there is no question that original western mining law was aimed at establishing private rights to water through appropriation, disputes over rights led to court cases, which in turn led to conflicts with the common law riparian doctrine. Judges were torn between their training, which taught them that decisions ought to "conform, as nearly as possible, to the analogies of the common law," and the western tradition, which held that law "ought to be based on the wants of the community and the peculiar conditions of things."[3] The tensions between the riparian and prior appropriation doctrines

33

are reflected in the findings of some courts that appropriative principles were "impractical" and the findings of others that cases "must
be decided by the fact of priority." The result was an interesting
and eventually harmful mix of eastern and western law. Webb captured the nature of the mix:

> The easterner, with his background of forest and farm, could
> not always understand the man of the cattle kingdom. One
> went on foot, the other went on horseback; one carried his
> law in books, the other carried it strapped round his waist.
> One represented tradition, the other represented innovation;
> one responded to convention, the other responded to neces-
> sity and evolved his own conventions. Yet the man of the
> timber and the town made the law for the man of the plain;
> the Plainsman, finding this law unsuited to his needs, broke
> it and was called lawless. (Webb 1931, 206)

From eastern law came such concepts as usufruct (the right to
use, rather than own, water), beneficial use, and reasonable use.
From the western mining camps and cattle ranges came absolute
property, equal footing for uses, and transferable ownership rights.
The riparian doctrine maintained an element of common property
by continuing to support the view that riparian owners have coequal
rights in the water; that is, when water is put to new uses, existing
riparian users may be required to reduce current uses to make way
for new ones. Because riparian rights were generally not transferable
apart from the riparian land to which they were appurtenant, the
possibility of market allocation was further restricted.

The prior appropriation doctrine, on the other hand, established
ownership rights that were clearly defined, enforced, and transferable. Rights were absolute and not coequal. As a result, markets
were left to determine the value of water. The California courts
asserted that "a comparison of the value of conflicting rights would
be a novel mode of determining their legal superiority."[4] As
McCurdy (1976, 257–58) stated, "Anyone might take and use water
flowing on the public domain for any beneficial use subject only to
the rights of any prior appropriators." The appropriation doctrine
gave no preference to riparian landowners, allowing all users an
opportunity to compete for water and to develop far from streams.
Appropriations were limited only by the means used to divert and
transport the water or the purpose of the appropriation.

34

In many cases, disputes arose and courts were called on to define rights. Cases were often complicated, but Judge Stephen J. Field of the California Supreme Court contended that "the courts do not . . . refuse the consideration of subjects, because of the complicated and embarrassing character of the questions to which they give rise."[5] The Field court continually worked to define and enforce rights to promote efficient markets. Even pollution, which frequently occurred in the mining process, was handled by having polluters pay damages to those users who received lower quality water. The impact of the Field court decisions can be summarized as follows:

> By converting the possessory claims of so many trespassers into judicially cognizable property rights, the California court effectively brought federal land-use policy into the realm of private, and, in some instances, constitutional law. . . . Moreover, the court also mobilized the still inchoate "public purpose" and due process doctrines to prohibit the miners' "primary assemblages," as well as the state legislature, from using the organized power of the community to divest the equitably acquired claims of men who had evinced a growth-inducing "incentive to improvement." . . . Field believed that only the courts were capable of resolving allocation problems so as to simultaneously protect property rights, release entrepreneurial energies, and provide all men with an equal opportunity to share the material fruits of a vigorously expanding capitalist society. (McCurdy 1976, 264–66)

The law that evolved in the West reflected the greater relative scarcity of water in the region. As the settlers devoted more efforts to defining and enforcing property rights, a system of water law evolved that (1) granted to the first appropriator an exclusive right to the water and granted water rights to later appropriators on the condition that prior rights were met, (2) permitted the diversion of water from the stream so that it could be used on nonriparian lands, (3) forced the appropriator of water to forfeit his right if the water was not used, and (4) allowed for the transfer and exchange of rights in water between individuals.

Private Water Development

While the doctrine of appropriation was evolving in the mining camps, private institutions were developing to capture and deliver the water where it was needed. One usually thinks of large federal

35

reclamation projects as the main impetus to western irrigation, but private development dominated the frontier.

American Indians

When the Spanish conquistadors reached what is now the southwestern United States in the 16th century, they found the Zūni and Hopi Indians diverting snowmelt from the mountains to their fields via canals and irrigating crops of corn, squash, and melons in fields located around springs.

> By building small stone walls to check the flow of water and sand, the Hopi were able to prevent flooding of their crops and to enhance soil moisture. Scale economies in the construction of the irrigation systems made communal production and ownership superior to private efforts. If water came from a constantly flowing spring, water rights could be privately owned, but the flood waters that came with less certainty and flowed through communal irrigation systems were shared. (Anderson 1995a, 33–34)

Other than decisionmaking by family groups or clans, no centralized authority over water existed (Worster 1985, 32–33).

The Papago Indians, or Bean People, who lived in the Sonoran desert, practiced floodplain irrigation. Whenever and wherever rain fell, they quickly planted a crop of fast-germinating beans and harvested them before the soil became bricklike again in the desert climate. The Papago carried out this *ak-chin*, or *arroyo-mouth*, farming as self-contained village or family units, "where individuals of more or less equal standing came together to do a common job" (Worster 1985, 33–34). They irrigated in this manner until the white man came on the scene.

Between 300 B.C. and A.D. 1200, the Hohokam Indians constructed an extensive canal system along the Salt and Gila Rivers in Arizona (Robinson 1979, 2). Capable of irrigating thousands of acres, the Hohokam canals extended more than 100 miles. The largest canals were 30 feet across, 7 to 13 feet deep and several miles long. They were excavated with wooden and stone tools. Rawhides and baskets were used to carry the dirt to the canal banks. Silt and bank erosion were kept at bay by regular maintenance.

Although the evidence is not conclusive, the extent of the irrigation system likely generated some form of centralized coordination or control among its components, if for no other reason than to deal with periods of flood or drought. Nevertheless, the Hohokam civilization abandoned its canals sometime around A.D. 1400, most likely because they were unable to overcome these two enemies of agriculture. It is also probable that the intensive irrigation resulted in increased salts and alkali in the topsoil, rendering it useless (Robinson 1979, 2; Worster 1985, 34).

The Settlers

Spanish water development in what later became the southwestern United States consisted of establishing missions and settlements (pueblos) near available water supplies and building an irrigation system for the surrounding lands. The construction and maintenance of *acequias* (canals) was a community effort, and each settlement elected a *mayordomo* (ditch chief) to oversee the efforts along with water distribution (Huffman 1953, 14; Dunbar 1983, 5–8).

The first English-speaking settlers to irrigate on a large scale in the United States were the Mormons, who began establishing town sites and digging irrigation ditches upon their arrival in the Great Salt Lake Valley in July 1847 (Baker and Conkling 1930, 6; Pisani 1992, 78). Communities were established by plotting out a townsite and surrounding it with small farm parcels. Each settler received a town lot and a 10- to 20-acre farm. To avoid monopolies, the church prohibited the ownership of more than one town lot per farmer and forbade farms larger than 20 acres. Although the climate was dry and the landscape harsh, many small streams flowing out of the mountains provided abundant supplies of water. The Mormons irrigated their fields by building small diversion dams and canals using makeshift tools and surveying instruments. Each settler contributed labor to the project according to the acreage he would cultivate. Stock in the community irrigation system was issued to settlers according to the labor they contributed and the number of acres they irrigated. Later, a local watermaster was elected by the farmers to supervise water distribution. In this manner, the Mormons irrigated 16,333 acres by 1850, 150,000 acres by 1865, and 263,473 acres by 1890 (Pisani 1992, 78; Dunbar 1983, 10–15; Robinson 1979, 4–5).

Cooperative colonies also made significant contributions to early irrigation development in the West. The Greeley Colony, founded in 1870 in Colorado and named after Horace Greeley, brought 32,000 acres under irrigation and set the stage for irrigation development in Colorado. The Anaheim Colony in California also demonstrated that private savings could finance the construction of irrigation canals. The main group involved in that cooperative stayed at their jobs in San Francisco to finance the venture while others worked the colony lands to produce crops on 20-acre, privately owned parcels irrigated by communally owned canals. Other irrigation colonies launched in California were successful in raising and selling high-value crops by pooling their resources to reduce the costs of farming. The most notable were Riverside, Redlands, Lompoc, and Pasadena (Pisani 1992, 81).

Commercial Irrigation Companies

Many different forms of business organization were used to develop western irrigation. For the smaller projects, especially in the mining districts, individuals and partners had sufficient funds to undertake the necessary investments. As set forth above, the cooperative ventures of the Greeley, Anaheim, and similar colonies irrigated thousands of acres by pooling resources to purchase land and construct irrigation systems.

In addition, corporations were formed to construct irrigation systems and sell the water to farmers. Initially, investors from eastern cities and Europe furnished capital in the hope of realizing huge returns once the settlers arrived and began farming. Diversion dams and canals capable of irrigating thousands of acres were built at great expense by companies such as the Northern Colorado Irrigation Company, which built the 85-mile High Line Canal to divert water from the Platte River; the Wyoming Development Company, which built a 2,105-foot dam and 2,380-foot tunnel to carry water from the Laramie River to irrigate more than 50,000 acres; the Pecos Irrigation and Investment Company, which built two dams and two canals 30 and 50 miles long, respectively, in southeastern New Mexico; the Idaho Mining and Irrigation Company, which constructed a diversion dam and canal to irrigate 600,000 acres; and the San Joaquin and King's River Canal and Irrigation Company, which built a canal capable of irrigating 16,000 acres (Dunbar 1983, 24; Worster 1985, 102).

Most of these commercial irrigation enterprises were built on watercourses flowing through federal lands. As a result, the land was not available to secure their promoters' investments. Some sought grants of land from the federal and state governments, but grants were often opposed by those who feared monopoly by such enterprises. When the corporations began to face financial difficulties, the optimism of their investors disappeared, and no further funds for irrigation development could be found (Pisani 1992, 90–91; Huffman 1953, 82).

Unfortunately, most of the commercial irrigation corporations went out of business for several reasons. First, their developers were ignorant of the actual amounts of water carried by streams and the amount of water necessary to irrigate a given quantity of land, as well as the effect of the often harsh and inconsistent climate on the water supply (Baker and Conkling 1930, 9–10). Those first to arrive on the frontier often had an unbridled optimism. Hence, in the race to establish a claim on the frontier, they arrived far ahead of a time when the land and water could really generate a profit.[6] Second, the corporations underestimated the cost of constructing and maintaining irrigation works (Allston 1978, 109). When settlers did not arrive in droves and immediately begin buying water for farming as expected, overhead costs quickly overwhelmed the irrigation enterprises. In the absence of further investment capital, they were driven into bankruptcy. Moreover, states began passing laws allowing county commissions to regulate the rates commercial companies could charge for water, which prevented them from recapturing their costs. Good came of the failure of these enterprises, however, in that thousands of acres were irrigated by the systems the companies built and many of the irrigation works were taken over by settlers who formed mutual companies or irrigation districts and continued their operation (Dunbar 1983, 24–27; Pisani 1992, 106).

Development corporations fared better than the large commercial irrigation companies. Development corporations purchased large parcels of land, built irrigation works to provide water for farming, formed mutual irrigation companies, and then subdivided and sold the parcels along with a proportionate number of shares in the mutual company. By the time all the land was sold, the purchasers owned the water company. Development corporations were so successful that thousands of acres in California were irrigated in this manner (Worster 1985, 100–102).[7]

Mutual Irrigation Companies

One of the more successful types of irrigation organization was the mutual irrigation company, or "mutual." Also known as canal companies or ditch companies, mutuals were private cooperatives formed by groups of irrigators for the purpose of providing water at cost (Dunbar 1983, 28). Shares of stock were issued to each member representing a percentage of the water supply, which was prorated each year according to stock ownership. The shares could usually be rented or sold and could be transferred anywhere within the service area of the mutual. The price of the shares was determined by the marketplace. Members either retained their water rights or deeded them to the mutual (Pisani 1992, 101; Smith 1984, 167).[8]

Upon forming the mutual company, the members elected a board of directors that was responsible for operating the organization in accordance with state law and the corporation's articles of incorporation and bylaws. Although not required to be, most mutual companies were incorporated. Incorporation provided several advantages, including the authority to enter into contracts, incur obligations, appear in court, and hold property as a separate entity. Unincorporated mutuals were required to obtain the consent of all members before taking any action (Huffman 1953, 71).

Mutual companies either built their own irrigation works[9] or purchased those of other irrigation companies.[10] They levied assessments against shares of stock for construction, maintenance, and operation and borrowed money secured by liens on the members' land for larger projects (Baker and Conkling 1930, 396–97).

The fact that mutual companies were so accessible and appropriate to water users rendered them the dominant institution for irrigation management in California, Colorado, and Utah. They were also widely used in other western states. While a few were large, such as the Twin Falls Canal Company of Idaho with 204,000 acres and the Salt River Valley Water Users Association with 228,000 acres, most were small, serving neighborhoods or communities. As of 1925, the average size of most mutuals was between 1,000 and 2,000 acres (Huffman 1953, 72; Baker and Conkling 1930, 396).

The structure of mutuals was especially significant, since it further contributed to the operation of private markets in the West. By using members' assets as collateral, mutuals could enter capital markets to obtain the investment funds necessary to develop irrigation projects. The transferability of stocks ensured that water could be moved to higher valued alternatives, further ensuring the success of the operation. These features, combined with the security of rights provided by the doctrine of appropriation, stimulated an effective marketplace.

Irrigation Districts

Irrigation proponents, however, considered mutual irrigation companies to be severely weakened by their inability to force irrigators to join them. When the benefits of irrigation became obvious in the 1880s, irrigators sought a means of coercing participation in community irrigation projects (Chandler 1913, 132). California's Wright Act, passed in 1887, was the first major legislation creating irrigation districts.[11] All of the western states later passed similar legislation. The districts were quasi-municipal corporations and political subdivisions of the state. As such, they had powers that went beyond those of private corporations. Irrigation districts could issue bonds and secure them by attaching liens to all lands within the district. Revenue to pay interest on the bonds and for maintenance and operation of irrigation works was raised from tax assessments levied against that same property. All property within the district was included in the district, whether or not the owner wanted to participate, and whether or not the property was irrigable.[12] Moreover, districts had the power to condemn water rights to provide a unified distribution system (Huffman 1953, 73–75; Chandler 1913, 133; Baker and Conkling 1930, 395).

Irrigation districts fared similarly to the commercial irrigation enterprises in their attempts to finance and construct large projects.[13] Nevertheless, they became widely used in the 20th century as a counterpart to mutual irrigation companies in the management of irrigation systems (Pisani 1992, 103–104; Dunbar 1983, 33–34).

The contributions of private reclamation projects should not be underestimated. By 1910, more than 13 million acres of land in the West were irrigated by private ventures. Between 1900 and 1910, the number of irrigated acres grew by 86.4 percent, with private enterprise accounting for almost the entire increase (Golze 1961, 6). See Table 3.1. While individual and partnership efforts were responsible for irrigating the bottom lands along rivers and streams by means of crude diversion dams and ditches, it was cooperatives and other business organizations that developed the fertile bench lands and nonriparian ground (Dunbar 1983, 20). By 1920, cooperative

41

Table 3.1
PRIVATE IRRIGATION DEVELOPMENT IN 17 WESTERN STATES, IN ACRES

Census	Total Irrigated Acreage	Furnished Government Water	Private Development
1890	3,631,381	—	3,631,381
1900	7,527,690	—	7,527,690
1902	8,875,090	—	8,875,090
1910	14,025,332	568,558	13,456,774
1920	18,592,888	2,388,199	16,204,769
1930	18,944,856	3,049,970	15,894,886
1940	20,395,043	3,800,239	16,594,804
1950	24,869,000	5,700,000	19,169,000

SOURCE: Golze (1961, 14). Reprinted with permission.

Table 3.2
AREA IRRIGATED IN 17 WESTERN STATES, BY TYPE OF ENTERPRISE

Item and Type of Enterprise	Primary Enterprises (acres)		
	1920	1930	1940
Individual and partnership	6,448,663	6,038,835	6,906,738
Cooperative, incorporated	6,569,690	6,271,334	5,706,606
Cooperative, unincorporated	—	—	907,242
Irrigation district	1,822,887	3,452,275	3,514,702
Reclamation district	—	—	59,052
Commercial	1,635,027	999,838	855,166
Bureau of Reclamation	1,254,569	1,485,028	1,824,004
Bureau of Indian Affairs	284,551	331,840	515,765
State	5,620	11,472	16,995
City and/or sewage	40,146	121,218	83,457
Other	531,735	233,016	5,316
TOTAL	18,592,888	18,944,856	20,395,043

SOURCE: Golze (1961, 99). Reprinted with permission.

ventures, including incorporated and unincorporated mutual companies, and irrigation districts had surpassed individuals and partnerships in numbers of acres irrigated. See Table 3.2. Even though public development greatly increased after passage of the Reclamation Act of 1902, private development continued to provide a significant portion of new irrigation development.

In spite of the financial failure of many of the initial private attempts at irrigation development, Elwood Mead, writing in 1903, concluded that corporate capital investment in canals

> has been the leading factor in promoting agricultural growth of the western two-fifths of the United States. It has been the agency through which millions of dollars have been raised and expended, thousands of miles of canals constructed, and hundreds of thousands of acres of land reclaimed. It has been the chief agency in replacing temporary wooden structures by massive headworks of steel and masonry, and, by the employment of the best engineering talent and the introduction of better methods of construction, has promoted the economy and success with which water is now distributed and used. (Mead 1903, 57)

In discussing the contractual benefits of the Colorado ditch companies, Mead, one of the leading irrigation experts of his day, concluded that "if the water of streams is public property, the public should show the same business ability in disposing of its property as those to whom its control is transferred. Colorado can learn something about the management of the water of streams by studying how canal companies dispose of the water which they appropriate" (Mead 1903, 167).

Conclusion

During the last half of the 19th century, the foundation was laid for effective water markets. Following the doctrine of prior appropriation, water rights were defined and enforced and made transferable. In part, it was a sense of justice that led the early settlers to allocate water rights on the basis of "first in time, first in right." Out of this doctrine grew an efficient set of institutions that allowed individual actors in the marketplace to determine the uses of water most beneficial to them at the time. Authority was linked to responsibility, giving water owners the incentive to seek out the highest and best uses of the resource. The scarcity of water increased the benefits of activities designed to establish and enforce exclusivity. Therefore, it is not surprising to find that in Montana, Wyoming, Colorado, and New Mexico, where rainfall averages 15 inches per year, the common law riparian doctrine was eventually abrogated, while in North Dakota, South Dakota, Nebraska, Kansas, Oklahoma, and Texas, it was retained in a modified form. The evolution of water law on the Great Plains was a response to the benefits and costs of defining and enforcing rights to a valuable resource.

With an efficient set of water institutions in place, individuals undertook projects to deliver water where it was demanded. Well-defined, exclusive land and water rights provided the necessary tenure security to stimulate private investment. A variety of organizational structures were used to mobilize the necessary capital for building dams to store water and aqueducts to deliver it. The leaders of the reclamation movement at the turn of the century were correct in asserting that without the application of water, lands west of the 100th meridian would not be very productive. They failed to recognize, however, how effectively private institutions and markets could serve this purpose. Thousands of miles of ditches were constructed and millions of acres blossomed as a result of entrepreneurial efforts to use water.

None of this should imply that water rights and markets are without defects. Resources had to be used to define and enforce water rights and to resolve disputes over those rights. Disputes continually arose over who was first in time and what quantities of water were claimed. Moreover, water markets operated in a region and time where information traveled slowly and risks were great. As a result, it was not easy to mobilize capital to invest in water development. The fact that the lands upon which most of the irrigation development occurred were not privately owned, and therefore could not be used to secure the contributors' investments, limited the pool of potential investors even more.

The western frontier was an experiment with the evolution of property rights. Because the actors in that experiment had to bear the consequences of their actions, they had an incentive to develop institutions that got the incentives right. Because water was a limiting factor in agriculture and mining, it was critical to provide incentives for private owners to invest in delivering water to where it was most productive. The prior appropriation doctrine effectively got the incentives right. Though water scarcity has increased during the 20th century, however, water institutions seem to have regressed in a way that has lost sight of the importance of individual incentives.

44

Notes

1. See Anderson and Hill (1995).

2. The doctrine of prior appropriation is that body of state law under which individuals can acquire a water right by diverting water from a watercourse and applying it to a beneficial use. One's prior right to water is determined by the date on which he or she first applied the water to a beneficial use, known as the priority date. In times of shortage, older, or senior, rights must be satisfied before newer, or junior, appropriators may take their water. The doctrine places no limitation on the place of use, and appropriative rights are transferable. Nonuse of a water right may be considered abandonment and result in its forfeiture. Although the doctrine arose in state constitutional and case law, eventually it was codified in state statutes and tailored to suit the needs of each individual western state.

3. *Hoffman v. Stone*, 7 Cal. 46, 48 (1957).

4. *Weaver v. Eureka Lake Co.*, 15 Cal. 271, 175 (1860).

5. *Butte Canal and Ditch Co. v. Vaughan*, 11 Cal. 143, 152 (1858).

6. For a discussion of the problem, see Anderson and Hill (1990).

7. See also Dunbar (1983, 31–32). The climate of land ownership in California was conducive to development corporations because speculators had acquired thousands of acres under the federal land laws such as the Desert Lands Act of 1877. Although the federal legislation was designed to convey land to individuals in 160-acre parcels, speculators used bribery, dummy entrymen, and manipulation of the laws to appropriate considerably larger tracts. As land values increased, these individuals sold and developed their holdings in various ways, including the use of development corporations (Worster 1985, 98).

8. See generally Smith 1984.

9. For example, the Tempe Irrigating Canal Company, organized in 1870, constructed irrigation works to distribute 11,000 miner's inches of water from the Salt River in Arizona (Dunbar 1983, 29–30).

10. The Big Ditch Company was organized to purchase a project constructed by the Minnesota and Montana Land and Improvement Company west of Billings, Montana, in 1900 (Dunbar 1983, 29–30).

11. Utah passed irrigation district legislation in 1865, but it did not give districts the power to issue bonds, thus leaving them powerless to raise revenue for construction of new projects (Worster 1985, 79; Huffman 1953, 75).

12. The basis for including in the district all land located within its geographical boundaries was that all property would increase in value once the surrounding lands were irrigated. Some states provided for exemption of property from the district if its owner applied to withdraw it (Wyoming), the land would not be benefitted by the district (California), or it was located in a town or city (Oregon) (Chandler 1913, 135).

13. But see McDevitt (1994), who presents evidence that state certification of irrigation and district bonds in California, beginning in 1913, strengthened the ability of districts to fund projects.

4. Politics and Water Don't Mix

The system of water rights that evolved during the late 19th and early 20th centuries was by no means perfect. When return flows were claimed by downstream users, conflicts resulted as upstream users changed the amount or location of diversion, leaving less water to flow downstream. Capital markets were in their infancy, so some economical water projects were probably not funded. Because of economies of scale and imperfect capital markets, owners of delivery systems no doubt had some market power. Third-party effects also existed on the frontier, where the first-in-time, first-in-right attitude often allowed pollution to foul downstream flows. In general, frontiersmen were experimenting with new institutional arrangements that were imperfect and could not possibly establish a set of water rights that took account of all contingencies.

The imperfections in the system, however, did not provide sufficient reason for the extent of governmental intervention that occurred during the 20th century. The early development of water institutions took place outside the framework of formal government where private contracting formed the basis of water rights and markets. Eastern institutions and laws were often not suited to the resource endowments of the American West and therefore were modified or abandoned by the pragmatists on the frontier. However, as formal courts and judicial procedures were established, lawyers brought with them the baggage of eastern law and the formal powers of the federal government. As a result, it was not long before the institutions that evolved through spontaneous order were changed. Perhaps the Colorado mining district knew what it was doing when it resolved that "no lawyer be permitted to practice law in this district under penalty of not more than 50 nor less than 20 lashes, and be forever banished from the district."[1]

Rent Seeking at the Water Trough

Economists define rent as the return from using a resource exceeding the value of that resource in other uses. Rents, therefore, provide a dynamic force for resource allocation because they motivate entrepreneurs to try to capture them by moving resources from lower to higher valued uses. Of course, successful entrepreneurs attract competition from others replicating the activity in an effort also to capture rents, and to the extent those competitors are successful, rents are competed away. It is this entrepreneurial activity and the competitive process that expand the size of the economic pie by improving resource allocation.

Consider rents in the context of water. Suppose that water from a river is being diverted to irrigate wheat and that an acre-foot of water applied in this way adds $20 to the value of the crop. Now suppose that an entrepreneur sees a way of applying the same water to another crop like grapes where its value is $50. By reallocating water from wheat production into grape production, the entrepreneur can capture $30 in economic rents. Of course, as soon as other farmers recognize the profit potential they will follow suit, expanding grape production, reducing wheat production, and driving up the price of water. This expands the size of the economic pie because water is reallocated from the lower valued wheat to the higher valued grapes.

Rents can also be obtained, however, by redistributing the economic pie using the coercive powers of government. Suppose, for example, that the government is willing to tax a segment of the population to provide a subsidy for an irrigation project that will allow grape production. If water is free to the grape farmer but costs taxpayers $60 per acre-foot and produces additional grapes worth $50, the grape farmer is clearly better off. Those who obtain the subsidized water from the project capture rents equal to the difference between what they have to pay and what the water is worth to them. In that process, taxpayers lose part of their income, but grape growers receiving the subsidized irrigation water enjoy an increase in their wealth. In other words, rents are created for the grape grower at the expense of the taxpayer. Because one side's loss is the other's gain, both will have an incentive to influence the political outcome. Taxpayers, if organized, would lobby against the project, and grape growers would lobby in its favor. This win-lose game of redistribution ultimately reduces the size of the economic pie in two ways. First, in many cases the cost of supplying the water is greater than the value of the increased production. For example,

water from the Central Utah Project that is in the process of comple-
tion will cost taxpayers approximately $300 per acre-foot but will
produce crops worth only $30 per acre-foot. Given that farmers will
pay only $3 for each acre-foot, irrigators will capture rents. Second,
rent seeking reduces the size of the pie by diverting resources from
productive activities toward influencing the political sector. Both
potential winners and losers will spend time and money fighting
for and against the redistribution, respectively. In the end wealth
will be redistributed but nothing more will be produced.

Of course there are legal barriers to governmental redistribution
such as the takings clause of the Constitution,[2] but it is impossible
to plug all the holes in the rent-seeking dam. Especially in the case
of water, special interest groups have found ways around rent-
seeking barriers. But rent seeking is always justified by arguments
that disguise the true intent of tax subsidies and water reallocation.
The justification has centered on the argument that water is unique,
that it is a necessity of life, and that scale economies in storage and
delivery require governmental involvement. As early as the writing
of legal commentator William Blackstone the stage was set for government ownership of water when he asserted that "water is a
moving, wandering thing, and must of necessity continue to be
common by the law of nature; so that I can only have a temporary,
transient, usufructuary property therein" (quoted in Webb 1931,
434). Building on this assertion, most states grant only usufructuary
water rights and hence retain extensive regulatory powers. John
Wesley Powell's 1878 survey of the arid West emphasized the importance of water to life and entrenched the idea that water is too
precious to be left to the vagaries of the market.

While it is true that water could make the "desert bloom even as
a rose" as John Wesley Powell said and that water is a moving,
wandering thing, it is not so remarkable that it requires government
to control its allocation. Water certainly is necessary for life. But
clothing and shelter are also necessities, and there is no justification
for having government control their allocation.

> This is not to deny that, as a commodity, water has its special
> features; for example, its supply is provided by nature partly
> as a store and partly as a flow, and it is available without
> cost in some locations but rather expensive to transport to
> others. Whatever reason we cite, however, the alleged unique

> *importance* of water disappears upon analysis. (Hirshleifer,
> DeHaven, and Milliman 1960, 4–5)

Nonetheless, it was this uniqueness that "led to the near-universal view that private ownership is unseemly or dangerous for a type of property so uniquely the common concern of all" (Hirshleifer, DeHaven, and Milliman 1960, 367).

Paraphrasing a section of the Water Rights Act of Iowa (substituting land for water), Hirshleifer et al. (1960, 367) illustrate the absurdity of the uniqueness argument:

> *Land* occurring in any valley, or along any water course or
> around any other natural body of water in the state, is thereby
> declared to be public *land* and the public wealth of the people
> of the State of Iowa and subject to use in accordance with
> the provisions of this act, and the control and development
> and use of *land* for all beneficial purposes shall be in the
> state, which, in the exercise of its police powers, shall take
> such measures as shall perpetuate full utilization and protec-
> tion of the *land* resources of the State of Iowa.

Although most people would not accept this reasoning for the control of land resources, it has been used to further government intervention into the water allocation process.

Can Markets Allocate Water?

Those who support government involvement in water allocation usually focus on three types of market failure: monopoly, imperfect capital markets, and externalities. If any of these actually exists, a case can be made for government intervention. But even then we must ask whether the cure is worse than the disease.

Monopoly

Early water reformers feared that private water supplies would constitute a natural monopoly, which would allow suppliers to charge high prices for the resource. William Ellsworth Smythe stated the fear clearly:

> If we admit the theory that water flowing from the melting
> snows and gathered in lake and stream is a private commod-
> ity belonging to him who first appropriates it, regardless of
> the use for which he designs it, we have all the conditions
> for a hateful economic servitude. Next to bottling the air and

sunshine no monopoly of natural resources would be fraught with more possibilities of abuse than the attempt to make merchandise of water in an arid land. (quoted in Allston 1978, 128)

Even though John Wesley Powell recognized that the cheapest and most dependable source of water was from water companies selling at a profit, he was concerned with "the danger of an evil monopoly which would charge an exorbitant price and force the homesteaders to pay a heavy tribute" (quoted in Aliston 1978, 129). This concern contributed significantly to the government's growing involvement in the control of water rights and distribution.

The fear of monopoly, however, has little empirical basis. While it is true that water companies sold a product whose demand was fairly inelastic, there is no evidence that these companies were earning substantial monopoly profits (recall the discussion in Chapter 3). If one company raised its price too much trying to appropriate settlers' rents, the settlers could, without too much trouble, move to lands irrigated by cheaper water. As technology was developed that allowed irrigation from groundwater sources, the possibility of competition was even greater. Further, those commercial companies that were the only suppliers of water to a region had, for the most part, only one group of buyers. This situation led to possibilities for a bilateral monopoly, wherein irrigation companies *and* farmers bargained over the price of water. Finally, water companies could effectively execute monopoly power only if they could withhold their product from the market, an action requiring large storage facilities. Companies may have been able to hold back enough water to keep prices up temporarily, but eventually the water would have to be released, even from the largest facilities. When this water was released, the courts held that the water was free to be claimed by others. Therefore, the possibility of increasing prices by restricting output was highly unlikely.

Inadequate Capital

Another reason given to support governmental alternatives to water allocation especially at the turn of the century was that capital markets were unable to provide the investment funds necessary for large projects. Alfred Golze (1961, 12) stated that "while private enterprise had managed to bring under successful irrigation an impressive and substantial acreage of land, a point had been reached where further development would need stronger support by the federal and state governments." In other words, additional and larger water projects would have to be subsidized by government. Even though water reformers recognized that capital markets had raised enough funds to build many irrigation projects, their visions encompassed reclamation on such a large scale that capital requirements were enormous. In 1902, it was difficult to envision a world capital market that would be as extensive as it is today. And even though capital markets have developed to support massive investments in infrastructure, they could hardly compete with federal reclamation projects, especially when the latter did not have to pass the cost-benefit scrutiny of the marketplace. As we will see below, those projects would not have been profitable for private enterprise and existed only because of public subsidies.

Externalities

The third argument for governmental intervention in water allocation has greater legitimacy: because of the physical nature of water, its use can produce third-party effects, or externalities. If one user pollutes a stream, the pollution moves downstream to affect other users. If one user pumps water from a common ground-water source, other users' pumping costs are affected. In some cases, such concerns are warranted, making the possibility of externalities one of the more powerful economic arguments used to justify government intervention.

The fact is, however, that the evolving system of water rights on the frontier was internalizing many of the external problems. In the case of pollution from mining operations, the courts "issued injunctions when debris buried the claims of miners below, destroyed the growing crops of preemption claimants, filled irrigation ditches and poisoned their fruit trees, or split the hoses of hydraulic miners downstream" (McCurdy 1976, 262). In *Jennison v. Kirk*, a California case in which a miner was held liable for damages when debris washed away the ditch of another appropriator, Judge Stephen Field ruled that "no system of law with which we are acquainted tolerates the use of one's property in that way so as to destroy the property of another."[3] Externalities do present real problems in any system of water allocation, but they are overused as an argument for governmental intervention in water markets.

Rent seekers who used the coercive powers of government to obtain control of water rights or subsidies for irrigation projects made very successful use of these arguments against water markets. Backed by such public reclamation entrepreneurs as John Wesley Powell, Arthur P. Davis, and Elwood Mead, politicians saw an opportunity to provide their constituents with rents. Rent seekers claimed that

> federal control would promote "scientific" management of land and water resources, simultaneously "conserving" and "developing" them; prevent the monopolization of water by corporations and "speculators"; streamline the system for establishing and enforcing water rights; and encourage the development of rural democracy by war veterans and other deserving pioneers. These policies received the strong backing of at least three presidents including the two Roosevelts and Herbert Hoover. (Cuzan 1983, 24)

Limits on the Prior Appropriation Doctrine

The American West was evolving an effective system of water rights, provisions had been made for definition and enforcement, and rights were transferable. All the necessary ingredients existed for an effective water market to allocate the scarce resource. Given this evolution, how and why did the transformation to centralized control take place?

The California court, under the direction of Judge Field, recognized the potential for "'using the organized power of the community to divest the equitably acquired claims of men who had evinced a growth inducing 'incentive to improvement'" (McCurdy 1976, 265). In spite of the court's insight, the divestiture of water rights began in the late 19th century, when inefficient restrictions began to be placed on the prior appropriation doctrine. State laws had come to recognize prior rights, but western state constitutions and statutes were moving toward the establishment of public ownership of water. Appropriators under those systems received only a usufructuary right (a right to use the water), not an actual ownership right, so state legislatures felt free to declare that the *corpus* of water was state property. Making that distinction contrasted sharply with existing land laws and created tension between use and ownership by making it much easier for rent seekers to exploit the potential for gain from regulation of water use.

State Administration of Water Rights

As population and demands for water in the West grew, so did the number of disputes over ownership. When water was abundant, it did not pay to get involved in disputes. But as the value of water rose, it became rational to devote resources to the fight. From the outset of the doctrine of appropriation, courts were involved in settling conflicting claims, with the costs being borne by those directly involved. But some found it profitable to have states subsidize the process. In 1874, for example, irrigators in Colorado "met in convention to demand legislation for public determination and establishment of rights of appropriation, and the state superintended distribution of water in accordance with the thus settled titles" (Lasky 1929, 173). The transformation from prior appropriation to administrative law eventually brought with it requirements for the filing of new claims, first at the county, then the state level; the limitations on the size of "excessive" claims and legal specifications on the duty of water;[4] attachment of water rights to specific land tracts; the disallowing of ownership to water by canal companies that did not irrigate lands of their own; regulation of canal company rates by states and counties; state encouragement of the formation of irrigation districts with the power to tax, condemn property, and sell bonds to finance construction of irrigation works and buy out water companies; legislative determination of what constitutes "beneficial use," along with the ranking of uses by classes; prohibition on sale of water rights beyond state or irrigation district boundaries; administrative allocation of water during periods of "drought;" and the establishment of the centralized bureaucracy headed by a state engineer or water commissioner to administer policies and judicial decrees and, in some states, undertake irrigation projects (Cuzan 1983, 21–22).

The Ubiquitous Riparian Doctrine

Judges also contributed to the erosion of the prior appropriation doctrine by failing to abandon the common law precedent of riparian rights used in the eastern United States. As defined in an 1845 Maine supreme court case, under the riparian doctrine,

every owner of land through which a natural stream of water
flows, has a usufruct in the stream, as it passes along, and
has an equal right with those above and below him to the
natural flow of the water in its accustomed channel, without
unreasonable detention or diminution in quantity or quality,
and to the reasonable use of the stream for every beneficial
purpose to which it can be applied, and none can make
any use of it prejudicial to the other owners, unless he has
acquired a right to do so by license, grant, or prescription.[5]

Some elements of the riparian doctrine led directly to more public
control of water allocation in the West. First, with riparian ownership
the resource is held in common, requiring regulations to prevent
the tragedy of the commons that accompanies open access. Second,
because diversions necessarily were prejudicial to other riparian
owners, farmers and miners sought and obtained "license, grant, or
prescription," in the courts and through legislation.

Miners had presented the courts with a fairly well-settled doctrine
for defining, enforcing, and transferring rights. But as disputes came
before the courts, riparian arguments were continually introduced.
As early as 1853, the California Supreme Court held in *Eddy v.
Simpson*[6] that "the owner of land through which a stream flows,
merely transmits the water over its surface, having the right to its
reasonable use during its passage. The right is not in the corpus of
the water, and only continues with its possession." Though the
ruling was subsequently overturned, a riparian precedent was established in California. Courts continued to hold that rights were only
usufructuary and that they were lost once the water left the possession of its appropriator. John Clayberg (1902, 97–98) saw how riparian principles were contributing to the evolution of the prior appropriation doctrine:

There never seemed any doubt in the mind of the court about
the true position to be taken, but it is almost amusing to read
their statements as to whether the principle announced was
in consonance with the common law, or in departure from
it, because of the conditions and necessities of the case. In
one case the court would say that they did not depart from
the common law but found principles there insufficient to
sustain their holdings. In another, the doctrine would be
announced that the common law was inapplicable, and that
the reasons of that law did not exist in California.

The inability of lawyers and judges to put aside riparian precedent and the resultant mixture of riparian with prior appropriation doctrine led to a confusion that stifled the effective establishment of private property rights in water. Without such rights, the confusion could only be resolved through legislation and administration.

The doctrine that had evolved through the decentralized actions of miners and irrigators was slowly degenerating to the status of state-controlled permits and licenses. As early as 1929, Moses Lasky declared that the principle of appropriation had reached its zenith. The water rights that evolved in the quasi-anarchistic setting of the frontier were replaced by permits to use state-owned water, with decisions on water use ultimately made by state officials. Lasky (1929, 162) argued that the changes were causing a move *away* "from various forms of extreme individualism and vested property rights of substance in water to . . . the economic distribution of state-owned water by a state administrative machinery through state-oriented conditional privileges of user."

Federal Involvement—Navigation, Commerce, and Reserved Rights

The commerce clause of the Constitution also contributed to increased governmental regulation of water rights because it granted the federal government the right to regulate navigable waters to protect interstate commerce. But the federal government's commerce clause power was much broader than just regulation of water for navigation.[7] Any action affecting interstate commerce on the nation's navigable waterways was subject to federal regulation.[8] A power known as the navigation servitude[9] empowered the federal government to ensure unimpeded navigation on navigable waterways and to remove obstructions or improve navigable waterways below the high waterline without compensating the adjacent landowner.

Whether waterways were subject to federal regulation under the commerce clause depended on whether the waterway was navigable. Navigable waterways were defined as those waters used or susceptible of being used in their ordinary and natural condition as highways for commerce over which trade and travel could be conducted.[10] Because the navigability test was so broad, large numbers of streams and rivers were subject to federal regulation and the navigation servitude (Goplerud 1995, 8).[11] Thus, expansive federal powers over navigation effectively prevented private parties from developing reservoirs or rivers. In 1957, Charles Corker noted the implications of the federal government's power over navigation:

> The Congress and the courts have been content to treat the word "navigation" as an open sesame to constitutionality. So long as Congress uses the word in a statute and the case relates to something moist, the Court takes at face value the declaration that the legislation is in furtherance of navigation. Moreover, the tests of what constitutes a navigable stream have been stretched to embrace most of the waters of the United States. . . . (Corker 1957, 616–17)

Another federal power that served to undermine water rights was the doctrine of federal reserved water rights. This doctrine arose under the property clause of the Constitution and involved the reservation by the United States government of vast tracts of land in the West for Indian reservations, national parks, and national forests. Accordingly, when the federal government retained land in the federal estate, it implicitly reserved to itself, as of the date of the land reservation, all unappropriated water on the reserved lands needed to fulfill the purposes for which the land was reserved (Sax and Abrams 1986, 494). Since 1908, the U.S. Supreme Court has upheld these claims.[12] Unfortunately, in spite of the accepted validity of the federal reserved water rights, most of the rights were not quantified in the late 19th and early 20th century when the lands were set aside.

To understand how the doctrine can cloud water rights, consider the context in which reserved water rights evolved. The federal government established the Fort Belknap Reservation in Montana in 1888 but did not quantify any water rights and did not divert water for irrigation, the main criterion for claiming an appropriative water right. Subsequently, settlers came to the area and developed irrigation systems, appropriating water from the Milk River, assuming that the water was unappropriated under Montana law. When the Indians began diverting water and disturbing the settlers' claims, the settlers built dams and reservoirs upstream of the reservation to ensure irrigation of their non-Indian lands. Those projects in turn reduced water availability for the reservation, prompting the U.S. government to sue the settlers in its capacity as trustee for the Indians. Eventually the court enjoined the settlers from diverting any waters that interfered with Indian water rights, finding that "when the Indians made the treaty granting rights to the United States, they reserved the right to use the water of the Milk River, at least to an extent reasonably necessary to irrigate their lands."[13] Rodney Smith (1992, 169) summarizes the ambiguities that ensued:

> The *Winters* decision set the parameters for Indian water rights litigation in terms of the amount of water "reasonably necessary for the purposes of the reservation." In assessing what constituted reasonably necessary, the court would not restrict itself to current uses but would also consider "future requirements." Without specific criteria for determining what constitutes "reasonably necessary" and "future requirements," the court raised the specter of complex factual inquiry into the economics of water use on and off the reservation and suggested possible consideration of the equitable interests of the parties.

Ever since, there has been a cloud over the quantity and security of water rights claimed under the prior appropriation doctrine when federal lands are involved. To make matters worse, the federal government has begun claiming reserved water for wilderness areas and national parks where it is even more difficult to quantify how much water was implicitly reserved.

The Public Trust Doctrine

A final limitation on the prior appropriation doctrine that threatens private water rights and water markets is the public trust doctrine. This common law doctrine, inherited by the United States from Great Britain, was used originally to protect the public's interest in commerce, fishing, and navigation on navigable waterways. More recently, however, the doctrine has been expanded beyond its traditional purposes and used to bring into question long-held water rights. In the 1983 Mono Lake case[14] in California, for example, the court found that the state had a trust responsibility to protect the environment. In that case, the city of Los Angeles was diverting so much water from the Mono Lake basin that aquatic and bird life was being affected. Although Los Angeles was entitled to the water under appropriative rights granted by the state in 1940, the court ruled that the state must reconsider its decision granting the rights in light of its responsibility to protect public trust values, which the court held now included environmental protection.

Six years later the court issued an injunction halting the city's diversions until the lake level rises 2 feet, and limiting them to 12,000 acre-feet per year until the level rises 16 feet, which it is estimated will take at least 20 years (Marston 1994, 15). Los Angeles now has to spend an extra $38 million a year to buy water from other sources. Although the state has agreed to kick in more than $36 million per year over four years for new water projects that will serve the city (*Economist* 1994, 31), the bottom line is that well-settled property rights have been abrogated in the name of an expanded public trust doctrine. If the public trust doctrine is permitted to extend beyond commerce, navigation, and fishing to the environment and trump prior appropriation water rights, there are almost no limits on how states can regulate water use and water marketing.

Administrative and Judicial Rules

By using legislative, administrative, and judicial rules, individuals have been able to regulate water rights and limit water marketing to capture rents. For example, using the argument that the prior appropriation doctrine is "unfair," junior users have persuaded some state legislatures to limit the transfer of water from agriculture by establishing a system of priorities other than first-in-time, first-in-right. Preference is usually given to domestic and agricultural uses, with commercial and industrial uses having a lower priority. Therefore, even if commercial and industrial users purchase senior water rights, those rights may not be transferred to nonagricultural uses.

Similarly, legislation requiring forfeiture of rights for nonuse has created the "use-it-or-lose-it" principle; if water is not diverted, it is considered abandoned and therefore available to other users. While such laws were passed in an effort to prevent waste, they have created waste by encouraging water owners to use all the water to which they own rights, even if less would be sufficient for their purposes. Water rights owners are discouraged from conserving water because of the risk of losing their rights to the amounts not used.

Perhaps the most obvious example of rent seeking occurs when allocative decisions are placed in the hands of a state agency or a court. With an agency or court empowered to allocate or reallocate water, users have an incentive to invest in influencing the agency's or court's decision. In the state of Montana, for example, the Board of Natural Resources and Conservation is empowered to reserve unclaimed water for future uses. Only governmental entities such as cities, counties, state and federal agencies, and irrigation districts are eligible to apply for reserved water. The board must reserve the water for future uses based on anticipated needs and can reallocate reservations at a later date if it feels that the water is more urgently "needed" for another use. Needless to say, the process for determining future needs involves considerable discretion on the part of the board. Therefore, the competing governmental entities invest considerable time and money to influence the board's reservation decisions. Ultimately the rent-seeking game is zero sum as one party's gain is another's loss.

Rent-seeking efforts have also placed restrictions on the transferability of water rights. Frank Trelease has argued that such restrictions had their roots in the "many early adjudications that gave the irrigators far more water than they really needed, so that the appropriator not infrequently sold his unused water to which he really had no right" (Trelease 1957, 315). Through restrictions on transferability, some water users were able to gain by obtaining those "excessive" water rights. Hirshleifer, DeHaven, and Milliman (1960, 235) have observed that "an attempt to correct past mistakes in vesting property rights by simple deprivation or confiscation may have only distributional effects (except insofar as insecurity of rights affects incentives of others) but freezing the right to the original use of water has an adverse efficiency effect from which the community as a whole loses." In Montana, for example, a statute in effect from 1979 to 1985 prohibited the transfer and sale of water for use in coal slurry pipelines, suggesting that the state's legislators somehow knew that coal slurry would never provide the highest and best use for water. And they may have been right, but limiting uses through laws and constitutional rules makes it very costly to adjust to changing market conditions. To the extent that restricted uses could compete with other uses, such provisions keep the price of water artificially low, providing a gain to some users at the expense of others.

Legal restrictions have essentially broken apart the foundation for an effective system of water rights that was built in the "lawless West," as noted by Cuzan (1983, 20–21):

> It is evident that the long-term trend of federal policy has
> been to mobilize financial, administrative, political, constitu-
> tional and judicial resources . . . to gain . . . control of western
> waters. . . . The appropriation doctrine has been undermined,
> water rights have been virtually expropriated and converted
> into licenses or permits, and control over western waters has
> been centralized in state and federal governments.

Instead of relying on markets, many water allocation decisions
have been turned over to a rent-seeking process that uses valuable
resources without guaranteeing efficiency or equity. If we are to
avoid a water crisis through a market solution, we must return to
the original principles of the appropriation doctrine.[15] Unfortunately,
this has been made all the more difficult by federal intervention in
the supply and allocation of water through subsidized irrigation
projects.

Reclaiming the West with Public Funds

Just as limits on the appropriation doctrine have hindered water
markets, public reclamation has replaced much private enterprise
and created a bureaucratic pork barrel that continues to thrive even
when other public funds are cut. What was the rationale for public
investment in reclamation? How did it come about? What are its
consequences?

In his *Report on the Lands of the Arid Region* in 1879, John Wesley
Powell expressed concern about water monopoly, writing, "[Water
rights] will be gradually absorbed by a few. Monopolies of water
will be secured, and the whole agriculture of the country will be
tributary thereto—a condition of affairs which an American citizen
having in view the interests of the largest number of people cannot
contemplate with favor" (Powell 1879, 43). This concern, coupled
with the argument that capital markets were not efficient enough
to fund reclamation projects, led bureaucratic entrepreneurs to seek
public funds for their large-scale plans to reclaim the American
West.

Two pieces of legislation provided the cornerstone for governmental involvement in reclamation. On the state level, the Wright Act
was passed in California in 1887, providing a statutory basis for
public ownership of irrigation facilities in the form of irrigation
districts. The act established a procedure under which an irrigation

61

district could be formed by a county board of supervisors upon receipt of a petition from 50 or more of the landowners in the area followed by a favorable vote of two-thirds of the affected electorate (Dunbar 1983, 33; Pisani 1992, 102). If half the landowners holding 50 percent of the affected land petitioned for a public irrigation district, county commissioners were directed to call a special election in which a two-thirds majority was needed to establish the district. Once established, the irrigation district's board of directors could incur financial obligations, impose property taxes, and establish water prices.[16] Even though the policies had to be approved by a majority of the voters, they paved the way for collective action to influence the distribution of benefits and costs of irrigation projects. When other western states adopted similar legislation during the next few decades, the door was open for rent seeking through irrigation districts. Unlike the private mutual companies, public irrigation districts could use property taxes to finance projects, creating the potential for income redistribution. Further, because neither the board of directors nor individual water users were residual claimants, the incentive for efficient pricing was greatly reduced. Irrigators who could keep the price of water below its opportunity cost received a subsidy paid for by water district taxes.

Between 1920 and 1950, public irrigation districts in California grew from 577,000 irrigated acres to 1,821,000 irrigated acres. During that time, the number of mutual irrigation companies and commercial enterprises declined (Smith 1983, 172). District organization reached its peak in the 1920s, while gross acreages of active districts remained fairly constant until 1910, grew dramatically until 1925, and stabilized thereafter.

Table 4.1 shows the increase in the amount of acres irrigated by irrigation districts for 17 western states between 1910 and 1978. Barton Thompson (1993, 689) summarizes the demise of commercial companies and the rise of governmental institutions:

> Although many private businesses supplied water to users up through the 1920s, commercial companies have long since been eclipsed by mutuals and governmental institutions, both of which are controlled by their customers. . . . [C]ommercial companies supplied water to approximately 10 percent of irrigated acreage in 1920, but they serviced only 0.5 percent of the acreage in 1978. Governmental institutions also dominate the market for domestic water. . . .

Table 4.1
HISTORICAL SOURCE OF IRRIGATION WATER BY IRRIGATED
ACREAGE
IN 17 WESTERN STATES (%)

Year	Self-Supplied	Mutuals	Commercial	Public Water District	Other
1910	—	79.3	10.6	3.8	6.3
1920	—	80.0	9.5	9.5	n/a
1930	8.4	44.5	7.1	24.5	15.5
1940	21.8	38.4	4.9	20.7	14.2
1950	39.4	38.4	2.9	20.4	5.3
1959	43.0	28.6	1.3	22.5	4.6
1969	41.6	26.5	1.2	27.9	2.8
1978	51.1	20.6	0.5	24.7	3.1

SOURCE: Thompson (1993, 690). Reprinted with permission.

Rodney Smith's empirical analysis of the choice between private and public irrigation ownership in California supports the hypothesis that public districts provided a means for obtaining rents.[17] While mutual water companies charge direct prices, public irrigation districts collect taxes, forming an implicit price. With mutual water companies, when individual water use increases, payments to the company increase, whereas with public irrigation districts, an increase in an individual's water use influences not only his own property tax liabilities but also the liabilities of all other landowners in the district. Therefore, a farmer in a public irrigation district receives a direct benefit, and the costs are diffused over the district population. Smith (1983) demonstrated that water demand in mutual water companies is much more responsive to direct charges than water demand in public irrigation districts is to indirect taxes. Pricing via taxes allows individuals to use public irrigation districts to redistribute income. Further, it promotes inefficient water use by allowing the irrigator to pay prices that do not reflect full costs.

Although the Wright Act provided a local mechanism for subsidizing water projects, the Newlands Reclamation Act of 1902 took the process one step further by launching the federal government into the water reclamation business in the West. By 1900, advocates of federal irrigation development had generated sufficient support to include federal reclamation planks in the Republican, Democratic, and Silver Republican parties' platforms. In 1901, federal reclamation legislation was drafted by Frederick H. Newell, chief hydrographer for the U.S. Geological Survey. Support in Congress for the legislation came from western senators and representatives led by Francis G. Newlands of Nevada. Not surprisingly, eastern and midwestern legislators opposed the reclamation bill as redistributive because it benefitted only a small portion of the population (the West) at the expense of the entire nation (Mayhew and Gardner 1994, 71-73). They also feared that farmers in the eastern states would suffer from the competition created by western agriculture made possible by federal reclamation. Moreover, farmers were already producing surpluses. Finally, the fear of monopoly of the federally developed irrigation water and reclaimed lands was ever-present in the reasoning of foes of national reclamation as it was in general in that Progressive era (Allston 1978, 73, 87, 109–115; Robinson 1979, 16).

Supporters of federal reclamation overcame the opposition by propounding classic Progressive ideals. Language was included in the reclamation legislation providing that the cost of the water projects developed by the federal government would be repaid from proceeds from the sale of public lands in the western states as well as by the actual recipients of the water (Mayhew and Gardner 1994, 83–84). The fear of monopoly was addressed by limiting delivery of project water to farms of 160 acres or less. Crops produced by federally reclaimed lands would be consumed locally or shipped to Asian markets rather than allowed to threaten eastern U.S. markets. In addition, reclaimed lands would serve as a safety outlet for surplus urban populations and create new markets for eastern manufactured goods and labor (Pisani 1992, 286–87; Penick 1974, 117). Key to the shift of western water development from private enterprise to governmental control, however, was the firm belief by federal reclamation proponents in the coordination, centralization, and extension of governmental authority in general, coupled with orderly development of the nation's natural resources through scientific management by disinterested engineers (Penick 1974, 121; Lilley and Gould 1966, 59).[18]

Although federal reclamation legislation failed to pass Congress in 1901, a year later the Newlands Reclamation Act of 1902 was enacted. Under the act, federal reclamation projects were to be funded from the proceeds of public land sales, with each western state receiving reclamation revenues according to its proportional contribution to the sales. Construction costs were to be repaid within 10 years by recipients of a project's water, though no interest charges were to be levied. By limiting water delivery to farms of 160 acres or less and making rights to the water appurtenant to the land, the act was intended to promote Jeffersonian democracy.

Those initial provisions were relatively harmless in subsidies to reclamation water users, because the program was to pay for itself. Nevertheless, some were skeptical about the act from the beginning.

> A New York Congressman estimated that the plan would ultimately cost the country billions of dollars. Dalzell of Pennsylvania believed it a plan to "unlock the doors of the treasury." Mr. Cannon of Illinois dubbed the bill a "direct grant in an indirect way." Payne of New York was of a like mind, while Hepburn of Iowa insisted "that this is a thinly veneered and thinly disguised attempt to make the government, from its general fund, pay for this great work—great in extent, great in expenditure, but not great in results. . . . " (Hibbard 1965, 442)

In retrospect, the critics were right. The Reclamation Act has provided substantial subsidies to irrigators from federal projects at substantial cost to the national treasury. In so doing, the act has also encouraged both irrigators and agents of the bureaucracy to engage in rent seeking.

In providing for interest-free repayment of construction costs over 10 years by water users, the Reclamation Act created a substantial subsidy for the farmers who settled on project lands. Rent seeking resulted when the farmers were unable to meet their obligations[19] and sought extensions of the repayment period. Several extensions and deferrals were enacted by Congress in the 1920s and 1930s, substantially increasing the subsidy created by reclamation projects. In 1914, the period of repayment was extended from 10 to 20 years, and a graduated repayment schedule was adopted (Baker and Conkling 1930, 394; Wahl 1989, 29). In 1921, 1922, 1923, and 1924, Congress used depressed agricultural prices to justify deferrals on payments of both the interest-free loans and project operation and maintenance costs. The 1924 act also modified repayment by classifying the lands within each project according to productivity and apportioning construction costs according to an "ability to pay" standard. The Omnibus Adjustment Act of 1926 extended the repayment period to 40 years. Further deferrals of repayment were granted in the Depression years, culminating in the Reclamation Project Act of 1939. This act provided for a 10-year "development period" following project construction during which no repayment was required and allowed for a 40-year repayment period. The 1939 act also allowed costs exceeding irrigators' "ability to pay" to be paid by revenues from other users of federal projects such as hydropower consumers (Wahl 1989, 29–33; Huffman 1953, 83–86).

Table 4.2 shows the subsidy created by interest-free repayment of project construction costs and its growth resulting from the legislation succeeding the Reclamation Act. The subsidy figures are based on the prevailing interest rate the government could have charged on repayment. The climb in interest rates in the 1970s and 1980s raised the value of the subsidy as high as 95 percent (Wahl 1989, 33).

It was not just irrigators who benefitted from increasing the value of the reclamation subsidy, however. The ability to lengthen the repayment period also produced rents for the Bureau of Reclamation in the form of long-term administrative control of projects because control was not to be relinquished until a certain percentage of construction costs were paid. In many cases this percentage has never been reached.

The Reclamation Act also promoted rent seeking by limiting the size of farms receiving project water to 160 acres or less.[20] Because enforcement of the limit determined the distribution of benefits from federal irrigation programs, irrigators attempted to alter its enforcement in several ways, including multiple ownerships within one family, deeding land to children, selling land and leasing it back, and establishing farm operations with the ownership distributed among several landowners, each owning 160 acres or less (Wahl 1989, 72). The Bureau of Reclamation, in turn, catered to its constituency by loosely and inconsistently enforcing the acreage limitation.

Changes to the original Reclamation Act that allowed a share of repayment to come from other project uses, especially hydropower, substantially added to the subsidies created by interest-free repayment and poor enforcement of the acreage limitation. Those other uses evolved in response to opposition to western irrigation projects

Table 4.2
INTEREST SUBSIDY FOR IRRIGATION CAPITAL COSTS EMBODIED IN GENERAL RECLAMATION LAW

Year	Prevailing Federal Borrowing Rate[c]	Repayment Period (Years)	Interest (%) subsidy[a,b] Assuming No Development Period	Assuming Ten-Year Development Period[d]	Legislation
			—%	—%	
1902	2.7%	10	14%	—	Reclamation Act
1914	3.3	20	42	—	Reclamation Ext. Act.
1926	4.0	40	51	—	Omnibus Adjustment
1939	2.4	40	36	50	Reclamation Proj. Act.[e]
1950	2.3	40	35	48	
1955	2.8	40	40	54	
1960	4.0	40	51	67	
1965	4.3	40	53	69	
1970	7.3	40	67	84	
1975	8.0	40	70	86	
1978	8.4	40	71	87	
1979	9.4	40	74	89	
1980	11.5	40	79	93	
1981	13.9	40	82	95	
1982	13.0	40	81	94	

continued

Table 4.2
INTEREST SUBSIDY FOR IRRIGATION CAPITAL COSTS EMBEDDED IN GENERAL RECLAMATION LAW (*continued*)

Year	Prevailing Federal Borrowing Rate[c]	Repayment Period (Years)	Interest (%) subsidy[a,b]		Legislation
			Assuming No Development Period	Assuming Ten-Year Development Period[d]	
1983	11.1	40	78	92	
1984	12.4	40	80	93	
1985	10.6	40	77	92	

SOURCE: Wahl (1989). Reprinted with permission.

Notes: Dashes mean not applicable. Specific project-authorizing acts may set repayment periods other than those listed here. The table does not reflect granting of deferred payment. Subsidy shown is for a project first placed in service in the year indicated. There would be an additional interest subsidy during the period of construction up to the in-service date.

[a]Value of interest-free repayment is calculated as the present worth of equal annual payments over the repayment period discounted at the prevailing federal borrowing rate. Subsidy to irrigators could exceed the amount shown if, under "ability-to-pay" criteria, repayment is made by other water users (see note e).

[b]Assumes payments are due at the end of each contract year.

[c]Long-term government borrowing rate (bonds with 10 years to maturity).

[d]It is assumed that no payments are made during the development period, which is also interest-free.

[e]The Reclamation Project Act of 1939 provided for a payment-free development period of up to 10 years and also allowed costs to be shared with other water users.

from the Department of Agriculture on the grounds that the projects would aggravate oversupply of farm products. The Bureau of Reclamation countered by introducing multipurpose projects such as Hoover and Grand Coulee Dams. The projects provided not only irrigation but also hydroelectric power, municipal water, flood control, recreation, and improved river navigation. Diversification gave the bureau support from other constituencies and enabled a further subsidization of irrigation. The magnitude of hydropower subsidies for irrigators is shown in Table 4.3.

Multiple-purpose projects fit nicely into the Progressive ideal because they involved development of natural resources, the economy, and society through "rational planning" by experts in the bureaucracy. The Columbia Basin Project exemplified those principles as well as the forces behind multipurpose water projects and the subsidies created by them. Although the CBP accomplished the goals of settling the region with farm families and turning desert into farmland, its costs far exceeded its benefits. The coalition of interests that pushed it through included politicians, business groups, farmers, and land speculators, who sought government allocation of resources with no concern for economic efficiency (Simmons 1994, 109–110).

Construction of Grand Coolee Dam on the Columbia River was authorized and begun in 1933 as part of Franklin D. Roosevelt's Public Works Administration Program. The dam was built to provide irrigation water to 500,000 acres of farmland in the Columbia Basin and hydroelectric power to the Pacific Northwest. As construction progressed, extensive planning for the development of project lands occurred between 1939 and 1942 and culminated with the Columbia Basin Project Act of 1942. That act supposedly provided for orderly settlement and protected against land speculation by transferring tracts of privately owned land exceeding the 160-acre limitation to a large number of settlers.[21] Like other federal projects, the CBP allowed farmers to repay construction costs over 40 years subject to their "ability to pay" (Simmons 1994, 98–104).

Not surprisingly, the CBP created unprecedented rent seeking by farmers who received the water but paid little for it. Simmons (1994, 108) summarizes the ways in which farmers were able to capture additional rents by circumventing the acreage limitation.

> With the help of lawyers, accountants, family, and friends, farmers used nominees, strawmen, trusts, corporate layering,

Table 4.3
THE POWER SUBSIDY

Project	Costs Allocated to Irrigation ($)	Costs to Be Repayed by Irrigators ($)	Irrigation Costs Subsidized by Hydropower Revenues (%)
Central Valley California	$682,152,000	$606,646,000	11.1
Chief Joseph Dam Washington[a]	11,083,200	6,050,000	45.4
Collbran Colorado	6,105,000	1,089,101	82.2
Columbia Basin Washington	745,111,398	135,916,400	81.8
Fryingpan-Arkansas Colorado	69,946,000	50,512,300	27.8
Rogue River Oregon	18,064,000	9,066,500	49.8
San Angelo Texas	8,853,904	4,000,000	54.8
The Dalles Oregon	5,994,000	2,550,000	57.5
Ventura River California	18,273,128	10,746,300	41.2
Washita Basin Oklahoma[b]	10,403,011	8,221,000	21.0

SOURCE: Rucker and Fishback (1983, 62). Reprinted with permission.
[a]Includes costs and repayments from Foster Creek and Greater Wenatchee divisions.
[b]Includes costs and payments from Fort Cobb and Fass divisions.

output contracts, and equitable interests to get around the acreage limitations. Titles often changed hands without the irrigation districts being notified. One method used by CBP farmers was to transfer title to friends, employees, or relatives who then transferred the land back to the original owner. The original owner, however, did not have the deed recorded. This allowed farmers to exceed acreage limitations without the Bureau of Reclamation's knowledge while retaining a protected interest in the land. Acreage limitations also were circumvented by lease-back provisions under which the original owner was given a lifelong lease on the property in exchange for listing his nonfarming children as the owners. Limited partnerships also allowed farmers to control a majority share in land and still qualify for project water.

As of 1959, 70 percent of the estimated cost of the CBP ($773 million) was incurred for irrigation facilities, but irrigators were required to pay only 15 percent. The remaining 85 percent of the cost was paid from hydropower revenues. Since then, additional construction has been completed, raising the cost of the project and the subsidy (Simmons 1994, 107).

Conclusion

Between court cases and public reclamation efforts, the market has been crowded out of many water allocation decisions. In most western states, water is the declared property of the state, the people, or the public. Only in Colorado and New Mexico is this declaration limited to unappropriated water. Writing more than 30 years ago, Hirshleifer et al. concluded (1960, 249) that

> the current trend . . . runs strongly against the development of a system of water law based on individual choice and the market mechanism. . . . The evidence is fairly clear that the tenor of the legislative and judicial edicts . . . is the product of the ignorance of even importantly placed and generally well-informed individuals today about the functioning of economic systems—and, in particular, it is the product of the common though incorrect opinion that the public interest can be served only by political as opposed to market allocation processes. . . . That there are defects in the present systems of private water rights is very clear; but to abolish property rights rather than cure the defects is a drastic and, we believe, unwise remedy.

With few exceptions, legislative and judicial actions have continued to erode the basis of private property rights in water. Lasky's concern in 1929 over the shift from prior appropriation to economic distribution of water by the state was certainly prophetic.

Large-scale federal involvement in reclamation has contributed to the demise of water markets and the promotion of inefficiency.[22]

71

Without proper information and incentives, alternatives to large-scale reclamation have not been considered carefully. For example, Rudolph Ulrich estimated that the costs of bringing desert land into agricultural production were five to fourteen times greater than the costs of clearing, fertilizing, and irrigating lands in the humid Southeast (Ulrich 1953). In 1924, Benjamin Hibbard (1939, 449) concluded:

> In passing the Reclamation Act in 1902 as a nation we clearly forgot those things which were behind, the millions of unoccupied acres of the Mississippi Valley, consisting mostly of fertile, well-watered land needing only to be drained or cleared. Had we really been concerned over the future food supply as we pretended to be, or being so concerned, had we calmly asked how to increase it in the cheapest and easiest manner, certain of the reclamation projects would still be undeveloped....

Reclamation may have made the desert bloom, but there is little economic justification for the blossoms.

Notes

1. Quoted in Beadle (1882, 468).
2. See Anderson and Hill (1980).
3. *Jennison v. Kirk*, 98 U.S. 453, 461 (1878).
4. The duty of water has been defined as the amount of water necessary to produce the maximum amount of crops normally produced on a given tract of land. The measurement necessarily varies with soil characteristics and cropping patterns, but some states administratively establish a uniform duty of water for purposes of considering water transfers and new appropriations. See the discussion in Chapter 5.
5. *Heath v. Williams*, 25 Me. 200, 43 Am. Dec. 265-75 (1845).
6. 3 Cal. 249, 252 (1853).
7. As stated in *United States v. Appalachian Power Co.*, 311 U.S. 377, 426–27, 61 S. Ct. 291, 308 _____ L. Ed. _____ (1940), _____.

> [I]t cannot properly be said that the constitutional power of the United States over its waters is limited to control for navigation.... In truth the authority of the United States is the regulation of commerce on its waters.... The authority is as broad as the needs of commerce.... The point is that navigable waters are subject to national planning and control in the broad regulation of commerce granted the Federal government.

8. For a more detailed discussion of the federal government's power over the waterways of the United States, see Washburn (1986).
9. The navigation servitude is generally considered a subset of Congress's broad power to protect interstate commerce under the Commerce Clause.

10. *The Daniel Ball*, 10 Wall. 557, 563, 19 L. Ed. 999 (1870).

11. For additional information on navigability, see Baughman 1992, 1028.

12. *Winters v. United States*, 207 U.S. 564 (1908). For an excellent discussion of this case and the impact it has had on prior appropriation claims see Smith (1992).

13. *Winters v. United States*, 143 F. 740, 749 (1908).

14. *National Audubon Society v. Superior Court of Alpine County* (Mono Lake case), 33 Cal. 3d 419, 189 Cal. Rptr. 346, 658 P. 2d 709, cert. denied, _____ U.S. _____, 104 S. Ct. 413, 78 L. Ed. 2d 351 (1983).

15. For a complete discussion, see Chapter 5.

16. See Huffman (1953, 73–75); Chandler (1913, 132–42).

17. But see McDevitt (1994), whose examination of primary data from irrigation districts and contemporary newspapers in California as well as from published sources supports a hypothesis supplemental to the traditional market failure and rent-seeking arguments for the demise of private irrigation enterprises and the rise of irrigation districts, namely, that a combination of agricultural, regulatory, and legal changes converged to increase the institutional advantages of irrigation districts relative to private irrigation companies.

18. According to Robinson (1979, 10), "A Federal reclamation law was viewed . . . as the first step in the evolution of progressive programs that would insure the availability of resources for future generations. Reclamation was the first rallying point for the progressive conservation movement that emerged in the early 20th century."

19. The inability of settlers to meet their obligations resulted from poor selection of projects, land speculation, greater than expected construction costs, and the time lag between construction of projects and actual crop production, coupled with farm surpluses (Huffman 1953, 83; Dunbar 1983, 54; Allston 1978, 109-115).

20. For purposes of clarification, the acreage limitation did not limit the size of private landholding within projects, only the number of acres eligible to receive federally supplied water (Wahl 1989, 71).

21. The acreage limitation for the CBP was originally established at 80 acres, but was increased to 160 acres in 1957 and later to 960 acres (Simmons 1994, 106).

22. For a thorough discussion of the impacts of federal water projects on agricultural efficiency, see Gardner (1995), Chapter 12.

5. Salvaging the Appropriation Doctrine

From the western frontier, especially the mining camps, came the doctrine of prior appropriation and the foundation for water marketing. As mentioned in Chapter 3, the Arid Region Doctrine that governed the ownership and use of water was based on "the recognition of discovery, followed by prior appropriation, as the inception of a possessor's title, and the development by working the claim as the condition of its retention" (Kinney 1912, 598). This system provided the essential ingredients for an efficient market in water wherein property rights were well-defined, enforced, and transferable. With the rights to water clearly assigned, the owner was forced to bear the cost and enabled to reap the benefits of good water allocation. Mistakes were undoubtedly made, but owners of water rights had an incentive to learn from their mistakes and improve on water allocation in the process.

As the demand for water grew, so did the likelihood that some costs and benefits would not accrue to the individual decisionmakers. Changes in water allocation by upstream users affected downstream users, and discharge of pollution into streams changed the quality of water for downstream recipients. Because of these third-party effects, legislatures, courts, and administrative agencies intervened in the market process by placing limits on water rights and on the ability of owners to transfer them. Since then, arguments alleging market failure and the recognition by special interest groups that government can be used to redistribute the water bounty have made governmental allocation of water an acceptable policy.

Can the prior appropriation doctrine be salvaged? Is there a legitimate rationale for restricting the transferability of water rights? Is it necessary to recognize ownership of water rights for nontraditional uses including the provision of instream flows to ensure environmental amenities? Can third-party effects be resolved apart from legislative, judicial, and administrative rulings? This chapter focuses on these questions.

Alleged Market Failure

Traditionally, natural resource economists have approached water allocation from a market failure perspective, generally accepting the idea that third-party effects dominate water resources and that legal restrictions on water transfers are necessary. Hartman and Seastone (1970, 2–3) describe how this perspective has manifested itself in water institutions:

> [T]he problem of externalities is widespread, and various organizational arrangements and regulatory measures have been adopted or proposed to cope with it. Laws have been written and established by courts to protect the third parties in water transfers. Special districts have been formed to internalize some of the externalities. The general tendency in institutional development has been to modify market procedures or completely replace them.

Allen Kneese, a natural resource economist with Resources for the Future, examined market failure in water allocation, claiming there was a growing conceptual and research basis for devising more efficient water transfer mechanisms. Nevertheless, he concluded: "It is not yet clear that the best means will be the exchange of water rights in markets because of the difficulty in arriving at reasonably certain definitions of rights when major third-party effects, resulting from water quality deterioration and return flow dependency, are involved. Perhaps the most satisfactory solution will be some mixture of market transfers of rights and administrative allocations" (Kneese 1965, 240).

More recently, Charles Howe, Paul Alexander, and Raphael Moses (1982, 383) argued that "if more than two users are involved, . . . any transaction between two users would ignore the return flow effects on the others." Because of these inescapable externalities, Howe, Alexander, and Moses (1982, 386–88) called for institutional reforms that would use nonmarket allocation. First, they claimed, a more flexible water ownership system would establish "an agency that files for (or buys) water rights under state laws and sells the water produced to another entity. . . ." Second, there should be an increased reliance on conservancy districts. Third, a state or interstate agency should be established to "make a market" in water rights: "Such an agency would stand ready to buy rights at a known schedule of prices and to sell rights to new users." Fourth, better climatic data and forecasting programs would improve regional water planning. Finally, more training of water users, especially irrigators, would lead to more efficient application of water.

These proposals suggest that the market process can be replaced with planners using "known" schedules of demand and supply. But such institutional reforms ignore the important role of information and incentives provided by the market.

The idea that markets are incapable of handling water allocation efficiently persists today. George A. Gould (1988) cites third-party effects and the difficulty of defining tradable water rights as significant impediments to water transfers. Gould's solution is substantial government involvement in water markets. Although David Getches acknowledges a place for markets in water policy, he views water as a public resource, the allocation of which must be regulated and even taxed to protect and promote the "public interest." In a recent work, Getches states:

> [E]conomics must be used in water policy with care and complemented with regulation to enhance overall public benefits from water. . . . The [prior appropriation] system now serves the narrow economic interests of those whose historical position gave them a legal right to use water. It creates a false simplicity that denies the physical, political, and economic realities of water use. . . . While no state has adopted truly integrated management of water, some have programs that are moving in that direction. To deal better with the complexity of water decisions, a few states have embraced comprehensive planning. (Getches 1993, 132, 134)

In *Searching Out the Headwaters: Change and Rediscovery in Western Water Policy*, Sarah Bates, David Getches, Lawrence MacDonnell, and Charles Wilkinson (1993, 185) advocate water markets, but in a role secondary to distribution of water for public use.

> A hard look at water policy should seek distributional fairness. . . . The public, through some acceptable process, must first decide which waters are for public use and which are available for private use within a market system. . . . [Private] appropriation ought to be limited to the amount that is not needed by the whole community for the satisfaction of public values.

Given the fact that much water in the western states is presently allocated via private water rights, giving the public the opportunity to decide which waters it will take and which it will leave to a market system will necessarily involve some divestiture of the private rights. Beyond that, Bates et al. (1993, 186) call for regulation of any private market that might exist in their system. "The use of waters appropriated for private use is subject to regulation like any other activity. For instance, regulation can limit pollution and define how markets operate. . . . State and federal agencies can further the principle of fairness in water decision making by creating new processes for comprehensive, integrated decisions. . . ."

The conclusion that market failure is pervasive in water markets is certainly nothing new. As discussed in Chapter 4, concerns about monopoly, imperfect capital markets, and third-party effects have been around since the late 19th and early 20th centuries when they were used to justify federal reclamation. Demands for governmental intervention have not been limited to water allocation, but such concerns did lead to some unique restrictions on water use, restrictions that have taken their toll on the market allocation process.

Frank Trelease (1976b), perhaps the foremost legal expert on the history of western water law, suggested that objections to the prior appropriation system fall into two categories. The first centers on observed examples of apparent market failure, such as excessive water use, duplicating ditches, dry streambeds, and erosion. Over the past few decades, the list has expanded to include water pollution, destruction of wetlands and wildlife habitat, extinction of aquatic species, spoiled aesthetics, and lost recreational values. In many of those examples, however, market failure is not responsible; it is, rather, the fault of resource owners placing different, subjective values on the resource. "The mistake in these cases is the assumption that because these examples of defects can be found the defects are inherent in the system. Most of these distortions and dislocations . . . could be corrected by small adjustment of the system or tighter administration of the law" (Trelease 1976b, 284).

Trelease's second category of objections includes three "recurrent reactions" to the prior appropriation system:

1. A dislike of the "property system": appropriators seize valuable interests in the public domain and enrich themselves at the expense of the public.

2. A mistrust of the "market system": a fear that under prior appropriation, water rights will become "frozen in the pioneer patterns," unsuitable for modern times and problems, and not subject to reallocation to new uses and needs.
3. A dislike of the "priority system": in a shortage an "all-or-nothing" rule gives one of two essentially similarly situated water users all of his water while his neighbor gets none. (Trelease 1976b, 284)

Objections of this nature are based on a failure to appreciate the flexibility and variety that markets, operating within the prior appropriation system, can provide to water allocation. The first objection is a reaction to the Lockean notion of homesteading wherein property rights begin with individuals. Hence, enterprising pioneers claimed a "right" to unclaimed water. Those who object to that appropriation believe that property rights emanate from government assigning usufructuary rights to individuals at its discretion. Under this view, that which is given can be taken back, thus diminishing the security of rights. The second and third objections question whether such other uses as fish, wildlife, and free-flowing rivers can compete in a market setting. The potential for secure water rights and markets to allocate water equitably to higher valued uses, including environmental uses, is often impaired because of legal restrictions flowing from the three objections.

Removing Laissez Faire from Water Markets

The many objections to a laissez-faire water market have resulted in restrictions on water rights and reduced efficiency of water markets. The restrictions are embodied in several forms, including the beneficial use standard, the no-injury rule, appurtenancy and diversion requirements, the use-it-or-lose-it rule, states' refusal to allow appropriators to keep or transfer conserved water, preferred uses, and federal reclamation restrictions.

Beneficial Use

Beneficial use restrictions are perhaps the oldest in the system of water rights, dating back to English common law. These restrictions found their way into the early mining camps in the West, where appropriators of water were required to put it to a beneficial use or lose it to other potential users. The ruling in an 1897 Nevada court case, *Union Mill and Mining Co. v. Dangberg,*[1] was typical of early decisions holding that "[u]nder the principles of prior appropriation, the law is well settled that the right to water flowing in the public streams may be acquired by an actual appropriation of water for a beneficial use" (quoted in Tregarthen 1976, 368). The list of uses generally considered beneficial included mining, domestic use, stock watering, and, later, irrigation.

In the early mining camps, the beneficial use standard may have made sense. It established a way of defining water rights that eliminated a need for complicated recordation. By defining the right according to use, it was clear enough who had water rights. The beneficial use criterion also encouraged application of water and discouraged speculation (acquiring a water right and leaving the water in the stream for future sale or use). If it were enough to claim water without putting it to use, individuals could have claimed entire watersheds by staking their claim at the mouth of a stream or river, thereby extracting monopoly profits from anyone hoping to use water upstream.[2]

Today, however, the beneficial use requirement, coupled with the use-it-or-lose-it principle, encourages the wasteful application of water because it locks water into historical uses that were considered beneficial when they were initiated but that now may be considered wasteful. For example, irrigating hay meadows may have been beneficial and even valuable in the late 19th century, but today using the same water to provide instream flows for fish may be much more valuable. If private provision of instream flows is not considered a beneficial use, however, as it was not for many years in the western states, the beneficial use standard will prevent efficient water allocation through the market process.

Beneficial use restrictions also encourage individuals to use the law to preclude competing uses. If a state is to enforce use restrictions, it must specify what constitute beneficial uses. Most western states do so in their constitutions or laws, defining beneficial use as "a use for the benefit of the appropriator, other persons, or the public," and listing specific uses as examples.[3] Such lists now typically include municipal, industrial, and hydropower uses along with domestic use, irrigation, and mining. In some cases, states have specifically excluded certain uses from being considered beneficial. For example, between 1979 and 1985, a Montana statute stated that use of water in coal slurry pipelines could not be considered a beneficial use.[4]

Until recent years, instream uses such as recreation and fish and wildlife were not listed as beneficial uses. For example, the Colorado Supreme Court ruled in 1965 that there was "no support in the law of this state for the proposition that a minimum flow of water may be appropriated in a natural stream for piscatorial purposes without diversion of any portion of the water 'appropriated' from the natural course of the stream."[5] Nowadays, most western states recognize instream flows as beneficial uses, but most allow only state agencies to maintain water claims without actually diverting the water.[6]

Beneficial use requirements substantially hamper water markets by obstructing the movement of water to its most valued uses. Apart from beneficial use restrictions (and the diversion requirement), instream flows would likely have become an accepted use of water long before now. And water kept in historically beneficial uses for no other reason than that newer, higher valued uses were not accepted by courts or agencies as beneficial would have been applied to more efficient uses. As long as beneficial use is determined in legislative, judicial, and administrative forums, a great deal of time, effort, and money will be devoted to the governmental process. "The doctrine of beneficial use, with its implications of judicial determination of need and nonuse in effect increases the uncertainty of title to rights in water, and therefore reduces their marketability" (Tregarthen 1976, 369).

Rather than lifting beneficial use restrictions, some scholars advocate expanding the concept in the name of the public interest at the expense of private water rights. According to David Getches (1993, 128–29),

> The beneficial use doctrine of prior appropriation law provides the legal foundation for incorporation of the public interest. The beneficial use requirement is a screening device for deciding which private uses of water will be allowed. Water rights are qualified property rights and once they are created, the states can use their authority to regulate the exercise of these rights for the welfare of the public just as the states do with other kinds of property. . . .
>
> All private water rights are conditioned on their being dedicated to a beneficial use. This principle provides a legal basis

for exercising the state's police power and enacting regulations to ensure that existing rights satisfy the condition. Thus,
*even the oldest water rights can be regulated to protect the para-
mount interests in water asserted by the public.* This regulatory
purpose justifies limiting water uses if they interfere with
water quality or jeopardize publicly important purposes like
fishing and recreation.

Applying property law principles developed in land use
cases, a court could allow governments to *regulate water rights
virtually without limit* if necessary to ensure that they are used
in accordance with contemporary notions of what constitutes
a beneficial use. Compensable takings would be rare [empha-
sis added].

The American Society of Civil Engineers, promulgator of the
Model State Water Rights Code, advocates broadening application
of the beneficial use requirement to include any useful or productive
purpose. Such a change could facilitate markets by lifting historical
limitations on what uses are considered beneficial. However, the
society's Model Code would go well beyond this to include within
the concept of beneficial use the goal of "maximiz[ing] social welfare
by considering instream and offstream uses as well as broader societal interests like the environment and conservation" (Matthews
1994, 191). As with the system advocated by Getches, such an expan-
sion would only foster more extensive governmental involvement
in water allocation decisions at the expense of private property rights
and water markets.

The No-Injury Rule

When water is diverted by an upstream user, that diversion can
affect downstream users either because there is a return flow that
is claimed by others or because there is a change in water quality.
If downstream claims are junior to upstream claims, the juniors must
take the quantity and quality of the return flow as given. However,
if an upstream user subsequently changes the point, time, place, or
use of the diversion, the quantity or quality of the return flow may
change. In that event, other water users on the stream could be
harmed. When the change is the result of a transfer of the water
right, the potential harm is known as third-party impairment or a
third-party effect because the affected water users are third parties
to the contract in which the owner of the water right transfers the

right to another person. The prior appropriation system has histori-cally considered such third-party effects but generally restricted claims of harm to water rights owners directly impacted by changes of use.

The possibility of third-party impairment prompted all western states to implement judicial or administrative procedures that must be followed before water use can be altered or water rights trans-ferred. Although the procedures vary from state to state, they typi-cally allow changes or transfers only if there is no injury to other water rights holders. This standard is known as the no-injury rule (Thompson 1993, 701). In Alaska, Arizona, California, Idaho, Kansas, Montana, Nebraska, New Mexico, North Dakota, Oklahoma, Ore-gon, South Dakota, Texas, Utah, Washington, and Wyoming, admin-istrative agencies are empowered by law to approve or disapprove changes. In Colorado, water courts determine whether changes in use or ownership should be allowed, but the same basic procedure is followed. If the owner of a water right wants to change the point of diversion or the method or place of use, he must petition the appropriate state agency or the water court for approval. The agency then studies the proposal to determine whether third-party effects are involved. Notice of the proposed change is published in a re-gional newspaper, to inform other users on the stream system. Objec-tions to the change may be filed, but generally objections are limited to only those who hold water rights.[7] Objections are resolved pri-vately between the parties involved or by hearing before the agency or water court. Transfer applications may be approved or denied as filed but are often approved subject to conditions that protect the interests of the objectors (Gould 1989, 464). Those disgruntled with the transfer decision may appeal either within the agency or to the state's courts.

Third-party impairment is a real problem that must be addressed when dealing with water transfers. The question is which process best solves the problem. Historically, states have dealt with third-party impairment through administrative or court hearings wherein potentially harmed parties can contest transfers. Montana law is representative. It allows changes in appropriative water rights when the appropriator proves by a preponderance of the evidence that the proposed new use will not adversely affect the water rights of other persons and the proposed use is a beneficial use.[8] While this process does protect third parties, it imposes high costs, delays, and uncertainty that can impede transfers, particularly small or short-term leases or trades, that promote water use efficiency.

Area-of-Origin Restrictions. Unfortunately, the legislative trend is toward increasing, rather than decreasing, statutory restrictions on transfers. The restrictions tend to go beyond the traditional definition of third-party impairment that included arm's length impacts of water transfers. Accordingly, third-party impairment has been stretched to apply to environmental impacts, local economies and cultures, and the "public interest" in general (Thompson 1993, 704, 708).[9] When regulations are expanded beyond traditional externalities to include more distant third parties, they enter the realm of rent seeking to protect status quo wealth from water reallocation that can improve efficiency.

Area-of-origin protection laws that limit transfers to other basins offer an excellent example of rent-seeking regulation in the name of third-party impairment. These laws may prohibit interbasin transfers, or limit them by imposing a tax on transfers as a type of impact fee or requiring payment of compensation to third parties in the area of origin. California allows an originating basin to recall the transferred water in the future if needed (Colby 1988, 738–41; Reisner and Bates 1993, 70–73). New Mexico transfer statutes require a reservation of a share of the originating basin's water supply but do not clearly define how large the share should be or under what circumstances it can be recalled (Colby, McGinnis, and Rait 1989, 713). Oregon requires a reservation to the state of 25 percent of any conserved water that is transferred out of a basin (Willey 1992, 403).

Area-of-origin laws are intended to protect the interests of people who interact with water owners rather than water owners themselves. In light of the fact that approximately 80 percent of western water is used in irrigation, transfers of water from irrigation to other uses could erode rural county tax bases, shut down businesses dependent upon agriculture, affect the local labor market, and threaten the social values and culture that have developed around the agricultural community. As a result, there is often support for legislation that prevents changes in water use in the name of third-party impairment.

To be sure, third parties do feel the impact of efficiency-enhancing water transfers, but that is always the case with market transactions.

If a new restaurant opens providing better service and food and attracting customers from existing restaurants, an argument can be made that existing restaurants are third parties that have been harmed by the competition. This impact is known to economists as a pecuniary externality that is part of the market process providing consumers with better products through improved resource allocation. Similarly, if a water owner sells his water to another user who values it more highly, efficiency is improved though others in the marketplace may be harmed. Naturally the third parties would like to restrict competition through legal restrictions such as area-of-origin legislation. The protection afforded by such legislation, however, is a far cry from the protection against direct third-party impairment originally taken into account by the prior appropriation doctrine.

Moreover, the extent to which there will be economic, cultural, and environmental impacts is often exaggerated. The impacts of transferring water from agricultural to urban uses need not dry up and shut down rural areas. In fact, such transfers can serve to strengthen rural economies. For example, the diversion requirement, the use-it-or-lose-it rule, and government subsidies give irrigators the incentive to apply their water to marginally productive lands and crops. According to Wahl (1989, 188–90), reduced production as a result of water markets is likely to be relatively small and limited to those least productive lands.[10] Agricultural water use could be reduced between 15 and 20 percent through conservation measures without significant decreases in production.[11] Thus, water markets could actually increase the economic stability of rural areas by encouraging improved agricultural efficiency and increasing incomes.

Wahl also makes a crucial point about prices and demand. Agricultural sector representatives often raise the argument that because cities can pay so much for water, municipal demands will put agriculture out of business if markets are allowed to operate. In response, Wahl states:

> As with most any commodity, the quantity consumers are willing to purchase is a decreasing function of price. Although growing municipalities are willing to pay high prices for some additional water, often hundreds of dollars per acre-foot, they would not be willing to pay similar prices for all of the great quantities of water currently used in

agricultural production. Also, as cities buy successive quantities of water from farms, the price for obtaining additional
amounts will rise. Eventually, a point of equilibrium will be
reached at which additional purchases become unattractive.
In other words, water has its value in food production also,
and, even though some water will be bid away, not all will
be. (Wahl 1989, 190)

There is also little support for the claim that out-of-basin water
transfers will deprive rural areas of cultural and environmental values. According to the Report of the Western Governors' Association
Water Efficiency Working Group, "It does not appear, westwide,
that water markets present the threat to traditional lifestyles or natural areas that is feared. There will just not be that much demand for
water to result in wholesale abandonment of rural areas or wholesale
destruction of natural areas" (Water Efficiency Working Group
1987, 110).

The Public Interest. Requiring consideration of the "public interest" in state water permitting and transfer procedures is another
method of rent seeking that goes beyond protecting third-party
water rights holders.[12] All western states except Colorado and Montana require water officials to consider the public interest in issuing
new permits to appropriate water, but many do not require such
consideration with water transfers. Nonetheless, the push toward
regulatory consideration of the public interest is increasing. Because
the public interest is never specifically defined, its use as a rent-
seeking tool can be expanded to include almost any special interest
under the guise of community values (economic, cultural, and
social), the environment (wetlands and other ecosystems, fish and
wildlife, and water quality), and recreational amenities, to mention
a few (Gould 1989, 446–48, 473; Ingram and Oggins 1992, 516).

Perhaps the most pernicious example of public interest regulation
is the public trust doctrine. This legal doctrine came to the United
States from English common law, where it served to protect the
right of the public to use navigable waterways for navigation, commerce, and fishing (Jaunich 1994). In recent years, the doctrine has
been broadened by federal and state courts to protect an expanded
range of public interests, including instream flows for fish and wildlife, recreation, and scenic values (Ingram and Oggins 1992, 523).
Application of the doctrine often trumps private property rights by

reallocating water rights to public uses without compensation.[13] The public trust doctrine has been touted as a potentially powerful tool in the fight for environmental restoration and as a means to insulate communities from the effects of "rapid debilitating change brought on by water rights transfers" (Ingram and Oggins 1992, 527, 530). Although great hope is held out for use of the public trust doctrine as a means to protect newly defined public interests, its record for accomplishing the sweeping goals laid out for it has not been established, and its future success is questionable in light of the Supreme Court's recent rulings on takings (see Burling 1994).

Appurtenancy

The appurtenancy requirement (attachment of water rights to the land on which the water was beneficially used) is another restriction on appropriative water rights that impedes water markets. This requirement arose in the late 1800s when private water development was at its peak and fear of speculation and monopoly was prevalent. Although the requirement was aimed at preventing speculation in water rights, there was so much demand for reallocating water to more productive lands that for all practical purposes it fell by the wayside (Clark, Beck, and Clyde 1972, § 411).

The Diversion Requirement

An especially problematic restriction in most western states is the requirement that water must be diverted from the watercourse to perfect a water right. As discussed earlier, the requirement provided an efficient means for a diverter to identify the location of his water right and notify others on the stream of his claim (Clark, Beck, and Clyde 1972, § 409.2). Now that most streams are fully appropriated and most western states have adopted other forms of notice, however, the diversion requirement is no longer needed. Nonetheless, the requirement remains a part of state water law systems and, where it is strictly enforced, discourages conservation because water rights holders fear losing their rights if they do not divert all the water to which they are entitled.

The Use-It-or-Lose-It Rule

Related to the diversion requirement is the use-it-or-lose-it principle that requires appropriators to use their entire water right or risk losing it through forfeiture and abandonment laws. This restriction encourages overuse of water and also frustrates water markets for several reasons. First, transfers to uses such as instream flows that do not require diversion or consumption may not be allowed by the state because of the use-it-or-lose-it rule. Second, with a temporary transfer such as a lease, a failure by the lessee to use the water may subject the lessor to loss of the right. Third, in deciding whether to allow a water right transfer, administrative agencies often look at historical use, that is, the amount of water actually used as opposed to the amount that could have been used under the paper water right. If historical use is less than the paper right, the agency may reduce the right to the amount of historical use. The risk of losing some of their "wet water" (the actual amount of water historically used) in the transfer process is enough to keep water rights owners from attempting to sell or lease their rights.

Limitations on Conserved Water

Rules prohibiting appropriators from keeping or transferring water salvaged from conservation efforts such as lining ditches, installing drip irrigation systems, or changing crops also discourage conservation. The restrictions are based on the belief that any conserved water must have been previously wasted and not put to a beneficial use. Hence the wasted water belongs to the watercourse from which it was originally diverted.[14] By not allowing appropriators to enjoy the fruit of their efforts, any incentive to conserve water through curtailing wasteful practices is eliminated (Clyde 1989, 442) just as it is under the use-it-or-lose-it rule. Unfortunately the restrictions remain in effect and reduce the incentive to employ water-conserving measures in all but three states, California, Montana, and Oregon.[15]

Preferential Uses

Legislative prioritization of uses is another restriction on appropriative water rights that limits water marketing. Early rulings by the California Supreme Court "asserted that 'a comparison of the value of conflicting water rights would be a novel mode of determining their legal superiority.' Thus, it became a fundamental axiom that each of the purposes 'to which water is applied ... stands on the same footing'" (quoted in McCurdy 1976, 257). In 1876 the Colorado state constitution declared that when water is used for the same purpose, priority and time would determine the superior right. But it also established a hierarchy among different uses under which, in times of shortage, domestic should be preferred over agriculture and agriculture over manufacturing (Trelease 1955, 134).

Most western states have followed Colorado by including preferred uses in their constitutions or legal codes. Although there is a wide variation in preferences, domestic and municipal uses are generally preferred over agricultural and industrial uses. Despite the appearance that preferences would require reallocation to preferred uses in times of shortage, courts have rarely interpreted them in that way because it would upset the prior appropriation system that is based on first-in-time, first-in-right. Some courts have even held that application of preferences would be a taking of property requiring compensation. In fact, all western states allow condemnation of water rights for municipal use, and many require eminent domain condemnation and compensation to effectuate preferential uses. (Getches 1984, 108–10; Clark, Beck, and Clyde 1972, § 408.4).[16]

In a market setting, if a water owner values his water more highly than does a competitor, market forces would ensure that he would not sell and that the water would remain in its highest valued use. With preferred uses and the power to condemn, however, competitors can obtain legally defined "inferior" water rights provided they pay "just compensation." In this setting, the value of the condemned water right and hence the compensation is determined by the judicial process where opportunity costs may be ignored. In the absence of mutual consent there need not be gains from trade or efficiency.

The power to condemn water rights from less preferred uses is exercised most often by municipalities, but fortunately preferred-use statutes are not widely used. Nevertheless, preferences have worked hand-in-hand with beneficial use and the other restrictions discussed earlier to reduce the security of water rights, reduce the potential for water marketing, and encourage rent seeking. Though these restrictions on water rights have been justified in the name of market failure, they have actually served to encourage market failure by weakening water rights established under the doctrine of prior appropriation and preventing markets from improving water-use efficiency.

Federal Control of "Federal" Water

When the Bureau of Reclamation entered the water storage and delivery business in 1902, the potential for water marketing was further undermined. The bureau began telling water users where, when, and how they could use the water from federal projects. Because government money was being used to provide the water, politicians and bureaucrats claimed that they had a right to dictate water allocation. The initial Reclamation Act of 1902 required repayment of construction funds for dams and delivery systems within 10 years, thereby limiting the period of federal control. But as the rent-seeking process encouraged the extension of repayment periods to more than 50 years, federal control was expanded and strengthened.

The vagueness of the various reclamation statutes about the transferability of federal project water coupled with the laws' restrictions, such as the appurtenancy requirement and acreage limitation, also fostered bureau control. In addition, the federal government obtained state water rights for project water and then entered contracts with irrigation districts that in turn delivered the water to its final users, creating uncertainty about whether districts or individual users had the authority to transfer it.

Charles Meyers and Richard Posner (1971, 20) have pointed out the extent of the Bureau of Reclamation's control over transfers.

> Even after repayment of its loans, the bureau, it appears, retains title to the dams and reservoirs constructed under the project and with them title to project water. In addition, many pay-out projects have rehabilitation contracts with the bureau, which give it a continuing interest in the financial integrity of the project. The bureau's interest in projects that have not paid out is clear, since it looks to the individual farmers or to the district . . . for recovery of the costs allocated to irrigation. At all events, whether by statute, expressed or implied contract, general understanding based on past and expected future favors, or some combination of these, the bureau's consent must be obtained for the transfer of any significant quantity of water, supplied by either a paid-out or nonpaid-out project, where the transfer involves either use on a different parcel of land or a different use; and this is so whether the transfer is within or outside project boundaries.

The bureau's control over water transfers creates tremendous potential for rent seeking. Bureaucrats can retain budget and power through their authority to grant or restrict transfers. Water users have an incentive to expend effort and resources in attempts to influence bureau decisions because they will affect their wealth positions.[17]

In the 1980s, the Bureau of Reclamation began to recharacterize its role in western water from dam-building to water management. To that end, in 1988 the Department of Interior (of which the Bureau of Reclamation is a part) published principles governing voluntary transfers of reclamation project water. Criteria and guidance for application of the principles followed in March 1989. The purpose of the principles was to clarify the Department of the Interior's policy governing water transfers and its intent to facilitate them.[18] The principles

1. acknowledged the primacy of state water law in allocation and management decisions;
2. outlined when the Department of the Interior would become involved in transactions for reasons such as federal contracts, federal water rights, legal obligations, or requests for involvement by nonfederal entities;
3. conditioned participation in or approval of transfers on adequate protection of third-party consequences[19] and on maintenance of the federal government's financial, operational, and contractual position following the transaction;
4. limited the department's participation to transactions that are in accordance with state and federal law and proposed by others;
5. considered irrelevant the fact that water involved in a transaction has been federally subsidized;
6. expressed an intent to allow transferors of project water to realize a profit without the bureau claiming some of that profit; and
7. stated Interior's commitment to comply with the National Environmental Policy Act and mitigate any adverse environmental effects arising from proposed transactions.

Although the Department of the Interior's principles were the first steps in the development of a federal policy favoring voluntary transfers of project water (see Smith and Vaughan 1991, 13), the reclamation statutes themselves remain the greatest restriction on federal water because they limit the uses to which project water may be applied and fail to establish a procedure for transfers. As a result, market activity in federal water has not increased significantly in spite of Interior's apparent change in policy.

In 1992, Congress took a step toward encouraging transfers when it passed the Central Valley Project Improvement Act.[20] That legislation authorized all individuals or water districts receiving Central Valley Project water under service, repayment, or exchange contracts to transfer all or a portion of that water to other California water users.[21] While the act apparently encouraged water markets, it effectively nixed trades by imposing 13 conditions on transfers, by favoring fish and wildlife interests at the expense of all other interests receiving CVP water under water contracts,[22] and by giving state and federal regulatory agencies power to achieve a "reasonable balance" among competing demands for CVP water. Such restrictions impede, rather than promote, efficient market allocation (Gardner and Warner 1994). The onus, therefore, still remains on Congress to revise reclamation legislation to facilitate markets to give teeth to any federal policy favoring transfers.

For the market to allocate water resources, rights to water must be well established and transferable. Legal institutions have interfered with both. To obtain a permit to use water, an individual must demonstrate that the water will be put to a beneficial use, the determination of which is left to the political and judicial processes. Market criteria are not the determining factors. Restrictions are placed on intra- and interbasin transfers of rights as well as on changes of use, encouraging rent seeking and distorting the true opportunity costs of water. The diversionary and appurtenancy requirements, preferred uses, and prohibitions on transfers of conserved water have outlived their intended purposes and severely restrict water transfers. Moreover, it is unclear whether water from federal reclamation projects may be legally transferred. As a result of all of the restrictions, markets may fail to allocate water efficiently, but the fault lies with politics, not markets.

Salvaging the System

The Gallison River

To understand how some simple changes could improve the efficiency of water markets, consider the following hypothetical example (see Figure 5.1).[23] The Gallison River is being used to supply water for municipal, agricultural, industrial, and recreational uses.

Figure 5.1:
HYPOTHETICAL GALLISON RIVER

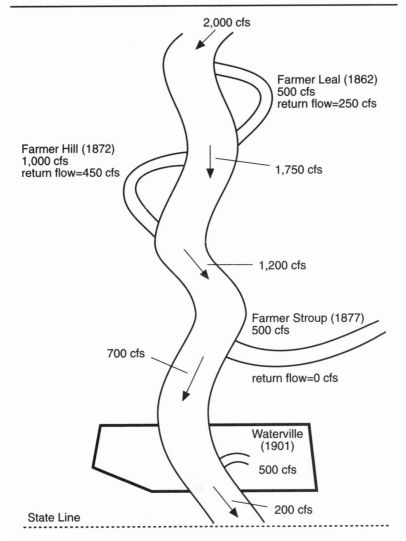

2,000 cfs

Farmer Leal (1862)
500 cfs
return flow=250 cfs

Farmer Hill (1872)
1,000 cfs
return flow=450 cfs

1,750 cfs

1,200 cfs

Farmer Stroup (1877)
500 cfs

700 cfs

return flow=0 cfs

Waterville
(1901)

500 cfs

State Line

200 cfs

The river is located in a western state where the doctrine of prior appropriation evolved from early mining and farming interests. Average annual flow in the Gallison is 2,000 cubic feet per second (cfs).

93

First settlement along the river came in 1862 when Farmer Leal began supplying agricultural products to nearby mining camps. At that time, he constructed an irrigation canal that diverted 500 cfs of water from the river. The crops he planted and the irrigation techniques he used resulted in a return flow of 250 cfs. In 1872, Farmer Hill settled in the Gallison Valley and constructed his own canal that withdrew 1,000 cfs and returned 450 cfs. The combination of withdrawals and return flows left 1,200 cfs of water unclaimed. Farmer Stroup arrived in 1877 and claimed 500 cfs, which he diverted through an ingenious canal system into a neighboring basin. Hence, the return flow from his withdrawal was zero.

By the time the town of Waterville was established in 1900, the procedure for establishing water rights had been turned over to the state water resources agency. The community's application for a permit to use 500 cfs for domestic consumption was not challenged. But when a cement plant located in the next basin sought a permit to divert the 200 cfs remaining in the river downstream from Waterville and transfer it out of the Gallison Basin, local residents protested, and the agency refused to grant the permit on the grounds that the transfer could jeopardize future development in the Gallison Valley and therefore would violate the state's recently enacted area-of-origin protection law. Eventually, the 200 cfs were claimed by a downstream user in the next state.[24]

As growth of Waterville led to increased municipal water demand, Waterville was forced to purchase water rights from other users. When Waterville attempted to purchase the 200 cfs from the user in the downstream state, that state's water engineer disapproved the transfer. Waterville then attempted to secure the water from upstream farmers but found them unwilling to sell at the price Waterville offered. The community thereupon exercised its eminent domain power and condemned 200 cfs of Farmer Stroup's water right, obtaining it at the price originally offered.

Farmer Stroup then attempted to purchase 1,000 cfs of water from Farmer Hill to replace the 200 cfs condemned by Waterville and to drown gophers in the fields he owned in a neighboring basin. The agency denied his transfer application, stating that if Farmer Stroup diverted and removed 1,000 cfs out of the Gallison Basin without returning 450 cfs as had Farmer Hill, third parties downstream would be impaired. Moreover, using appropriated water to flood gopher holes was not considered a beneficial use under state law.

To further complicate water rights in the Gallison Valley, Leal, Hill, and Stroup formed the Gallison Conservancy District and successfully transferred their water rights to the district in exchange for transferable shares. Then they lobbied for congressional authorization to construct a Bureau of Reclamation dam on the Gallison River just above Waterville. As the dam would leave 900 cfs in the river, its construction would cause no third-party impairment. In 1935, congressional approval of funds for dam construction was forthcoming, with the standard provision that the funds be repaid by the conservancy district. A repayment period of 40 years was established in the water service and repayment contract between the bureau and the district, but bad crops and low prices led the Bureau of Reclamation to grant several grace periods during which payments were not required. Until repayment was completed (and very likely beyond), the bureau would retain ownership of the water rights and dam works, and would levy annual operation and maintenance charges on the district.

When a sprinkler irrigation system salesman came through the Gallison Valley and demonstrated that the farmers could cut their water consumption in half by installing sprinkler systems, Farmer Hill almost signed on the bottom line. However, after learning that neither he nor the conservancy district would have any right to the water conserved as a result of his increased efficiency, he abandoned the idea as a waste of money.

After several bad years, Farmer Hill decided to sell his shares in the district to Waterville to avoid bankruptcy. Although the bureau was willing to approve the transfer, Waterville backed out of the deal because the dam's authorization act was vague concerning transfer of water outside the project area and use of project water for purposes other than irrigation. In addition, the Gallison Valley Conservancy District fought the transfer because Farmer Hill refused to give the district any share of the profit he would realize from the sale and because it was unclear whether the town would continue paying Hill's share of operation and maintenance costs.[25] The bad economic conditions facing the farmers in the district, however, did lead to another grace period during which repayment was suspended.

A More "Perfect" World

The Gallison River example illustrates how water transfers are restricted. Everything from intrabasin transfers to interbasin transfers to changes of use must wend its way through judicial or administrative processes before being allowed. The question is, could these transfers be efficiently handled through the market process without third-party effects?

✓ The cement plant's petition for unclaimed water for transfer to another basin was a signal that it had a use of higher value than any in the Gallison Valley. It is easy to understand, however, why Gallison Valley residents might protest the transfer to keep the water in their basin *in case* they might want it in the future. By limiting competition from outside sources, water prices will be kept lower for users in the basin. Unfortunately, it was state law, rather than market forces, that prevailed, resulting in an inefficient allocation.

Waterville's attempt to obtain additional water through market exchanges implied the town was willing to pay for more water. If a downstream user in another state were willing to sell to Waterville, the implication is that municipal uses had a value in excess of the water's opportunity costs (assuming the political process reflects municipal value). Upstream users were unwilling to sell their water at the price being offered by Waterville, suggesting that the agricultural value was greater than the municipal value. By allowing Waterville to condemn rights, either water was being transferred to a lower valued use or Waterville residents were obtaining their water for a price that was less than they were willing to pay. In the first case, inefficiency would result; in the second, value (rents) would be transferred from farmers to municipal residents.

The state's policy of not allowing water users to keep or sell water conserved or salvaged by increased efficiency removed all incentive for Farmer Hill to install a sprinkler irrigation system. As a result, water that could have been applied to other agricultural, municipal, or environmental uses and sold to increase Hill's revenue was locked into its current, less efficient use.

Farmer Hill's attempt to sell his shares in the conservancy district also reflects the potential for an efficient water transfer. It is only logical that the Bureau of Reclamation would want to protect its financial interest in having the construction costs repaid, and approval of the transfer would have increased the likelihood of repayment, especially given Farmer Hill's precarious financial position. Moreover, repayment from Waterville would likely have been larger than it would have been from Farmer Hill, due to the fact that under reclamation law, payments for municipal and industrial use of project water bear interest, whereas those from irrigation generally do not (Wahl 1989, 181).[26] Unfortunately, the transfer did not happen in spite of the Bureau's support because the vagueness of the reclamation statutes created legal risks that might invalidate the purchase and because the conservancy district opposed the transfer.

What about transfers that alter the return flow and affect downstream users, such as Farmer Stroup's endeavor to buy Farmer Hill's 1,000 cfs? Can a case be made that state intervention is necessary when return flows are altered by changes in use or diversion? As discussed earlier in the chapter and throughout the economic literature, externalities resulting from ill-defined property rights are viewed as pervasive because water can be used and reused along a stream basin. Any transfer may affect the return flow available to others (Johnson, Gisser, and Werner 1981, 273–74). Judicial and administrative frameworks are certainly capable of addressing and even eliminating externalities of water transfers. However, they do so by imposing restrictions and controls. The greater the restrictions, the more any prospect for market allocation is reduced.

While many scholars give lip service to facilitating water markets, they simultaneously advocate increased governmental control of transfers as the answer to avoiding third-party impairment. They would expand the list of parties with an interest in a water transfer beyond immediate water rights holders to include the broader local community, environmentalists, recreationists, and anyone else even remotely touched by water allocation decisions (see Bates et al. 1993, 182-92). Advocates of area-of-origin protection, public interest criteria, and the public trust doctrine are motivated by a distrust of markets and a belief that more regulation is necessary to solve problems not addressed by markets. They believe scientific management by "disinterested" bureaucrats can handle allocation of resources and care for the environment better than can markets (Huffman 1994b, 427–28).

To be sure, there are real third-party effects that must be taken into account before transfers are allowed, and administrative reviews offer a mechanism to do this. For example, suppose Farmer Hill changes his water use by applying it to a new crop that is much more water intensive. This will alter the return flow from irrigation and potentially impair downstream users whose rights depend on return flows from Hill. Or suppose that Farmer Stroup moves his point of diversion upstream, making it more difficult for other water users to divert water. In cases where stream conveyance is affected, third parties have a right to cry foul. Similarly cases of pollution are examples of third-party impairment that should be guarded against. In all three of these cases, there is a well-identified third party whose clear legal right has been impaired. Administrative procedures that regulate transfers to prevent harm to such third parties are justified on both equity and efficiency grounds.

Extending the web of rights to the general public, however, is a reach with little basis in the common law of torts, nuisance, and trespass and is likely to impede efficiency-enhancing transfers. Granting the public power to intervene in water transactions removes any limits on claims of third-party impairment. Such an extension of rights necessarily takes rights from existing owners and transfers them to new potential rights holders. When environmental groups successfully expanded the public trust doctrine in the Mono Lake case, senior water rights holders lost their ability to divert water and environmentalists gained protection of the things they valued. In finding that the public had a right to use water to protect environmental amenities, the court opened a Pandora's Box that invites other special interest groups to seek water reallocation on the grounds that they are a harmed third party. Not only is rent seeking encouraged in the legal arena, potentially efficiency-enhancing trades are discouraged because parties to trades are not certain of their water rights.

Rather than increasing restrictions on water transfers to protect against third-party effects, state transfer processes can work to facilitate water markets. For example, most water rights are specified in terms of the amount of water diverted. It is also possible, though not always easy, to determine what proportion of the water is actually consumed. This determination is necessary because return flows are almost always claimed by others who would potentially be harmed if the entire diverted water right were transferred. Once the amount of consumptive use is determined, that amount can be transferred.

The determination of consumptive use clarifies water rights and greatly reduces the potential for objections to transfers. Of course, allowing only transfers of consumptive use rights will not solve all third-party effects. Problems related to changes in the timing of return flows, changes in the ability of a stream to convey water, or changes in water quality must also be accounted for in the state transfer process.[27] Definition of consumptive use, however, is one means by which state agencies can aid rather than impede water markets.

Defining consumptive use also encourages water conservation. An individual who diverts 50 cfs and consumes 35 has an incentive to discover conservation measures. By reducing his consumptive use needs, the water user can free up water that he can transfer or apply to some other use (assuming state law allows it).

States' Efforts to Stimulate Water Markets

Colorado provides an example of what happens to water transactions when consumptive use rights are not clear. In Colorado, water rights owners are not entitled to transfer the quantity of water appropriated but are allowed to transfer only that amount historically applied to a beneficial use (MacDonnell 1989, 788). In order to determine the transferable quantity of water from an irrigation use, the courts have focused on the "duty of water," defined by the Colorado Supreme Court as

> that measure of water, which, by careful management and use, without wastage, is reasonably required to be applied to any given tract of land for such period of time as may be adequate to produce therefrom a maximum amount of such crops as ordinarily are grown thereon. It is not a hard and fast unit of measurement, but is variable according to conditions....[28]

The problem is determining the duty of water. Technical data such as those found in Table 5.1 can be useful. In Colorado, consumptive use is determined on a case-by-case basis following submission of evidence of the transferable quantity of water by all parties involved in the transfer proceeding. The adversarial nature of Colorado's transfer proceedings, coupled with the looseness of the definition of the quantity that may actually be transferred, results in

Table 5.1
SEASONAL CONSUMPTIVE USE CROP COEFFICIENTS FOR IRRIGATION

Crop	Consumptive Use Coefficient
Alfalfa	0.80 to 0.90
Bananas	.80 to 1.00
Beans	.60 to .70
Cocoa	.70 to .80
Coffee	.70 to .80
Corn (Maize)	.75 to .85
Cotton	.60 to .70
Dates	.65 to .80
Flax	.70 to .80
Grains, small	.75 to .85
Grains, sorghums	.70 to .80
Oilseeds	.65 to .75
Orchard crops	
Avocado	.50 to .55
Grapefruit	.55 to .65
Orange and lemon	.45 to .55
Walnut	.60 to .70
Deciduous	.60 to .70
Pasture crops	
Grass	.75 to .85
Ladino white clover	.80 to .85
Potatoes	.65 to .75
Rice	1.00 to 1.10
Soybeans	.65 to .70
Sugar beets	.65 to .75
Sugar cane	.80 to .90
Tobacco	.70 to .80
Tomatoes	.65 to .70
Truck crops, small	.60 to .70
Vineyard	.50 to .60

SOURCE: U.S. Department of Agriculture (1971, 11).
Note: The lower values are for the more humid areas, and the higher values are for the more arid climates.

transactions costs that are higher than for many other states—averaging $187 per acre-foot. Likewise, the time delays are greater, averaging 29 months, as compared with 9 months in Utah (Colby 1990,

1189, 1191). Moreover, historical consumptive use ("wet water") may be substantially less than the appropriative, or "paper right," resulting in risk to buyers when they purchase water rights (Reisner and Bates 1993, 99). For example, when the city of Denver sought to purchase water rights whose appropriated total was nearly 400 cubic feet per second, the Colorado court allowed only the transfer of 80 cubic feet per second (Hartman and Seastone 1970, 23–24).

New Mexico has performed better. As in Colorado, the quantity of transferable water is limited to the consumptive use. However, in New Mexico, consumptive use is fixed by a state administrative agency based upon basin-wide average consumptive uses (Colby 1988, 737). While parties who disagree with the transferable quantity established by the state may bring evidence to prove some other amount is appropriate, reliance on a standard quantity of transferable water has resulted in transactions costs of $54 per acre-foot in New Mexico, an amount substantially lower than in Colorado. Likewise, the average time delay of 4.3 months in New Mexico is much less (Colby 1990, 1188, 1191).

The distinction between diversionary and consumptive use rights in state transfer processes results in more clearly defined water rights. For example, when the Public Service Company of New Mexico purchased 10.23 acre-feet of water and changed both its location and its use, the new water right was described as follows: "(2) This dedication is for 6.82 acres of irrigated land having a diversion right of 20.46 acre-feet of water per annum and having a consumptive use of 1.5 acre-feet per irrigated acre for a total of 10.23 acre-feet per annum for consumptive use" (quoted in Johnson, Gisser, and Werner 1981, 285). Such a specific definition of a water right is common in the New Mexico system.

Other western states have adopted means of streamlining their transfer procedures. Wyoming statutes attempt to reduce the cost of determining consumptive use rights by establishing a presumption that return flows from irrigation are 50 percent (Gould 1988, 37). Nevada gives objectors to water transfers the option of filing either formal or informal protests. Formal protests require a hearing, while informal protests do not. Nevada also uses a unique method for resolving protests that often results in settlement. The formal field investigation enables parties to meet with the agency official at the site of the proposed change, which in turn lends clarity and understanding of the issues involved in the proposed transfer, as well as less formality to the process as a whole (Colby, McGinnis, and Rait 1989, 702–03).

In 1980, California enacted legislation providing for trial transfers, under which transfers could be approved without firmly showing no third-party impairment subject to future modification or revocation after the effects of the transfer are observed. Use of trial transfers was limited to situations where substantial injury was unlikely to occur (Gould 1988, 36). Before they could prove their usefulness, trial transfers were abolished by the California legislature in 1988, due to opposition from appropriators who feared such transfers might undermine their current water rights (Thompson 1993, 707).

Water banking, used in Idaho since the 1930s and in California during its recent droughts, is another means to streamline water transfers. In Idaho, banking allows reclamation water users to place unused supplies in the bank on a yearly basis. The bank leases storage space in Bureau of Reclamation facilities, accepts surplus water, and sells it, generally to power companies or other irrigators. The leases are not subject to state transfer procedures because the bureau holds the overall state right to the water within its projects, although state legislation does authorize the water rentals (Wahl 1989, 133–35).

Water banks were used in California in 1977 and 1991 as a response to severe drought conditions. The 1977 bank was established by the federal government, which spent $2.3 million to purchase 46,438 acre-feet of water from the California State Water Project and from the bureau's Central Valley Project water contractors. This water was then sold to irrigators experiencing critical shortages. Prices were set so that administrative and transport costs were covered, but no undue benefit or profit was permitted to accrue to the sellers (Wahl 1989, 136–38).

The 1991 water bank was established by the State of California rather than the federal government. It purchased more than 800,000 acre-feet of water from users under both the State Water Project and federal reclamation projects at $125 per acre-foot and sold nearly 400,000 acre-feet at $175 per acre-foot.[29] The buyers were mainly municipal and agricultural users.

Although successful in quickly moving water to higher valued uses under drought conditions, these examples of water banking are not perfect examples of water marketing. Tom Graff, economist for the Environmental Defense Fund, criticized the California water bank for failing to facilitate a true market because the state was the only buyer as well as the arbiter of who got the water. The California bank also established the prices at which the water would be bought and sold, rather than allowing the market to determine prices (Hayward 1991, 47). Despite the criticisms, even these flawed examples of water banking facilitated short-term transfers during times of drought and encouraged water conservation and efficiency by enabling users with surplus water to lease it to the bank for sale to higher valued uses.[30]

Finally, water transfer proceedings may be streamlined by emulating special water districts, such as irrigation and conservancy districts and mutual companies, within which active markets often exist. As discussed in Chapter 3, water districts are defined geographically, hold water rights under state law, and issue stock to shareholders. Shareholders receive delivery of water from the district on a pro rata basis depending on the number and class of shares held. Delivery of water to shareholders according to the number of stocks held is considered a contractual right, the transfer of which is not usually subject to state laws governing water transfers unless the district's water rights are affected (Thompson 1993, 712). In addition, because conveyance losses are proportionately shared and return flows are a part of the district's system as a whole, third-party effects are minimal and easily avoided. As a result, transaction costs for transfers are very low, allowing markets to thrive.[31] Moreover, prices are often set by the market, thus promoting efficient allocation and encouraging conservation.

The Northern Colorado Water Conservancy District is known for its very active internal water market. About 30 percent of the district's 310,000 shares move through its rental market each year. Prices have varied over the years, reaching close to $3,000 per acre-foot in the late 1970s and averaging $1,000 per acre-foot in the late 1980s (Shupe, Weatherford, and Checchio 1989, 423). Districts in other states, particularly Utah and California, also have very active internal markets (Thompson 1993, 714).

Creative Water Transfers

Water transfers are not limited to outright sale of water rights or entitlements, but include short- and long-term leases and sale-leasebacks that involve purchase of land and water rights followed by lease of the land and water rights back to the sellers, keeping agricultural lands in production. Cities in New Mexico, Arizona, and Colorado have used sale-leasebacks to secure future water supplies. Subordination agreements are another type of transfer that can be used to benefit environmental and recreational interests. Under subordination agreements, water rights holders with senior priority dates agree to subordinate their senior status to junior rights in dry years, essentially agreeing to share water shortages (Shupe, Weatherford, and Checchio 1989, 420–23).

The Metropolitan Water District (MWD) in southern California constantly faces deficits in its water supply because of the dry climate and continuing population growth. For years, MWD was unable to acquire water from nearby sources because of restrictions on transfers under California and reclamation law. As a result, the district was forced to develop and import water from new and often distant projects. In the past decade, however, the California legislature has changed the state's water code to facilitate and encourage transfers, and Bureau of Reclamation policy has become favorable to transfers. This new atmosphere has enabled MWD to look closer to home for additional supplies and spawned some creative transfer agreements, the most well-known of which is the water salvage agreement between MWD and the Imperial Irrigation District (IID).

The IID receives its water from the Colorado River via federal reclamation projects. Ninety-eight percent of the water goes to irrigation. Problems with drainage have plagued the district for years, raising allegations of waste. When IID faced judicial and administrative orders requiring conservation of substantial amounts of water in the 1980s, it began negotiating an agreement with MWD under which MWD would pay for ditch lining and other conservation projects within IID in exchange for the 106,100 acre-feet of water per year that would be salvaged. The Water Conservation Agreement was signed in 1989 and has an effective period of 35 years.

MWD has initiated other transfer arrangements that illustrate the variety of forms water transfers can take. In 1992, MWD began a two-year land fallowing program with farmers in the Palo Verde Irrigation District. MWD agreed to pay farmers $620 per acre per year not to grow crops. The water generated from the program is estimated to be 93,000 acre-feet per year at a cost to MWD of approximately $315 per acre-foot. MWD also negotiated a dry-year option with the Arvin-Edison Water Storage District in the Central Valley, under which MWD paid to store 115,000 acre-feet of its State Water Project entitlement under Arvin-Edison lands. In dry years, MWD also will pay Arvin-Edison to pump and use that water within the storage district in exchange for up to 128,000 acre-feet of the district's entitlement from the federal Central Valley Project. The cost to MWD of the water is $90 to $100 per acre-foot (Wahl 1994, 60). MWD has entered similar dry-year option agreements with the Coachella and Desert Water Agency (National Research Council 1992, 245).

Conclusion

The belief that the doctrine of appropriation contains a great deal of potential for market failure is pervasive but largely unfounded. Though the doctrine is not without transaction costs, the allocation problems in many western states are not so much the fault of prior appropriation as they are the fault of restrictions placed on appropriative water rights and markets. Administrative agencies and courts continually interfere with the definition and enforcement of water rights and thereby encourage rent seeking.

To salvage the appropriation doctrine, many of the restrictions on water transfers must be removed. When the diversion and use of water cannot be changed, higher valued alternatives are forgone at a cost to both the water right owner and society. If agricultural water users in northern California could transfer their rights or federal contractual entitlements to southern California municipalities, it is likely that water with low value in agriculture would be shifted to higher valued municipal uses, assuming the political process representing urban demands reflects actual values. The success of the California State Water Bank in 1991 is proof. When drought diminished water supplies within the state to critical levels, most of the water sold to the bank came from farmers who fallowed their land or replaced their supplies with ground water or stored water. The buyers consisted primarily of municipalities and water districts in southern California. Moreover, the transfers were accomplished in less than 100 days and even accommodated instream uses and water quality concerns (Gray 1994). The water bank concept could also be used in other contexts such as addressing shortages within the Colorado River basin or accommodating fisheries in the Columbia River basin.

Burness and Quirk (1980, 133) assert that "often what appears to be a shortage of water is actually the manifestation of restrictions on water rights transfer." Innovative water transfers are possible only if state water law and federal reclamation law become less restrictive. The past decade has seen substantial progress toward streamlining water markets. Markets have been accepted as a good way to address water allocation problems resulting from drought and changing societal attitudes toward the environment. States have taken steps to streamline their transfer processes while protecting third parties.

If irrigators are permitted to sell their water, they would have the incentive to consider more water-efficient irrigation technologies and cropping patterns. Unfortunately, the advocates of increased governmental restrictions on transfers are driven by a market failure perspective that fails to take into account the flexibility of the prior appropriation system and the significance of incentives. Rather than giving water users the incentive to increase efficiency by minimizing restrictions on transfers and thereby freeing up water to be applied to newly valued uses, market opponents seek to regulate water away from current users under the guise of fairness to third parties with no standing in the prior appropriation system. This chapter has demonstrated that efficient water allocation may be achieved by salvaging the appropriation doctrine rather than imposing more and new institutions. The problem is that existing bureaucratic agencies lose power when allocation is turned over to the market process. For water markets to develop, ideas must change and new political coalitions must reduce, rather than increase, the power of bureaucracies. When this happens, the doctrine of appropriation will provide the institutional foundation for efficient water markets.

Notes

1. 81 F. 73, 94 (C.C. Nev. 1897).
2. For a more complete discussion of why beneficial use made sense in the early West, see Anderson and Johnson (1986) and Sprankling (1994).
3. Montana Code Annotated § 85-2-102(2) (1993).
4. Montana Code Annotated § 85-2-104, passed in 1979 and repealed in 1985.
5. *Colorado River Water Conservation District v. Rocky Mountain Power Company*, 158 Colo. 331, _____, 406 P.2d 798, 800 (1965).

6. See Chapter 6 for a detailed discussion about instream flows.

7. Some states require consideration of whether the public interest will be impaired by the change or transfer (Colby, McGinnis, and Rait 1989, 718). Inclusion of these public interest factors or criteria in the transfer process is discussed later in this chapter.

8. Montana Code Annotated § 85-2-402 (1993). Applications for changes in water rights must be approved by the state Department of Natural Resources and Conservation. Additional criteria for changes to water rights include adequacy of the proposed diversion works, proof that no injury to the water quality of other appropriators will occur, and, when the proposal involves 4,000 acre-feet or more, application of public interest criteria.

9. The trend also embodies the standard reaction of many environmentalists to externalities—internalize them through command-and-control regulation. See Huffman (1994b).

10. The Western Governors Association Water Efficiency Working Group even went so far as to say that *benefits* to rural areas can result from water transfers away from rural areas: If land removed from production as a result of a transfer was marginal and if the revenues from the transfer remain at least in part within the transferring area to modernize irrigation operations or to diversify the local economy, benefits can result (Water Efficiency Working Group 1987, 109).

11. For example, the Metropolitan Water District of southern California acquired 106,100 acre-feet of salvaged water per year for the next 35 years by paying to line irrigation canals and other projects to improve water use efficiency in the Imperial Irrigation District (IID). The irrigated acreage within the IID was unaffected by the agreement (National Research Council 1992, 82–83, 243).

12. See Bates et al. 1993, 152–98.

13. See *National Audubon Society v. Superior Court of Alpine County* (Mono Lake case), 33 Cal. 3d 419, 189 Cal. Rptr. 346, 658 P.2d 709, *cert. denied,* 464 U.S. 977, 104 S.Ct. 413 (1983), discussed in Chapter 4.

14. An additional rationale for this restriction is that conservation efforts may reduce return flow and adversely affect other appropriators. But this problem can be guarded against by allowing only consumptive use rights to be bought and sold. See Johnson, Gisser, and Werner (1981).

15. Case law in Colorado and Utah also indicates that salvaged water can be transferred in those states (Gould 1989, 470).

16. For some uses, known as true preferences, no compensation need be paid upon condemnation. See Trelease (1955, 133).

17. The magnitude of the rent-seeking potential in the reclamation system was discussed in Chapter 4 in the context of extensions of the reclamation subsidy and circumvention of the acreage limitation.

18. Before issuing the principles, the various regions of the Bureau of Reclamation had been inconsistent in dealing with transfers of project water, thus generating confusion and uncertainty about the legality of such transactions.

19. The criteria and guidelines defined third parties as "those entities who may have some identifiable interest in the exchange, and would have a legal standing in an adjudication process in an appropriate State forum" (Bureau of Reclamation 1989, 4).

20. Pub. L. 102-575, Title XXXIV, 106 Stat. 4706 et seq., October 30, 1992, discussed briefly in Chapter 1.

21. The CVPIA also established a three-tiered pricing system for federal agricultural water that requires irrigators to pay increased rates for CVP water (up to the full cost of any water above 90 percent of the contract allocation). Although the increased

prices will encourage conservation and reduce the subsidy long enjoyed by irrigators, unrestricted transfers of project water would be still more efficient, because "[t]ransfers at market-determined prices would allocate water to highest value uses and provide the same incentives for water conservation as does the three-tiered system" (Gardner and Warner 1994, 7).

22. The CVPIA set aside 800,000 acre-feet of Central Valley Project water per year (about 13 percent of the total) for fish, wildlife, and environmental restoration. By allocating such a substantial amount of project water to environmental purposes, the act elevated fish and wildlife to a status above the uses represented by water contracts, because the former are not required to compete in the market for water resources like municipal, industrial, and agricultural uses (Gardner and Warner 1994, 7). The act also established a $50 million restoration fund to carry out environmental and wildlife mandates included in the act. The money for the fund will come from surcharges on CVP water users (CQ Almanac 1992, 269).

23. For a similar example, see Meyers and Posner 1971, 9–14.

24. This creates a potential political problem if the two states dispute who has first claim to the water. Ultimately such disputes can be resolved through interstate compacts, but they are very costly to negotiate.

25. For an in-depth discussion of the incentives of irrigation districts in relation to water transfers, see Thompson (1993, 724–39). Among others, Thompson discusses how (1) state law governing irrigation and conservancy districts often does not allow them to realize a profit from operations; (2) restricting the market for any surplus water to district members limits competition and keeps prices low; (3) district managers desire to avoid the controversy that surrounds external transfers; (4) managers fear additional administrative costs generated by external transfers; and (5) managers jealously protect their districts' water, which is the collateral for their political clout.

26. Under the Bureau's 1988 principles, when reclamation water is transferred from irrigation to municipal and industrial uses, transferees are required to pay interest on the repayment obligation assumed from the transferors (Gray, Driver, and Wahl 1991, 931).

27. For a detailed discussion of the ways return flow may be altered to the detriment of other water users, see Gould (1988, 13–19). Gould also criticizes redefinition of water rights in consumptive use rather than diversion as tremendously complex, expensive, time-consuming, and wasteful (because most water rights will never be transferred). Moreover, redefinition would fail to internalize the return flow externalities of transfers listed in the text (Gould 1988, 25–28). As stated earlier in the chapter, Gould's solution to third-party impacts from transfers is to refine administrative transfer processes to address such externalities. Gould also falls into the camp of those who advocate broadening transfer proceedings to include consideration of environmental and public interest concerns.

28. Farmers Highline Canal and Reservoir Co. v. City of Golden, 129 Colo. 575, 272 P.2d 629 (1954).

29. The remaining water was picked up by the State Water Project (Economist 1992b, 24).

30. California reactivated the state water bank during the summer of 1994, because of dry conditions once again. The state's goal was to purchase up to 300,000 acre-feet of water at a price of $50 per acre-foot to supply critical needs (U.S. Water News 1994a, 1).

31. In contrast, transfers of water out of a district or mutual affect the organization as a whole because of conveyance losses and loss of return flows. Such transfers are subject to state transfer procedures, since they affect the organization's water rights. Often, they are also either prohibited or opposed by the organization.

6. Privatizing Instream Flows

When the doctrine of appropriation was evolving in the American West, there was little need to consider who had the rights to instream flows. In the West water was primarily diverted for mining or agriculture, and flows were usually adequate to meet those demands. The only instream use of any consequence was navigation. To ensure sufficient flows to meet navigation demands, the commerce clause of the Constitution was invoked, thus preventing anyone from interfering with interstate commerce on rivers and other waterways.[1]

Over time, the demand for instream uses grew to include hydropower generation, waste disposal, and recreation. First water wheels and later hydroelectric generators were turned by instream flows; industrial effluent was discharged into rivers and lakes; and higher incomes and more leisure time increased the demand for aesthetic values. Hence, instream uses began to compete directly with uses that required diversion, making it impossible for the institutional structure to ignore instream flows. Judicial and administrative agencies generally responded by centralizing control over instream flows in governmental agencies rather than allowing markets to develop.[2]

Is the governmental action used to reallocate water from diversion uses to instream uses necessary? Can markets be allowed to resolve the conflicts? Before answering these questions, it is important to recognize that instream flows have two dimensions. The first deals with the quantity of water available for recreation, fishing, waterfowl, and scenic purposes. The second concerns the quality of water available for pollution dilution. Because water flows downhill, it is a natural medium for disposing of effluent. Unfortunately, as the flow of water decreases, the ability of the stream to assimilate effluent declines, increasing the cost of pollution to downstream users. Institutional changes necessary to increase the role of markets in maintaining sufficient instream flows are the topic of this chapter. Water quality issues will be taken up in Chapter 7.

Market Failure or Government Failure?

Most policy discussions begin with the presumption that instream flows have characteristics of public goods and therefore must be provided by government. Public goods are defined by two characteristics: (1) nonpaying users cannot be excluded from consuming the good, and (2) once the good is provided to one individual, it can be provided to others at no additional cost. Consequently, institutional arrangements for allocating such goods depend on collective action.

Consider the costs of excluding nonpayers from consuming a public good. If users cannot be excluded, private firms will have no incentive to produce the good because in doing so they will incur costs but receive little or no revenue. The ability to exclude nonpaying consumers depends on how much the supplier is willing to spend to keep people out. A rancher owning land along a fishing stream may find it costly to deny access to nonpaying fishermen. Fences, signs, and game wardens provide some measure of enforcement, but they also cost money. Whether they cost too much and prevent private provision of fish habitat depends on many variables including the technology of enforcement and the value of the resource. If the costs of exclusion decline or the value of the fishing experience rises, riparian landowners will invest more in exclusion and be more likely to privately supply the fish habitat including the necessary instream flows. The prospect of exclusion is diminished further if, as in Montana, law guarantees public access to streams.

The scenic value of a stream creates a more difficult exclusion problem. When a traveler on a public highway enjoys the sight of a beautiful stream surrounded by changing fall colors, there is little doubt that the view provides positive value. But the owner of the land and water resources that provide the view would be hard put to collect from every traveler who enjoys the scene.

To compound the problem, existence values may be associated with instream amenities; that is, some people derive satisfaction from simply knowing an amenity is there. A New Yorker, for example, may enjoy knowing that a wilderness area exists in Alaska, even if she has no intention of ever visiting it. She receives a positive value from the amenity without paying for it, and it is impossible to exclude her from enjoying its existence value. The argument is not unique to amenity resources. Its logic can also be applied to many privately produced goods. A discussion of existence demands at a staff meeting of the U.S. Fish and Wildlife Service demonstrates how far the argument can be pushed:

> One of the staff people said, "I feel very strongly about wilderness even though I may never visit one of these areas. I want to know that people can enjoy that kind of resource, that it is there, and that it is preserved and is available even though I may never be able to use it myself." One of the other participants responded, "That's strange—I feel the same way about Raquel Welch." (Greenwalt 1976, 622)

An element of existence value is attached to almost any good, but it does not necessarily preclude private production of that good.

The second characteristic of a public good, that once it is supplied to one individual it can be supplied to others at no additional cost, relates closely to scenic and existence values. Providing the view of a beautiful river to one individual does not preclude another from enjoying it at the same time unless there is a crowding problem at some vista. Economic efficiency dictates that the price of the good should equal the marginal or additional cost of producing it. If the additional cost of providing the view for an extra person is zero, the implication is that a zero price should be charged. If so, however, a private producer is unable to achieve a rate of return necessary to stimulate production.

The classic economics example of this element of a public good is the lighthouse. As the argument goes, once a lighthouse is built and lighting the way for passing ships, the additional cost of guiding another ship is zero. Thus, lighthouses must be public goods. As Ronald Coase (1974) has pointed out, however, private lighthouses have been in existence for many years and innovative contractual arrangements have evolved to allow private entrepreneurs the return necessary to produce the service.

Private Solutions to Public Good Problems

Though instream flows may have some public good characteristics, it does not follow that private markets cannot provide those uses. The free-rider problem can be overcome by innovative contractual arrangements. Private groups, such as Trout Unlimited, Ducks Unlimited, and The Nature Conservancy, have demonstrated that private resources can be devoted to the provision of some public

113

goods. During the winter of 1989, for example, The Nature Conservancy and the Trumpeter Swan Society acted to enhance instream flows for the benefit of wildlife on the Henry's Fork of the Snake River in Idaho. The resident population of trumpeter swans on the river was near starvation, its aquatic food supply cut off by river ice. Additional water from an upstream dam was desperately needed to open a channel and allow the birds access to their food. Through voluntary donations, releases of water from the reservoir, valued at $20,000 to $40,000, were acquired to enhance the flows in the river and save the swans (Anderson and Leal 1991, 108).

In Colorado, the Pittsburgh and Midway Coal Mining Company donated rights to 300 cubic feet per second of water in the Gunnison River to The Nature Conservancy. Because private entities are not allowed to hold instream flow rights in Colorado, the Conservancy donated the rights to the Colorado Water Conservation Board. The donation agreement, which is a binding contract under Colorado law, required the board to file an application to change the water right to an instream flow right. Before finalizing the agreement in 1992, The Nature Conservancy and the board negotiated with other water rights owners on the Gunnison, securing their consent to the change of use (Sims 1993, 12–10).

The market process can foster solutions to the free-rider problem because free riders represent opportunities for entrepreneurs who can devise ways of collecting from them. Environmental entrepreneurs in organizations such as The Nature Conservancy, Trout Unlimited, and the Environmental Defense Fund play an important role in creating private rights and capturing the benefits of the environmental amenities of instream flows.

Government Failure

If markets can help augment instream flows at a time when amenity values seem to be rising, why are they not used more? According to James Huffman (1983, 268), it is not because of market failure, but rather because of deficiencies in states' water rights systems. Existing water law seriously limits private acquisition of instream flow rights. As a result, we cannot be sure from experience that the assumption that water is a public good is accurate and therefore markets are incapable of providing instream flows (Huffman 1983, 268).

In many western states, the institutional (legal and administrative) structure precludes private ownership of instream flows. In some cases, the list of accepted beneficial uses does not include instream flows. In 1917, the Utah supreme court ruled on the disputed ownership of instream flows for the purpose of supporting a duck population. The court held:

> It is utterly inconceivable that a valid appropriation of water can be made under the laws of this state, when the beneficial use of which, after the appropriation is made, will belong equally to every human being who seeks to enjoy it. . . . [W]e are decidedly of the opinion that the beneficial use contemplated in making the appropriation must be one that inures to the exclusive benefit of the appropriator and subject to his dominion and control.[3]

This language suggests that the state was unwilling to allow individuals or groups to appropriate rights for the "public good."

The requirement that water must be diverted to perfect a water right has also interfered with the potential for using markets. For example, when the Colorado legislature authorized the Colorado River Conservation District to reserve water for instream purposes in any natural stream large enough to support a fish population, the Colorado Supreme Court ruled that there was "no support in the law of this state for the proposition that a minimum flow of water may be 'appropriated' in a natural stream for piscatorial purposes without diversion of any portion of the water 'appropriated' from the natural course of the stream."[4]

When the West was being settled, the diversion requirement served the purpose of notifying users on a watercourse of the amount of water controlled by an appropriator as well as the location of the claimed water right. Diversion requirements also prevented speculators from claiming water for future sale. When states established record systems for water rights, the diversion requirement became obsolete but was nevertheless retained as an element of many states' appropriative water law systems. Unfortunately, as long as water use requires diversion, there is no way that property rights can be established for instream purposes.

Another facet of the prior appropriation system that prevents establishment of instream flow rights is the use-it-or-lose-it rule. In most states, water rights may be deemed abandoned or forfeited if the water is not "used," that is, if it is left in a stream to provide a beautiful view or fish habitat. The law of forfeiture and abandonment of water rights is related to the beneficial use standard in that it is designed to ensure that appropriated water is reasonably used and not wasted. Like the diversion requirement, it is also aimed at preventing speculation in water. For example, if an individual were to claim a right to water from a stream in the hope that its value would rise, the water would not be used (diverted and consumed). The argument against speculation in water is that it causes valuable resources to remain idle and unproductive, thus inhibiting economic growth. This argument made sense when the West was being settled, resources were abundant, and economic development was the common goal. The same argument makes little sense, today, however, because the individual appropriating a water right bears the cost of not consuming the water; his actions imply that he believes the water is more valuable left instream than diverted. By threatening water rights holders with loss of their rights if they do not consume the water, the law of forfeiture and abandonment stifles the establishment of instream water rights and discourages these valuable instream uses.[5]

As we will see in the next section, some states are beginning to break down the barriers to markets for instream flows, but the beneficial use standard, the diversion requirement, and state forfeiture and abandonment laws continue to discourage market transactions. As long as rights to instream flows cannot be defined and enforced, markets cannot provide instream uses. Eliminating the obsolete elements of the prior appropriation doctrine discussed here and in Chapter 5 would lower the institutional barrier to private provision of instream flows. If the beneficial use requirement cannot be eliminated, it would help to expand the categories of uses considered beneficial to include more instream uses.[6] Explicitly recognizing that nonconsumptive instream flows are not abandoned water rights would also be a step in the right direction. Unfortunately, the norm is to rely on governmental provision of instream flows rather than freeing up appropriative water rights systems to include private instream flow rights.

Instream Flows in Western States

Because most western states have declared in their constitutions or by statute that all waters within the state belong to the state and

116

grant only usufructuary rights to water, and because instream uses have some public good characteristics, it is not surprising that the standard approaches to the maintenance of instream flows have involved public action. Rather than allowing private entities to acquire, hold, and transfer rights to instream flows, states have more commonly chosen to maintain instream flows by reserving water from appropriation, establishing minimum stream flows by bureaucratic fiat, conditioning new water permits, or directing state agencies to acquire and hold instream flow rights.

Idaho

In 1978, the Idaho state legislature passed a law that established base flows on the Snake River and authorized the Idaho Water Resources Board (WRB) to appropriate water for instream uses. The law authorized the WRB either to initiate action or to respond to private requests for instream appropriations. It also subjected the WRB's actions to legislative approval and vested water rights owned by private individuals. While actions of the WRB are subject to technical constraints, such as past flow records and minimum flows necessary for the preservation of fish and wildlife habitat, recreation, navigation, aesthetic beauty, and water quality, the board still has a great deal of discretion to act in the public interest. As of 1993, however, instream flows had been appropriated by WRB on only 288 miles of Idaho streams.

The board has been more successful at protecting instream flows under the 1988 Idaho Protected Rivers Act that calls for designation of specific river reaches as either natural or recreational. These designations effectively create minimum stream flows by prohibiting construction, diversion, and alteration activities on the watercourse. The studies used to determine whether to designate rivers as protected are also used by the WRB as a planning vehicle in seeking instream flow permits (Beeman 1993, 13–15). Between 1988 and 1993, more than 580 river miles were designated as protected under the act and at least 70 miles were added in 1994.[7] Nevertheless, as a percentage of Idaho's total stream miles, the number of protected instream flows remains minimal.

Washington

The state of Washington has attempted to maintain instream flows by giving its Department of Ecology the power to grant, deny, or

117

WATER MARKETS

condition permits for water appropriation. Since 1949, water rights on approximately 500 streams in the state have been denied or conditioned with instream flows (Slattery and Barwin 1993, 20–3). In 1967, the Washington legislature gave the Department of Ecology added authority to establish minimum stream flow requirements for wildlife habitat, recreation, and environmental purposes upon request from the state departments of fisheries or wildlife. This program was largely superseded, however, by the Water Resources Act of 1971, which required the Department of Ecology to set base flows in all perennial streams in the state. By 1993, most of the heavily used streams in eastern Washington and the Puget Sound area had instream flow requirements established for them (Slattery and Barwin 1993, 20–24). As a result, those streams were effectively closed to additional appropriation. The Department of Ecology established the flows by administrative rule based on the quantity of water necessary to sustain a stream during extended dry periods. In so doing, the Department carried out instream flow incremental method studies that collected and analyzed historical stream flow records and determined the impact of stream conditions on fish and fish habitat.

Unlike the Idaho system, where politics plays an important role, the Washington State system depends primarily on technical experts. Except for a few limited exemptions from minimum flow requirements for nonconsumptive, nondiversionary uses, or certain domestic or municipal uses,[8] there is little room in the Washington system for economic criteria in the establishment of instream flows. Moreover, where ambiguities in the instream flow legislation exist, the Department of Ecology has resolved them in favor of instream flow protection over future diversionary uses (Slattery and Barwin 1993, 20–6, 20–7, 20–18).[9]

In 1986, Washington's Department of Ecology suspended its efforts to establish new minimum stream flows and undertook an in-depth review of its instream flow program, part of which involved preparation of a program environmental impact statement under the State Environmental Policy Act. Legislation passed in 1988 called for more policy reviews and recommendations for statutory changes. In 1991, representatives from virtually all water interests in Washington State met and drafted the Chelan Agreement on Water Resources, an unsigned document setting forth recommendations for state

118

water policy. The recommendations have been followed by the Department of Ecology in carrying out the state's instream flow policy. However, the recommendations favor regional planning and rulemaking by the Department of Ecology, and voluntary transfers for increasing instream flows are only a sidelight.

Colorado

In Colorado, the Colorado Water Conservation Board is authorized to apply for rights to unappropriated water to maintain instream flows or to acquire existing rights by grant, purchase, bequest, devise, lease, exchange, or contractual agreement (Shupe 1988, 863). The board is specifically prohibited from acquiring rights by eminent domain. The Colorado system has two important characteristics: first, like any other appropriator, the board must have evidence that its requests for water constitute a beneficial use.[10] Second, when the board purchases existing rights, it must pay the market rate. Though the state's budget constraint is considerably different from that of any private user, the system does force the state to consider the costs of instream flows. In a state such as Colorado, where most water rights have already been claimed, the market approach is probably the only viable alternative to forced reallocation by the state. However, Colorado falls short of creating a true market for instream flows because only the Colorado Water Conservation Board is permitted to hold instream flow rights.[11]

California

California establishes instream flows by denying or conditioning applications for appropriative water rights to leave water in the stream. The California Water Resources Control Board also retains jurisdiction over water rights and may modify them to protect instream flows. In addition, changes of use, including water transfers, are subject to instream flow protection conditions imposed by the board. Other indirect means available to the Water Resources Control Board to protect instream flows include water quality requirements and enforcement of the state's constitutional requirement that water be used in a reasonable manner and not wasted (Gray 1993).

The California system has been criticized as inadequate for protecting instream flows because it essentially depends upon case-by-case review of water rights and applications for water rights, which in turn depend upon the discretion of the Water Resources Control

Board. Changing times and personnel on the board inevitably lead to inconsistency. Granting appropriative rights for instream flows in the same manner as for consumptive rights would provide security for instream uses and allow for transfers of consumptive uses to instream flows.

Oregon

In 1987, Oregon passed a law creating instream flow rights. The law provides several ways to acquire the rights, including claiming unappropriated water for instream uses and purchasing, leasing, or donating existing water rights for instream flows.[12] All instream flow rights are held by the Water Resources Department in trust for the people of the state of Oregon. Thus, while an individual or organization may purchase, lease, or accept donation of a water right for instream flows, the state essentially co-owns or co-leases the right. Although only state agencies can apply for instream flow rights in unappropriated water, anyone can convert existing rights to instream flows (Kaufman 1992).

Oregon's new law has enabled individuals and organizations such as the Oregon Water Trust to use the marketplace to purchase existing water rights and convert them to instream flows. In 1994, the Oregon Water Trust leased water rights from a ranch on Buck Hollow Creek, a steelhead-spawning tributary of the Deschutes River, and left the water in the stream. Late in 1994, the Trust received some $400,000 in grant money to spend on leasing additional water rights for instream flows. According to Janet Neuman, president of the Trust, the Trust's modus operandi is to operate in a noncontentious, cooperative manner to provide incentives for leaving water in the streams (Laatz 1994; Cockle 1994).

Montana

Montana has maintained instream flows primarily by reserving water from private appropriation. The 1973 Water Use Act authorized federal, state, and local governments to apply to the Board of Natural Resources and Conservation for water reservations for existing or future beneficial uses including the maintenance of minimum stream flows. The Board of Natural Resources and Conservation's most ambitious undertaking was its consideration of applications for reservations on the Yellowstone River in a single proceeding.

Because private water users could not apply for reservations, the board sought to assure that the reservations that it granted did noi tie up all of the water and thus prohibit any future private development of water. However, the variable nature of the stream flow and the inadequacy of much of the data available to the board raises some doubt about the prospects for future private water development. (Huffman 1983, 264)

Though the board granted numerous reservations for consumptive water uses by municipalities and irrigation districts, by far the lion's share of Yellowstone River water was reserved for instream flows. The instream flow reservations were granted on approximately 2,078 stream miles in the Yellowstone River Basin. Those flows constitute 60 to 70 percent of the average annual flow in the basin and approximately 12.5 percent of Montana's total stream miles (McKinney 1993, 15–16).

Because the reservation system allows little room for economic criteria and little flexibility once the reservations are made,[13] market mechanisms have been introduced into the law. In 1989, Montana passed legislation providing for a temporary leasing program.[14] The legislation authorized the Department of Fish, Wildlife, and Parks (and only FWP) to apply to the Board of Natural Resources and Conservation for designation of up to 20 stream reaches eligible for leasing to maintain or enhance stream flows. FWP could then seek permission from the Department of Natural Resources and Conservation to lease existing water rights on a designated reach for instream flows. The FWP was required to provide detailed information on the stream reach and a stream flow measuring plan. Authorization for the lease could be granted only after notice of the application was published and all objections were resolved.

Although the leasing program was a step in the direction of a market for instream flows, its success has been limited. By 1994, five years after the program's inception, only two leases had been negotiated. Two factors explain the limited success of the instream leasing program: (1) only FWP can lease water and its budget for leasing is limited, and (2) instream flow uses are not politically popular in the rural areas of Montana where agriculture is predominant. That political sensitivity is exacerbated by the fact that farmers and ranchers must deal with FWP. This creates a problem because

121

the bureaucracy is in a monopsony position as the sole buyer of instream flows and because bureaucrats within agencies have little experience with market transactions.

Legislation was introduced in 1991 that would have allowed public or private entities to purchase water for instream flows. The bill faced strong opposition from agricultural interests, however, and was killed before reaching the floor of the Montana senate (McKinney 1993, 15–33). Fortunately, a coalition of environmental and agricultural interests laid down their swords in 1995 and successfully passed legislation allowing temporary transfers of water to instream uses and short-term (maximum of 10 years) leasing by private parties. Agricultural interests would not accept outright sales of water rights for instream uses for two reasons. First, they feared long-term consequences for the future of the agricultural community. Second, they feared that instream rights owners would have standing to object to agricultural water transfers, which are common in the state. The first concern was overcome by limiting private instream transactions to leasing instead of outright purchases, and the second by explicitly precluding instream flow lessees from objecting to transfers on the grounds that they are harmed third parties. Montana's statute paves the way for innovative alternatives in other states.

Which Works Best?

Comparing six methods of maintaining instream flows used by Idaho, Washington, Colorado, California, Oregon, and Montana provides insights into whether governmental action promotes efficient water allocation. The Idaho, Washington, and Montana systems exclude some waters from private appropriation. California denies or conditions water right applications and directly regulates existing rights. To the extent that water cannot be appropriated, these systems depend on "wise administrators" who must know the appropriate amount of water to withhold from private appropriation to maintain instream flows. The systems are fraught with problems of governmental failure (see Chapter 2). When prices do not exist, values are difficult to determine; when voluntary trades do not determine use, opportunity costs are ignored; and when the political process is used to determine allocation, well-organized special interests tend to preempt diffuse general interests. Even where administrators or legislators are not subject to political pressures, it is unlikely that they will have enough information to make efficient tradeoffs among water uses. In the absence of prices, valuing the water in alternative uses is difficult, if not impossible.

Efficiency is further impeded because administrators and legislators do not have to face the opportunity costs of their actions. When water is reserved for instream uses so that consumptive uses are precluded, the decisionmakers do not bear the cost of the forgone alternative uses. To complicate the process, agricultural, mining, industrial, and municipal users will compete with instream users to make their political voices heard. There is no guarantee, however, that political expressions of preference will mirror economic values. The Colorado approach has a slight advantage over the others in that it forces voters, legislators, and bureaucrats at least indirectly to consider the opportunity costs of instream uses. As long as existing consumptive rights must be purchased, state revenues will have to be provided. Nevertheless, it is important to remember that the state budget is a common pool, and individuals seeking revenues to purchase water rights will still be able to ignore the full opportunity costs of their actions (Baden and Fort 1980).

It should also be remembered that political decisionmakers determine future as well as present water use, and that to do so they must be able to accurately predict future values of water in a changing world. Once water is reserved for instream uses, the political process makes it difficult to change that use. The fear that instream flows will prevent future development of water resources is justified where flows are designated or reserved by the state. If instream flows are embodied in freely transferable water rights, however, flexibility both to and from diversion uses is more likely.

With governmental allocation of water resources, rent-seeking costs can be considerable as individuals and groups invest in trying to obtain preferential treatment. Idaho's legislative process encourages people with an interest in instream flows to try to influence their legislators. The reservation process in Montana is extremely costly when viewed in the time and money spent on hearings and court cases. California's case-by-case approach to instream flow protection provides a myriad of opportunities to influence government decisionmakers. The Mono Lake case, discussed in Chapter 4, represents a successful attempt by environmental groups to persuade a

123

court to reallocate water resources from vested water rights to instream flows without compensation. And the federal Endangered Species Act has empowered state and federal agencies to force water users in California to leave water in the stream to protect endangered fish (Dunn 1994). Under these systems, the cooperation found in the marketplace is replaced with challenge and conflict, and what could be a productive exchange is transformed into a negative-sum game.

Oregon's instream flow rights law and the new Montana legislation open the door to greater protection of instream flows through water marketing. By allowing private parties to purchase or lease consumptive water rights for instream purposes, many of the problems of governmental allocation can be avoided. Of course, defining instream flow rights may be more costly than measuring traditional diversionary water rights, but these costs are minimized to the extent consumptive water rights are already well specified. Furthermore, as the value of instream uses rises and technologies for monitoring water use improve, the definition problem will become less significant (Anderson and Leal 1988, 320).

Although newly appropriated instream flow rights are junior and therefore afford relatively little protection in relation to other appropriative water uses, markets allow instream interests to acquire senior consumptive water rights with greater priority to the available water on a stream system. Innovative contracts between consumptive and stream flow rights holders may also be used to protect both existing diverters and instream flow interests while enhancing stream flows. For example, an environmental group could contract with a water right owner to move his diversion point downstream from a reach that would benefit from increased flows (see McElyea 1989, 1094).

Markets for Instream Flows

The evidence suggests that if legal obstacles to establishing instream flow rights were removed, private provision of instream uses would develop. On small streams, for example, where some of the legal restrictions do not apply, private owners are gainfully providing fishing. Along the Yellowstone River south of Livingston, Montana, several spring creeks begin and end on private land and are wholly appropriated by the landowners. Because access to the streams can be monitored inexpensively, landowners can collect a

124

fee from fishermen. The fee, as much as $50 per day, gives the owners the incentive to develop spawning beds, prevent siltation, and keep cattle away from the streams to protect bank vegetation and cover. Owners limit the number of fishermen per day so that crowding does not diminish the value of the experience. Spring creeks in the Gallatin Valley near Bozeman, Montana, are also protected privately. Recreational values have risen sufficiently so that fishermen are purchasing land along these creeks, removing or fencing off livestock that trample streambank vegetation, and reclaiming the fish habitat. In contrast, comparable spring creeks near Lewistown, Montana, where public access is permitted, are characterized by crowding and reduced fish population (Anderson and Leal 1991, 109).

The results of private ownership of fishing rights are being noted all over the world. On the southwest Miramichi River in Quebec, for example, the owner of a fishing camp describes how he turned his leased section into the perfect place for salmon fishing:

> I *made* it perfect by rafting a bulldozer in here. . . . We cleared away the gravel bar that kept fish from going up the tributary . . . dug the hundred-yard-long pool . . . and shoved a big-as-a-house boulder in place at the head of it. . . . With all due respect for Mother Nature, that pool was built by men and machines, and it seems to be as good now as it was the first year. (quoted in Zern 1982b, 87)

In much the same way, Dale Miller, Bob O'Brien, and Greg Koonce, founders of Inter-Fluve, Inc., are improving neglected trout streams. By repairing streambeds, shoring up banks, planting willows, encouraging native grasses, and creating other elements of trout habitat, Inter-Fluve has increased the fishing quality and the aesthetic value of streams in the United States, Mexico, Argentina, and New Zealand, and its success is attracting other firms to the industry (Dempsey 1991). The company converts irrigation ditches into fertile streams complete with spawning beds, reclaims rivers from mined-out waste lands, and creates spring creeks where there were none (Brooks 1991, D1).

Inter-Fluve sales gross several million dollars each year, and their clients are diverse. Ted Turner hired Inter-Fluve to reclaim trout streams on two of his Montana ranches. Inter-Fluve rehabilitated 1.5 miles of stream near Butte, Montana, for Atlantic Richfield by

redirecting flows away from mining tailing ponds and stabilizing
banks, all of which resulted in lower water acidity (Brooks 1991).
These "stream doctors," as they are sometimes called, actually created more than two miles of new trout streams for an exclusive
residential development in Idaho. The project plan was in large part
responsible for the granting of water rights to the development.
Inter-Fluve also prepared a five-year plan for trout habitat improvement on several miles of a high-altitude tributary to the Colorado
River for the Vail Chapter of Trout Unlimited. And the Montana
Department of Fish, Wildlife, and Parks often retains Inter-Fluve to
do inspections and other consulting work.

Other instances of instream flow protection by private individuals
and groups have begun to dot the landscape. On the Darlington
Spring Creek in Montana, the Madison-Gallatin Chapter of Trout
Unlimited helped deepen pools and create riffles and runs, dramatically improving the fishery. A similar effort took place in Oregon,
where the Klamath County Flycasters, a group of Boy Scouts, members of the Klamath Tribe, and state and federal officials worked
together to plant willow trees along the Williamson River to cool
river temperatures for trout.

In Nevada, The Nature Conservancy has spent $1.5 million since
1990 to purchase water from farmers in the federal Newlands Project
to leave instream in the Carson River.[15] The beneficiary of the instream flows is the Stillwater National Wildlife Refuge into which
the Carson River empties. At one time, the Refuge was a huge marsh
covering an average of 100,000 acres in the Lahontan Valley at the
base of the Sierra Nevada Mountains. The marsh was a major stop-
over for hundreds of thousands of migrating birds. But irrigation
diversions by the Newlands Project gradually reduced it to 3,100
acres in 1990. The Nature Conservancy's water purchases were made
possible by the federal Truckee-Carson Water Rights Settlement Act,
which instituted a program of voluntary purchases of water rights
from willing sellers. The Conservancy's response to the plight of the
Stillwater Refuge clearly demonstrates that the demand for instream
flows to preserve wetlands and protect wildlife can be met by private entities.

Such efforts to leave water in streams and improve stream systems,
if they are to be successful, require some security of rights to instream
flows. The fact that individuals and groups are taking the initiative

to maintain and enhance streams for their instream flow amenities, even when rights to the flows are less than certain, is a good indication of the ability of markets to facilitate the demand for instream flows. However, these efforts remain limited in the face of the institutional obstacles to private instream flow rights discussed early in this chapter.

The rights to instream flows in England and Scotland have long been well established and encourage efficient instream uses. The tradition of trout fishing in Great Britain has led some owners to maintain their fisheries even though they have not marketed the fishing rights. As the value of fishing rights has risen with the demand, however, "there are few land owners . . . who can afford to ignore the commercial aspect of the sporting rights which they own" (Southerland 1968, 110). As a result, Clarke (1979, 219) notes that angling associations have been formed to purchase rights to instream flows and charge for fishing: "In the 1960s and 1970s smaller, privately managed fisheries that offered exclusivity in exchange for higher rod fees began to break out like an aquatic rash around [England]. Now every city and major town . . . has first-rate trout fishing within easy reach, and at an affordable price." In Scotland,

> virtually every inch of every major river and most minor ones is privately owned or leased, and while trespassing isn't quite as serious a crime as first-degree murder or high treason, it isn't taken lightly. . . . Many of these stretches, which may be 100 yards of one bank of a river or several miles of both banks, are reserved years in advance, with a long waiting list. (Zern 1981, 120)

But this does not mean that privately owned streams where fees are charged are solely the domain of the wealthy. As with any market, there is a range of quality and price. You can pay as much as $1,000 per year to join a "rather 'starchy' and exclusive syndicate that provides the right to fish one day a week," or you can pay approximately $50 per year to join a "coarse" fishing club (coarse fish include pike, bream, and chub) (Shaw and Stroup 1988, 35). You can even fish by the day at publicly owned reservoirs for as little as a few pounds.

Even communities have recognized the value of fishing to the economy. In Grantown-on-Spey, the angler can "join the local

127

Angling Association by paying a weekly fee of about $25, and be free to fish any of seven miles of Association water. Sometimes, too, hotels and inns own or lease a stretch of river for their guests or can make arrangements with a local owner of fishing rights" (Zern 1981, 120).

When individuals or groups can own water for instream uses, they have an incentive to manage and improve the fishing habitat. To capture a return on their investments, owners must invest in enforcing their property rights, so the British hire private fish and game managers.

> To maintain their houses as homes, they retained housekeepers. To keep a proper garden and park, they had groundskeepers. Gamekeepers for stag and grouse. Then, as keepers of the kept, even gatekeepers to further secure things. And eventually, it was for the British to devise the ultimate in the art of maintenance—the riverkeeper.
>
> Now, the name itself could easily be misinterpreted—as it has from time to time by our American "riverkeepers," whom we call "the Corps of Engineers." To keep a river from doing what it is supposed to do would be noxious to the British, as it is to many anglers. (Zahner 1980, 16)

In the United States, where private rights to instream flows generally cannot be established, having a private riverkeeper is virtually unheard of. Most people believe that this role must be left to the state. But when the role of riverkeeper is turned over to a governmental agency, such as the Bureau of Reclamation or the Corps of Engineers, the agency tends to "keep the river from doing what it is supposed to do."

Establishing private property rights generates many innovative ways of enforcing those rights. In England, for example,

> one large estate owner . . . who was considerably troubled by poachers, solved his problem by inviting the most hardened poacher to form a fishing club, and provided two locks and a stretch of river for the purpose. It proved highly successful. The club members themselves contributed to the restocking of the water and the landowner's private rights were assiduously respected. (Southerland 1968, 114–15)

Owners of fishing rights in England may also sue upstream polluters whose effluent adversely affects their fishing resource. In 1948, the Anglers' Cooperative Association was formed and began helping members—individual anglers and clubs—obtain injunctions or damages in pollution cases.

> The Association won its first major pollution case in 1951 against two chemical companies and the city of Derby for pumping untreated sewage, hot water, and tar products into the River Derwent. It has lost only [two cases] since and in 1985, for example, returned £25,000 in damages. Most cases are settled out of court with the polluters' insurance companies. Claimants are paid the cost of restocking the river or lake plus costs reflecting the "loss of enjoyment." (Shaw and Stroup 1988, 36)

The liability rules under the English common law system provide an effective means of enforcing and protecting instream water rights. The same could have been true in the United States had the common law of nuisance and water law not become restricted by environmental statutes such as the Clean Water Act. According to Meiners and Yandle (1994b, 4), advances in pollution control technology and in understanding the consequences of pollution as well as changes in society's attitude about the acceptability of pollution would have encouraged further development of a common law standard of strict liability for polluters—which is close to what existed before the CWA.[16]

The British system illustrates how the United States might restructure its institutional arrangements to encourage the preservation of instream flows. Where instream flow rights are well-defined, enforced, and transferable, enviro-capitalists will come up with new contractual arrangements to promote efficient allocation. The value of such rights will increase to reflect the costs of enforcing and enhancing the amenities they produce as well as the demand of society for instream water uses. Fishing rights in Scotland, for example, sell for as much as $220,000, giving stream owners an incentive to enhance instream flows (Zern 1982a, 23). To do otherwise would be to destroy wealth. Southerland has noted:

> [There is no doubt] that sporting rights are a desirable amenity ... but it must be remembered that without careful preservation much of the amenity would not exist. The good-natured farmer who allows anyone to shoot over his land, and does nothing to preserve his stocks, will soon find out

there is nothing left to shoot. . . . [i]f he invests in improving his sporting amenities he is surely entitled to make what profit he can from his enterprise. That this should result in the rationing of the commodity by price is no more deplorable than the fact that Dover sole costs more than herring. (Southerland 1968, 113–14)

Until private rights to instream flows are allowed in the United States, property owners will have no reason to recognize these amenity values, authority will not be linked to responsibility, and efficient instream uses will not be encouraged.

Conclusion

It is commonly believed that markets in instream flows cannot work because of the public good characteristics of instream flows or because instream flow interests cannot compete in a market with those who divert and consume water. State institutional structures dealing with instream flows reflect this misconception. By refusing to allow private entities to hold instream flow rights and by holding on to obsolete elements of the prior appropriation doctrine, such as the diversion and beneficial use requirements and the use-it-or-lose-it rule, states have thrown obstacles in the way of markets. The result is governmental control of instream flows, fraught with rent seeking, constraints on future development, and limited budgets. States have established only a minimal amount of instream flows when compared with the total capacity of watercourses in the West. It is ironic that constraints on future development and insufficient provision of instream flows are the very things feared of markets.

While some states have taken steps toward markets, the remaining obstacles inhibit market solutions to instream use conflicts. With these barriers removed, we could move a long way toward efficient water allocation and use. British water institutions that promote a higher quality fishing experience and give owners an incentive to guard against stream pollution suggest that markets can play a greater role in preserving instream flow amenities in the United States.

Part of the opposition to water markets comes from fears in both the agricultural and environmental communities. Farmers are afraid that markets will allow environmentalists to buy up enough water to drastically change traditional agriculture. Environmentalists do not believe fish and wildlife can compete in a water market with consumptive users.

Neither position is realistic. The agricultural industry needs to understand that some reallocation of water from consumptive uses to instream flows is inevitable. The question is how the reallocation will take place. It may be achieved voluntarily through market transactions where current users will be compensated for conserving and transferring water to environmental uses. Alternatively, environmental interests will force reallocation by involuntary, uncompensated state regulation, the public trust doctrine, or the Endangered Species Act. If reallocation comes through market transactions, the amount of water actually reallocated is likely to be smaller than if reallocation comes through uncompensated takings. In the latter case the demands are insatiable. In the former, they are constrained by the pocketbooks of the demanders.

Environmentalists need to understand the inconsistency of their argument that fish and wildlife cannot compete in a market with consumptive water users such as agriculture. On the one hand, environmentalists argue that the agricultural industry, which uses most of the water in the West, contributes only a small percentage to western states' economies. On the other hand, environmentalists claim they cannot compete in a market with agricultural water users. It is true that agriculture is a struggling industry. Agricultural water prices are often low because of subsidies. If water is not valuable in agriculture, then environmentalists and recreationists should be able to purchase a lot of water for a little money. Indeed, most data show that a small percentage of water used in western agriculture would yield significant flows for instream flows and other uses. Couple this with the fact that many environmentalists and recreationalists have above average wealth, and it seems unlikely that they would not be able to compete for water in the marketplace.

In short, markets are unlikely to cause the economic and cultural upheaval expected by interests on all sides of the water allocation debate. Until markets are given a chance to work, however, instream flows will continue to be a political football in the United States and are unlikely to be adequately protected.

Notes

1. For a more detailed discussion of the Commerce Clause and the federal navigation servitude, see Chapter 4.

2. For a discussion of early judicial and legislative decisions on instream flows, see Anderson and Johnson (1986).

3. *Lake Shore Duck Club v. Lake View Duck Club*, 50 Utah 76, _____, 166 P. 309, 310–11 (1917).

4. *Colorado River Water Conservation District v. Rocky Mountain Power Company*, 158 Colo. 331, _____, 406 P.2d 798, 800 (1965).

5. Even in the states that now recognize instream flows as beneficial uses, the use-it-or-lose-it rule discourages changes from diversion uses to instream uses.

6. New Mexico still does not recognize instream flows as a beneficial use. Montana lists fish and wildlife and recreation as beneficial uses, but not enhancement of riparian vegetation or wetlands.

7. Personal communication with Frank Sherman, Idaho Department of Water Resources, 8 December 1994.

8. Existing appropriative water rights are also exempted.

9. Again, existing water rights take priority over newly established instream flow regulations.

10. As of 1973, instream flows were recognized as a beneficial use in Colorado (Sims 1993, 12-2).

11. Recently, the Colorado supreme court recognized the right of entities other than the Colorado Water Conservation Board to appropriate water for nonconsumptive instream uses by controlling the water in its natural course (Clifton and Zilis 1993, 988). Because the holdings of the two pertinent cases, however, depended upon control of the water in the watercourse, it remains to be seen how the cases will apply in situations where water is simply left in the watercourse for instream flow uses.

12. State law also requires that 25 percent of all conserved water be reserved to the state for instream flows. This water may be converted by the state into an instream flow right. The same is true of the 75 percent retained by the water user.

13. Reservations must be reviewed at least once every 10 years, to ensure that the objectives of the reservation are being met. Reservations may be modified to reallocate all or a portion of the reserved water to another use if the board finds that all or a portion of the reservation is not needed for its designated purpose, and if the other use outweighs the need for the original reservation. Montana Code Annotated § 85-2-316(10) (1993).

14. Montana Code Annotated § 85-2-436 through 885-2-438 (1993).

15. A total of over 14,000 acre-feet have been purchased by The Nature Conservancy, the U.S. Fish and Wildlife Service, and the Nevada Division of Wildlife.

16. See Chapter 7, "Troublesome Pollution," for a more detailed discussion.

7. The Solution to Pollution

The problem of water pollution is pervasive the world over. Releases of polluted effluent from industrial facilities, otherwise known as point source discharges,[1] are largely uncontrolled in developing nations. In Chile's Maipo River basin, for example, only a small percentage of waste discharges are treated. The same was true of the Rhine River in Europe until the 1980s, when discharges were reduced and treatment improved (World Resources Institute 1990, 163–64). In 1969, the Cuyahoga River in Cleveland, Ohio, was so full of chemicals it caught fire. The Nashua River in Massachusetts used to change color from the dye discharged by paper mills located along its banks.

Salt and other nutrients have leached into surface water and ground water from irrigated soil for thousands of years, but improved agricultural productivity since World War II has increased pollution from pesticides and fertilizers. As a result, irrigation runoff causes one of the most widespread of all water quality problems, particularly in industrialized nations such as Great Britain and the United States (World Resources Institute 1990, 161–64; *Economist* 1992a, 11).

But agriculture is not the only source of polluted runoff, otherwise known as nonpoint-source pollution. In many third world countries, urban sewage often is not treated. As a result, diseases associated with filthy water kill more than five million people per year. Cities contribute to water pollution when storm water drains off streets and overflows sewage systems and when oil spilled by residents on their driveways washes into storm sewers along with fertilizer from urban lawns (Parfit 1993, 84).

Water pollution is generally blamed on economic development and markets, but, like water allocation problems discussed in earlier chapters, pollution results from a lack of markets for clean water. As with water quantity problems, well-defined and enforced property rights can encourage water quality. The most obvious way that

133

markets can improve water quality is to facilitate increased allocations to instream flows to dilute the pollution. But markets can
also be an effective means of controlling discharges into streams
and lakes.

Unfortunately, most water policy has focused on command-and-
control rather than market incentives. In the United States, water
pollution control has been governed by the 1972 Clean Water Act.[2]
The CWA unrealistically called for total elimination of discharges
into the nation's streams and lakes by 1985. It has been criticized
by economists for ignoring the costs of stopping all discharges. But
economists who have called for benefit-cost analysis to find the
optimal level of pollution have not considered the institutional environment of laws, property rights, and regulations that together can
enable market forces to achieve a balance between nature and economic development.

Solving water pollution problems with markets requires thinking
about pollution as a matter of whether and whose rights are being
violated. This means that rights must be defined and enforced. Before
passage of the CWA in 1972, common law courts were defining
property rights in land and water in lawsuits based on trespass,
nuisance, and other torts. The reasonable-use doctrine of riparian
water law protected those who had a right to clean water from
pollution[3] while allowing upstream water users to dump effluent
into a stream so long as downstream users' right to reasonable use
of the stream's water was not violated (Meiners and Yandle 1994a,
88).[4] If effluent was dumped into a river or lake, common law courts
asked who was harmed, who was causing the harm, and how much
harm was done. In this way, land rights, riparian water rights, and
appropriative water rights were protected as the courts required
polluters who violated these rights to pay damages or stop polluting,
or both.

Though the no-discharge goal of the 1972 CWA embodied the
notion that no one has the right to pollute the nation's waters, the
act's 1977 amendments stepped back from this unrealistic goal. The
amendments shifted the emphasis from stopping all pollution to
setting water quality standards that implicitly acknowledged the
inevitable existence of some pollution (Brown and Johnson 1984,
952). Subsequently, the 1987 amendments to the CWA shifted the
focus from control of point sources of pollution to control of nonpoint

sources. Tradable pollution rights, or TDPs (tradable discharge permits), were touted as an efficient tool to achieve nonpoint source reductions, but environmentalists protested their use on the grounds that they would give polluters a right to pollute. Nevertheless, the idea of tradable discharge permits gained credibility. Markets in tradable emissions rights were incorporated into the Clean Air Act in the Clean Air Act Amendments of 1990. In 1989, a market structure for trading water pollution rights formed the basis for a nutrient reduction program implemented in North Carolina's Tar-Pamlico River basin. The success of the strategy, even in its early stages, prompted the U.S. Environmental Protection Agency (EPA) to encourage its use in other basins.

Achieving meaningful reform in water pollution regulation will require innovative institutional changes. This chapter explores the potential for using common law doctrines to help define property rights to clean water. Where rights to clean water cannot be defined, tradable pollution rights have the potential to achieve clean water from another direction by incorporating market incentives into the current regulatory process.

The Command and Control Approach to Water Pollution

The Clean Water Act

The CWA was passed in 1972 with the overall objective of restoring and maintaining the chemical, physical, and biological integrity of the nation's waters.[5] On the way toward achieving that objective, the act established the goals of rendering the nation's waters fishable and swimmable by 1983 and eliminating the discharge of water pollutants by 1985.[6] The process for achieving those goals focused on controlling water pollution from point sources by regulating the amounts and types of pollutants that could be released. The act directed the EPA to establish uniform effluent limits for all point sources in each industrial category nationwide. The limitations were technology-based, meaning they limited pollution discharges to levels achievable using the best pollution control technology available. Individual permits issued to each point source incorporated the effluent limitations in the form of specific discharge limits based on the technology requirements (Toft 1994, C6).[7]

The 1977 amendments to the CWA shifted its emphasis away from technology-based effluent limitations to water quality standards. The

135

amendments required the EPA or states to establish standards for water bodies regardless of whether the technology existed to achieve compliance.[8] Although relatively few water quality-based standards have been imposed, recent court cases demonstrate that states and the EPA will be pushed to adopt them (Toft 1994).

Since passage of the CWA in 1972, pollution from point source dischargers has been dramatically reduced, but not without cost. As of 1987, U.S. businesses, government, and individuals had spent more than $300 billion for water pollution control (Conservation Foundation 1987, 87). According to a cost-benefit comparison published by Resources for the Future in 1990, the average annual benefits of federal water pollution control between 1979 and 1988 were $15 billion while annual costs averaged $23.2 billion. These data do not mean that all expenditures on water pollution control have been unnecessary, but the magnitude of the numbers does suggest that we may have gone overboard with efforts to clean up some rivers and streams while others remain neglected.

Not only is the CWA pollution control scheme costly, it "relies heavily on punishment, i.e., the threat of fines or imprisonment, rather than on economic incentives to induce industries, municipalities, and other waste dischargers to reduce the pollutants they discharge into public waters" (Brown and Johnson 1984, 952). Section 309 of the CWA,[9] for example, provides for fines of up to $250,000 and up to 15 years in jail for violations of the act or discharge permits. In *U.S. v. Weitzenhoff*,[10] the Ninth Circuit Court of Appeals affirmed the convictions of two sewage treatment plant managers for violation of the terms of their permits. The court held that because the CWA is a public welfare statute, a court may apply criminal sanctions when a defendant knowingly engages in conduct that results in permit violation regardless of whether he is aware that he is violating the law (Cohn-Lee 1994, 1357).

The coercive regulatory process used to control point source dischargers has addressed only part of the nation's water pollution problem. The 1987 amendments to the CWA[11] began the first coordinated assault on nonpoint sources, currently the chief cause of surface water quality problems. Nonpoint sources of pollution include erosion from plowed land, runoff containing pesticides, herbicides, and fertilizers from farms and suburban lawns, and toxic metals and chemicals from streets and highways (World Resources Institute

1993, 40; Riggs 1993, ii). Though some advocate treating nonpoint sources the same as point sources (Davidson 1989, Foran et al. 1991), the difficulty of detecting and monitoring pollution from these diffuse, ill-defined sources, as well as the overwhelming number of human activities that would be affected by controls on nonpoint source pollution, has prevented application of the command-and-control approach.

The 1987 amendments required states to develop programs for assessing and managing nonpoint source pollution (Malik, Letson, and Crutchfield 1993, 959). By 1993, 44 states had received EPA approval of their nonpoint source management programs, the majority of which provided for voluntary implementation of best management practices (World Resources Institute 1993, 40; Foran et al. 1993, 480). Best management practices are management methods for agricultural operations and other nonpoint sources aimed at reducing water pollutant loadings. An example of a management practice aimed at protecting water quality is farmers' planting grass buffer areas along streams and wetlands. Such zones filter runoff from farm operations and prevent soil erosion. The Monsanto Company sponsors a program called "Operation Green Stripe." The program provides educational grants to chapters of Future Farmers of America that recruit farmers to plant 16-foot-wide buffer strips along streams, rivers, and lakes. In most cases, farm cooperatives donate the seed to plant the buffer zones, and farmers are enthusiastic about the program (*U.S. Water News* 1994b). Operation Green Stripe is a good example of voluntary implementation of best management practices by the agricultural industry to control nonpoint source pollution.

Along with voluntary best management practices, states and the EPA are also considering and implementing trading programs as a means of controlling nonpoint source pollution. The potential of such programs is discussed later in this chapter.

Issues in the Reauthorization of the CWA

The CWA was up for reauthorization once again in the 104th Congress, after unsuccessful efforts to reauthorize it in the prior three sessions (*U.S. Water News* 1995b). Reauthorization proposals have been opposed by industry and agriculture as unreasonably onerous and by environmental groups as insufficient. The key issues being considered have been watershed management, fees on point source discharge permits, reduction of toxic chemical use by industry, stronger attempts to control nonpoint source pollution, and regulation of wetlands.

Managing water quality on a watershed basis, as opposed to political boundaries, has generated significant interest, particularly as nonpoint source pollution has come to the forefront. Watershed management involves addressing the cumulative effect of all activities that generate pollution within a water basin, including both point and nonpoint sources. A prime example of a watershed management approach is the cleanup of the Chesapeake Bay. In 1983, a cooperative public-private effort to restore and protect the bay was launched. The Chesapeake Bay Program involves three states, the District of Columbia, and the EPA in coordinating efforts to reduce nutrient and toxic loadings into the bay and restore native vegetation that is essential to the estuary's health. The state of the bay has significantly improved since the program's inception, but nonpoint source pollution remains the number one cause of pollution in the bay.

Not surprisingly, watershed management has not been embraced by everyone, despite its obvious benefits. States are wary of it because they fear the primacy in water quality management they have enjoyed under the CWA[12] may be undercut by federal watershed mandates. Farmers fear it as a first step toward a permit system for agricultural nonpoint sources.

On the other hand, environmental groups like the idea of watershed management. They would like to see it become mandatory rather than voluntary. And because they fear the approach would allow states to ease up on point source dischargers, they are insisting on strong EPA oversight of watershed programs (Rubin et al. 1993).

Watershed management is a necessary step in the direction of markets in tradable discharge permits. In a basin where both point sources and nonpoint sources contribute to pollution loading, trading within and between both groups provides multiple opportunities for economically efficient pollution reduction. The House of Representatives acknowledged as much when it passed H.R. 961, the Clean Water Amendments of 1995. H.R. 961 included a provision encouraging states to use voluntary watershed management programs. States would be granted flexibility in issuing point source permits under watershed management plans, which in turn would facilitate permit trading.

Proposals to impose fees on point source discharge permits have also been included in reauthorization bills. Supporters of fees see them as a means of funding the costs of permit administration as well as other CWA programs. Though industry is not opposed to the concept of fees to underwrite administration of the CWA's permitting program, it is not eager to pay them (Ember 1992, 20).

In an effort to further reduce toxic discharges, the 1992 massive rewrite of the CWA proposed by Senators Max Baucus (D-Mont.) and John Chafee (R-R.I.) called for a ban on the discharge of eight toxic substances. Industry opposes such prohibitions, claiming they lack sound scientific basis. Because a ban on toxic discharges would also force changes in manufacturing processes, industry views it as an attempt by government to control industrial processes with the potential to seriously disrupt efficiency (Ember 1992, 20).

Stronger controls on nonpoint source pollution have been included in all of the reauthorization proposals. Environmental groups and their advocates in Congress want federally prescribed and mandated BMPs incorporated into the CWA. But states oppose such proposals, on the grounds that it would be impossible for states to review, approve, and monitor hundreds of BMP programs tailored to individual agricultural operations. States would rather be required to meet water quality standards in a timely manner but be free to determine how to meet the standards (Dean 1994, 35).

Another source of nonpoint source pollution targeted in CWA reauthorization bills is combined sewage overflow caused by the combination of sewage and storm water runoff in municipal sewage systems. The combined systems can overflow during rainstorms, sending untreated sewage into streams and rivers (Ember 1992, 19). Most reauthorization proposals provide grant money to states to help them overhaul combined sewage overflow systems.[13] While states would like to double the amount of grant money available, current reauthorization bills before Congress generally change the grants to loans and cut the amounts available (*U.S. Water News* 1995b).

Wetland regulation is a particularly controversial issue in the CWA reauthorization debate. Both urban and agricultural development can disrupt wetlands by draining and filling them.[14] While not intuitively related to water pollution control, wetlands are environmentally important because they purify water, protect against floods

139

and erosion, recharge aquifers, and provide fish and wildlife habitat (Hanson 1994, 39). Wetlands are included in the CWA definition of "waters of the United States" over which the federal government has jurisdiction. Wetlands protection began in the 1960s and was strengthened in 1972 under section 404 of the CWA.[15]

Under its regulatory authority, the U.S. Army Corps of Engineers and the EPA may limit or prohibit development of property that includes wetlands. Because many wetlands are located on private property, landowners claim that such regulation decreases the value of their property, entitling them to compensation under the Fifth Amendment to the Constitution. The 1994 CWA reauthorization bill would have provided some financial incentives for wetlands conservation, but environmental groups and key White House officials oppose compensation measures, claiming they would raise serious fiscal problems. Environmental organizations also argue that protecting wetlands cannot constitute a taking because the importance of conserving wetlands supersedes any individual's economic interests (Hanson 1994, 39). These arguments notwithstanding, the 1995 Clean Water Act Amendments passed by the House again included compensation provisions.

The debate over wetlands and takings brings to the fore the importance of determining whose rights are being violated when it comes to environmental protection. When property rights are clearly defined and enforced, governmental agencies are forced to become more circumspect in their regulation, and individuals are held accountable when their actions harm the rights of others. Thus constrained, both regulators and private property owners must carefully weigh the costs and benefits of their actions. The common law of nuisance, negligence, and trespass helps in this definition and enforcement process.

The Common Law Approach to Water Pollution

What Is Common Law?

Before passage of the CWA in 1972, the common law governed water pollution. The common law is the body of law made up of the decisions of judges as opposed to statutes enacted by legislatures (Black 1983, 144). Common law rules are asserted in lawsuits brought against polluters, in which individuals damaged by pollution seek compensation or an injunction to stop the pollution, or both. Historically, nuisance and negligence law and the rules governing water rights have been the most frequently raised claims in water pollution cases. Trespass has also been used, although not as often (Davis 1993).

Common law water pollution control is based on protection of property rights.[16] Just as property owners are protected from unreasonable interferences with the use and enjoyment of their property (nuisances) or from unauthorized physical invasion of their property (trespass), riparian and appropriative water rights owners are protected from a diminution of water quality. If any of these rights are violated by water pollution, the common law provides a remedy. However, it takes more than petty inconveniences to support a plaintiff's claim. Liability can be imposed only with sufficient and credible evidence of harm. Riparian water users, for example, are required to prove that a polluter's use of the water in a stream is unreasonable in relation to the stream's other users. Nuisance law requires plaintiffs to prove not only that the defendant's conduct is unreasonable, but that the harm it has caused plaintiffs is substantial. Trespass requires proof that an intrusion was unauthorized and either intentional or negligent, or that it involved abnormally dangerous activity (Buchele 1986, 612–13, 616–17).[17]

In contrast with statutory law, the common law relies on evidence of injury in a specific situation to determine the "right" level of pollution. If a discharge causes no injury, the pollution may be acceptable. But if a pollutant causes an injury, the pollution must be ended or reduced to a nonharmful level and damages must be paid (Meiners and Yandle 1994b, 7–8). By addressing pollution in specific cases, the common law holds polluters directly accountable to those they harm.

Under the common law system, individuals whose property is damaged by polluters have an incentive to minimize or stop the pollution because they are directly harmed and because they have standing in court to do something about it. For example, in Great Britain, ownership of fishing rights enables anglers to protect water quality via common law nuisance and trespass actions. As discussed in Chapter 6, it is possible in England to own fishing rights in a stream. Because a healthy salmon or trout fishery requires clean water, owners of fishing rights have an incentive to monitor water quality. In 1948, the Anglers' Cooperative Association was formed to fight pollution on behalf of angling clubs in England and Wales. Since then, the ACA has grown to 17,500 members and brought 2,000 actions of which only two have been lost and in the remainder has won hundreds of thousands of pounds in damages. Significantly, the polluters they defeat are often enjoined from further polluting activities. Because the English common law provides protection of fishing rights and forces polluters to pay and/or cease polluting, few pollute the same stretch of river twice (Bate 1994, 14).

Common Law Water Pollution Cases

In the United States, common law cases also have successfully addressed water pollution problems. In a 1906 Louisiana case, a riparian landowner successfully sued International Paper Company for polluting a stream that ran through his land, ruining his fishing business and reducing the value of his property.[18] In *Sammons v. City of Gloversville*,[19] a New York court issued an injunction against a town's sewage disposal system. The court found that the town's practice of emptying its sewers into a creek that flowed through a farmer's land caused filth to accumulate on the creek's bed and along its banks, and held that this act constituted a trespass of the farmer's property rights. The town was enjoined from further sewage disposal into the creek in spite of the public necessity of the sewage works and the great inconvenience and cost that could result from the injunction. The court specified that the injunction would not become operative for a year, however, giving the town reasonable time to establish a different sewage disposal system or obtain legislative relief (Brubaker 1995, 32).

More recently, in 1983, the State of New Jersey held two corporations liable for creating a public nuisance by dumping mercury-laden waste material on their property and into a creek. The corporations were ordered to abate the nuisance by removing and cleaning up the mercury pollution and to pay damages to the state.[20]

The 1906 case of *Missouri v. Illinois*[21] is a perfect example of the proof required in common law cases. In that case, Missouri tried to enjoin Illinois from allowing Chicago to dump raw sewage into the Desplaines River that ultimately flowed into the Mississippi River, becoming St. Louis's drinking water supply. Missouri alleged that the sewage carried typhoid-causing bacteria downriver to St. Louis, resulting in almost 200 deaths per year. However, the evidence in the case showed that the bacteria could not survive the trip. Because the evidence did not support Missouri's claim, the injunction was denied (Meiners and Yandle 1994b, 5).[22]

Strengths and Weaknesses of the Common Law

The requirement that harm be proven is both a strong point and a weak point in the common law approach to pollution control. Proof requirements protect accused polluters from frivolous lawsuits and claims that can be very costly. On the other hand, the proof requirements can also be an obstacle to recovery in legitimate cases. For example, when multiple sources contribute to the pollution of a stream, it is difficult to pinpoint responsibility and to prove a causal connection between the defendant's actions and the damage suffered by the plaintiff. It can also be difficult and costly to prove harm from pollution when a large number of individuals each suffer only a small amount of damage. Such victims tend to become free riders on legal actions brought by someone else against the polluter(s). Class action suits, of course, can greatly reduce the magnitude of this problem, and associations such as the ACA may be formed to help overcome it. Property owners' associations are common among landowners, and could be common among water owners if property rights to clean water were well-defined and enforced.

The transaction costs associated with using the common law to control pollution decline as our knowledge of the effects of pollution advances, making it easier to prove the cause and extent of injury. With knowledge comes responsibility in the form of tougher liability standards on polluters. According to Meiners and Yandle (1994b, 4),

> [T]he common law, not restricted by statutes, might have provided more ecologically and economically sound pollution control than has occurred under the CWA. Advances in pollution control technology and in understanding the consequences of pollution as well as changes in society's attitude about the acceptability of pollution would have encouraged further development of a common law standard of strict liability for polluters—which is close to what existed before the CWA.

In addition, the common law provides for injunctions against pollution activities so as to eliminate harm, even if it means a polluter must be shut down. Under the CWA, on the other hand, dischargers who violate their permits are merely ordered to comply with the law and possibly pay a fine. Penalty amounts are usually trivial when compared with the cost of compliance and the damage that may have been inflicted on others. Moreover, the penalty is paid to the government, not to the damaged individuals (Meiners and Yandle 1994b, 8).

A criticism of the common law approach as opposed to a legislative-regulatory approach is that the former is sporadic and ad hoc. When individual judges in different areas of the country decide cases based on unique facts and state law, the legal standards that develop may be difficult to apply in other cases. Moreover, water pollution often involves highly technical issues that can make it difficult for a court to understand and rule upon evidence (Buchele 1986, 620).[23]

Perhaps the most often raised critique of the ability of the common law to address pollution problems adequately is the seeming lack of pollution control prior to passage of the CWA in 1972. If the common law works so well, why did the Cuyahoga River catch fire in 1969? Why weren't the victims of pollution suing polluters and winning large damage awards and deterring other polluters? The answer is not entirely clear, but we can speculate about some possibilities. First, it is costly to coordinate individuals who may be harmed to bring suit against the polluter. Second, especially in the case of nonpoint sources of pollution, it can be costly to identify who is responsible for the harm. Third, even before the CWA, various federal and state statutes reduced the incentives of private parties to enforce common law restrictions on water pollution (Beck and Goplerud 1988, 204.2). Fourth, the common law was not perceived to be adequate to the task of curtailing environmental harms in the 1960s and early 1970s.[24] And finally, a growing body of evidence suggests that the demand for environmental quality is positively related to income. Without a doubt it was during the late 1960s and early 1970s that Americans began to express their demand for cleaning up the environment on a broad scale.

The Common Law and Clean Water Act Compared

Though the common law did not perfectly control water pollution, it was largely supplanted by passage of comprehensive federal water pollution legislation (the 1972 CWA), which effectively preempted many incentive-based enforcement mechanisms and "the polluter pays" principle. Although the CWA contains a clause preserving state law and other remedies against polluters, it has been narrowly construed by the Supreme Court in the face of the comprehensive nature of the act's regulatory scheme.

In *Milwaukee v. Illinois,* the high court held that federal common law was preempted by passage of the CWA, because in passing the act Congress filled the field of water pollution control with legislation, removing the need for federal court-made common law. As a result, Milwaukee's dumping sewage into Lake Michigan could not be enjoined as an interstate nuisance. So long as Milwaukee complied with its CWA discharge permit, Illinois was left without a federal common law remedy.

Six years later, the Supreme Court limited state common law by holding that Vermont could not apply its own nuisance law to impose liability on a New York discharger located on Lake Champlain, or to require the discharger to comply with more stringent controls than those imposed under a CWA discharge permit issued by New York.[25]

The CWA was enacted to protect people from the effects of pollution, but it actually limits the rights of citizens to seek protection and redress from polluters (Meiners and Yandle 1994b, 7). Under the CWA, regulators establish the acceptable level of pollution when they promulgate effluent limitations and issue discharge permits. "This statutory approach presumes regulators are correct in their knowledge about how much pollution is 'right'" (Meiners and Yandle 1994a, 91). No matter how well intentioned or informed agency officials may be, however, it is impossible for them to determine the optimal level of pollution in every case. They are subject to political pressures, and, in promulgating regulations, they set uniform standards that are applied over a broad range of pollution contexts. Moreover, the CWA's technology-based regulations sometimes require pollution control equipment to be used even if the pollutant is harmless. Worse, technology-based standards can allow emission of a harmful pollutant if the best control technology currently available is inadequate (Meiners and Yandle 1994b, 8). When compared with the common law, which determines the "right" level of pollution based on evidence of injury in individual cases, the statutory

145

method of setting uniform pollution standards breaks the connection of accountability between polluters and citizens affected by pollution.

Not unlike other environmental statutes, the CWA does allow any citizen to bring a civil action against a polluter who is in violation of effluent limitations or standards or of the polluter's discharge permit.[26] Citizens may also sue the EPA for failing to enforce the CWA. Citizen suits are limited to enforcing effluent limitations, standards, or permit requirements and may include imposition of civil or criminal penalties, an order requiring the polluter to comply with its permit and the act, and a possible award of costs and attorney's fees to the prevailing citizen. The CWA contains no provision for any payment of damages to parties injured by the pollution.[27] This limitation reduces the incentives of injured parties to seek redress that would carry with it the benefit of a general reduction in pollution and environmental damage (Meiners and Yandle 1994a, 91).

The CWA requires individuals who intend to bring a citizen suit to give 60 days' notice to the discharger. If the polluter is able to bring itself into compliance within the 60 days, the suit cannot proceed unless the violation is alleged to occur intermittently.[28] No such grace period exists under the common law. If harm giving rise to a cause of action is inflicted, a suit for damages may be brought at any time within the applicable statute of limitations.

In short, the CWA does not provide the same remedies to those adversely affected by water pollution as does the common law. At best, the enforcement provisions of the CWA bring point sources into compliance with their discharge permits, but compliance will not necessarily alleviate the pollution problem or make the harmed party whole. In contrast, the common law makes polluters directly liable for damage caused by pollution, giving them the incentive to develop better control technology and methods, and giving injured parties the incentive to sue for damages and an injunction. The deterrent effect of potential liability is particularly effective, as the work of the ACA in Great Britain demonstrates.

A Case Study: Knee Deep Cattle Co. v. Bindana Investments Co.

The strengths of the common law become evident when compared with the regulatory structure of the CWA. A lawsuit pending in

Oregon is illustrative. The Stevenson family owns the Knee Deep Cattle Co. near Coburg, Oregon, where they run 1,000 head of cattle that drink from the Little Muddy Creek. When developers built a recreational vehicle park next to a hotel near the Stevenson ranch, Mike Stevenson wondered if the motel's sewage treatment plant would be able to handle the additional volume. His fears were confirmed when untreated (and unreported) sewage was dumped from the plant into the stream (*U.S. Water News* 1995b, 7). When Stevenson's cattle began to get sick, he brought a CWA citizen suit against the hotel and recreational vehicle park owners. In the same suit he filed state common law claims of trespass, nuisance, negligence, and strict liability. The Stevensons estimated their economic damages at $350,000 and the decrease in their property value at $568,000. They also sought $2 million in punitive damages.

The CWA citizen suit was dismissed by the federal district court on the ground that Oregon's Department of Environmental Quality had diligently prosecuted the hotel/recreational vehicle park owners for violating their permit.[29] When the sewage dumping was reported, the DEQ entered into an agreement with the defendants requiring them to upgrade their facility. Although the defendants violated interim discharge limits established in the agreement and were assessed penalties, the court held that the agreement was a shield against further enforcement liability under the CWA citizen suit provision. The court also stated that citizen suit plaintiffs are not entitled to a personalized remedy.[30] The Stevensons appealed the district court decision to the 9th Circuit Court of Appeals because of defendants' continuing violation of the terms of their discharge permit and their agreement with DEQ.

At this time, the appeal remains pending. The trial on the common law claims has been delayed by pretrial motions. The Stevensons believe they can prove that the pollution from the hotel's sewage treatment plant damaged their cattle operation. Because the Stevensons got nowhere under the CWA, their only recourse lies in the common law.

Given that the common law has been eroded and replaced with a regulatory approach that is costly and inefficient, the question is whether a middle-of-the-road solution is available through legislative reform. One possibility is to establish water quality standards for a river basin and allow the users of that basin to use market mechanisms to meet the standards collectively at the lowest cost. Tradable pollution rights are a tool being considered and implemented to achieve this goal.

The Market Approach to Water Pollution

Though the CWA does not specifically authorize markets in pollution permits, permit markets arise under the act's directive to states to come up with plans to control nonpoint source pollution (Bartfeld 1993). States are drawn to incentive-based market schemes for controlling nonpoint sources as a positive alternative to the CWA's technology-based regulatory approach. While command-and-control can reduce pollution, it is unnecessarily burdensome because it pays little attention to the costs borne by regulated firms and their consumers. Command-and-control is based on uniformity, which makes the bureaucrat's job of monitoring and enforcement easier (Yandle 1994, 187). But the cost of pollution control to individual point sources varies with the nature of their locations and operations. By failing to take this variation into account, uniform regulation such as the CWA's technology requirements is far more expensive than it need be.

Moreover, as many point sources have already achieved significant effluent reductions, the cost of achieving additional controls is now much higher than the cost of implementing nonpoint source controls. Further point source reductions would contribute less toward water quality in many basins in light of the fact that point source effluent discharges now constitute a much smaller percentage of pollutant loadings than discharges from nonpoint sources. For example, before implementation of a trading system in North Carolina's Tar-Pamlico basin in 1989 (discussed later), more than 80 percent of the nutrient pollution entering that watershed came from nonpoint sources (Hall and Howett 1994, 27; Riggs 1993, i).

In short, nonpoint source pollution must be addressed if further progress toward clean water is to be realized. But by their very nature, nonpoint sources are dispersed and numerous and therefore not amenable to uniform technology-based regulation (Willey 1990, 575). In addition, attempts to control politically the extensive activities that cause nonpoint source pollution, such as agriculture, construction, and urban runoff, are not likely to be well received (Battle and Lipeles 1993, 422).

148

Because of the potential efficiency gains, all roads lead to markets in discharge permits. Tradable discharge permits (TDP) offer an incentive-based system by which regulatory agencies can achieve pollutant loading targets. . . . Unlike the [technology-based regulatory] approach, TDP's allow a degree of economic flexibility and ensure a least-cost allocation of discharge reduction across sources. (Weinberg and Willey 1991; Willey 1990, 542)

The Mechanics of Markets in Tradable Pollution Rights

What are TDPs, and how do markets in pollution rights work? Tradable pollution rights are essentially an assignment by a governmental agency of a right to discharge a specified level of pollution into a water body or watercourse. Discharge permits represent a "bubble" approach to pollution control. The bubble theory, which originated under the Clean Air Act, treats sources within a designated area as if they were all under an imaginary bubble. The total level of discharge into the bubble is determined politically, but within the bubble, sources allocate discharge levels among themselves according to relative economic efficiency.

In the context of water pollution, bubbles can be placed over a watershed within which the sum of all point and nonpoint discharges must meet established water quality standards. Under a trading program, if it is too expensive for a point source discharger to further reduce his discharges, he can buy additional discharge rights from other point sources or from nonpoint sources by funding nonpoint source controls (Bartfeld 1993, 60). Point sources with lower control costs would have the incentive to clean up more than is required of them, creating tradable discharge rights. Higher-cost dischargers would buy discharge rights and clean up less. Either way, the net amount of discharge would not exceed the allowed amount, which, again, was established in a command-and-control process (Yandle 1994, 188).

Differences in pollution control costs will create incentives for gains from trade, thus enhancing efficiency. If all sources in a basin had identical abatement costs, the net gains from trade would be zero and trading would present no advantage (Riggs 1993, 30). But differences in control costs can be substantial among point sources and between point and nonpoint sources. For example, point sources in North Carolina's Tar-Pamlico basin estimated the cost of further

149

effluent reductions required by pending legislation to be $50 to $100 million, while costs for nonpoint source reductions were estimated at $11.7 million. At one location in the estuary, additional point source reductions were estimated to cost $860 to $7,861 per pound of nutrient pollution eliminated. Nonpoint source reductions of the same pollutant from farms in the watershed would cost $67 to $119 per pound (Yandle 1994, 193).[31] The difference was substantial enough to motivate the point sources to form a basin association and set up a trading system under which they could trade pollution credits among themselves and also create tradable pollution rights by funding best management practices to reduce nonpoint source pollution.

To create a market in TDPs it is necessary, first, to determine the amount of pollution currently being discharged into a water basin and the impact of the pollution on water quality. This information, known as the baseline, allows the relationship between pollutant loadings and water quality to be established. The baseline is the level of pollution from which water quality improvements are measured (Bartfeld 1993, 64).

The second step is to establish target levels of pollutant loadings for individual pollutants in the basin.[32] Those targets will depend on the capacity of the water body to assimilate pollutants and must be translated into individual load allocations for all pollution sources within the basin. Credits or TDPs are created when a source discharges less than its allocation and is permitted to sell the credit to other polluters who wish to discharge higher loads than their permits allow (Riggs 1993, 20).

The initial assignment of TDPs is controversial because it determines who pays whom; in other words, it determines the distribution of wealth. Discharge permits can be apportioned among point sources based on each facility's historical discharge under its CWA permit as a percentage of the basin's total allowable discharges. Load limits might also be allocated among nonpoint sources as well as point sources. Where there are large numbers and a wide dispersion of nonpoint sources, Willey has suggested issuing pollution rights to geographical units such as irrigation and drainage districts or urban storm water districts (Weinberg and Willey 1991; Willey 1990, 543).[33] Discharge permits also can be auctioned to the highest bidder (Willey 1992, 416, 418). Each of these methods for allocating TDPs has very different distributional consequences.

150

Once TDPs are assigned, it is important that they be transferable. Indeed, regardless of the initial assignment, it is transferability that allows resources to move to higher valued uses. If TDPs are not transferable, a well-functioning market for the permits cannot evolve. It is especially important that TDP transactions not be burdened by lengthy administrative hearings and legal hurdles lest the net gains from trade be reduced sufficiently to discourage trading (Yandle 1994, 189). Rather than encumbering trade, governmental agencies can facilitate it by gathering data on water pollution, maintaining an efficient TDP title registry, and consistently enforcing contracts between rights holders (Ackerman and Stewart 1988, 184). Individuals must be free to seek willing buyers and sellers and to consummate trades through efficient administrative channels. Brokers can play an important role in orchestrating trades, and basin associations may act as brokers because they are likely to possess information necessary to expand gains from trade.

TDPs also must not be restricted by technology-based requirements that dictate how discharge levels are to be achieved. By setting standards and granting participants flexibility in achieving them, markets create a discovery incentive wherein dischargers will seek the most cost-effective methods of abating pollution to minimize costs and maximize profits. In addition, when they can profit by finding cheaper ways to reduce discharges, they have an incentive to discover and apply new technologies (Riggs 1993, 29; Yandle 1994, 188). Leaving the means of pollution abatement to those with time- and place-specific information about control costs and effectiveness gets the incentives right.

Monitoring and enforcement of discharges under a TDP market is no less important than it is under a regulatory system. Under the CWA, the EPA and states rely heavily on polluters to provide the bulk of data on discharges. Not surprisingly, dischargers are reluctant to report their own violations, and regulators lack the budgets or manpower to address all violations even when they are aware of them.

> For example, a General Accounting Office investigation of 921 major air polluters *officially deemed in compliance* revealed 200, or 22 percent, to be violating their permits; in one region, 52 percent were out of compliance. Even when illegal polluters are identified, they are not effectively sanctioned. For

151

example, the EPA's Inspector General in 1984 found that it was common practice for water pollution officials to respond to violations by issuing administrative orders which effectively *legitimize excess discharges*. (Ackerman and Stewart 1988, 182, emphasis added)

In contrast, markets provide strong incentives for private monitoring and enforcement, because property rights have value only when enforced. For TDPs to be of value to their holders, they must be defendable as well as capable of being divested. Both individuals and groups such as basin associations have more incentive to monitor and enforce discharge permits than a governmental agency because they have a stake in maintaining the value of their TDPs. The association can hire water quality managers to monitor and report on water quality, to prosecute violators among its members, and to pinpoint pollution originating outside its boundaries.

By requiring compliance with water quality standards and allowing markets to enforce pollution rights, agencies can reduce their monitoring burden. Rather than being responsible for ensuring that numerous pollution sources comply with their discharge permits,[34] TDP markets allow regulators to concern themselves with establishing and enforcing water quality standards, which become the binding constraint on the basin association and, hence, define the market. The focus shifts from requiring installation of certain pollution control technology, which may or may not result in clean water, to the actual condition of the environment.

Obstacles to TDP Markets

Although markets have terrific potential to reduce water pollution, they are not without flaw. Perhaps the greatest obstacle to implementing TDPs is the difference in the nature and timing of pollution between point sources and nonpoint sources. Because of these differences, initial markets are likely to address pollutants such as nutrients (nitrogen and phosphorus) that are common to both point sources and nonpoint sources. Although this may seem to be a severe limitation, in reality, "nutrients (primarily phosphorus and nitrogen) represent the largest common pollutant problem between point and nonpoint sources, . . . and are among the most common nationwide causes of degradation to lakes, rivers, and estuaries" (EPA [1992] cited in Bartfeld 1993, 49).

The second obstacle to TDP markets lies in the difficulty of defining and monitoring nonpoint source controls. Because nonpoint source pollution comes from hundreds of acres within a basin and varies according to the weather, the lay of the land and land use practices, it is more difficult to track than pollution from the end of a pipe. The uncertainty of the effectiveness of nonpoint source controls gives rise to the need for a trading ratio between point and nonpoint sources. That is, market administrators must establish the number of units of nonpoint source loadings that must be reduced to produce a pollution credit for a point source (Bartfeld 1993, 66).

In light of uncertainty about the relationship between point and nonpoint sources, the trading ratio tends to be set higher than one-to-one. A two-to-one ratio, for example, requires a point source to secure more than one unit of reduction in nonpoint source loadings to create a TDP for itself (Malik, Letson, and Crutchfield 1993, 960). In the case of Dillon Lake in Colorado, a two-to-one trading ratio was established for phosphorus reductions. This ratio was designed to provide an environmental safety margin due to nonpoint source uncertainty as well as to account for any increase in nonpoint source loading due to growth.[35]

Other implementation problems faced by markets in pollution rights include the cost of collecting the data necessary to track pollution within watersheds and the inevitable politics involved in the initial allocation of permits. The latter is especially a problem because it determines distribution and the value of TDPs.

These problems notwithstanding, TDP markets provide the best means of switching our focus from regulation and pollution control technology to environmental quality. As stated by Jerome Milliman:

> The evidence is fairly clear that the present policy of detailed direct regulation of discharges is expensive, wasteful, and ineffective. . . . Effective and efficient water pollution control policy requires a commitment to make greater use of markets and the price system as instruments of social policy. Even more basic, however, is a commitment to a goal of efficiency in environmental policy itself. (Milliman 1982, 193–94)

The Tar-Pamlico Trading Program

The nutrient trading program established in the watershed of the Tar and Pamlico Rivers in North Carolina is a good example of the incentives and organizational decisions involved in creating a market in pollution rights.[36] When the Pamlico estuary was declared Nutrient Sensitive Waters by the North Carolina Department of Environmental Management in 1989, point sources in the area were faced with the prospect of additional regulation that would require them to reduce pollutant loadings at an estimated cost of $50 to $100 million. Although nonpoint sources were responsible for 85 percent of the nutrient loads in the basin, point sources were targeted by default given the political and technological constraints of detecting, monitoring, and enforcing nonpoint source controls.[37] In response, the point sources formed the Tar-Pamlico Basin Association and with the help of environmental groups and the Department of Environmental Management developed an alternative plan for reducing the eutrophication-causing nutrient levels.

At its core, the plan consisted of a trading program between point and nonpoint sources. On the way to trading, however, the strategy called for development of a computer model of the basin that would enable tracking and monitoring of pollutant loads. Point sources also were required to evaluate their facilities and make minor operational and capital improvements. Once point source facilities were physically optimized, the association was given the option of trading discharge levels among themselves or trading with nonpoint sources by funding best management practices that would be implemented via the existing North Carolina Agricultural Cost Share Program. Best management practices used to reduce nonpoint source discharges in the basin included building animal waste treatment lagoons on farms, planting strips of vegetation along the borders of fields and along streams to prevent erosion and filter runoff, fencing livestock away from stream banks, and converting cropland to permanent vegetation.[38]

Pollutant loads were allocated by the association according to each member's permitted pollutant load under its Clean Water Act permit as a percentage of the association's total permitted load. If the association as a whole exceeds the allowable level of nutrient discharge, it must purchase nonpoint source reductions at a rate of $56 per kilogram of excess nutrients discharged. The $56 figure represents a three-to-one ratio for best management practices on cropland and a two-to-one ratio for best management practices for livestock operations (Bartfeld 1993, 87).

The association is required to self-monitor by conducting weekly samplings of water discharged from each facility, which are submitted to the Department of Environmental Management annually. The Department of Environmental Management checks for accuracy and completeness and uses the reports to determine whether the association has complied with or exceeded its total discharge limit. If the discharged loads are greater than the association's total allocation, the figures are used to calculate the excess loading payment due the Agricultural Cost Share Program. Fines and penalties may be imposed by the Department of Environmental Management for false monitoring reports, providing an incentive for accuracy.

Association members have been able to meet almost 80 percent of the nutrient reduction target by operational changes alone. Between 1989 and 1993, nutrient loading within the basin was reduced by 28 percent in spite of the fact that the average monthly flow into the watershed increased by 18 percent. The concentrations of nitrogen, the primary pollutant of concern, in effluent have decreased from 14.4 milligrams per liter to 8.9 milligrams per liter. The program has been touted as a success by members of the association, state regulators, and the EPA, all of whom point to it as a model for cost-effective and innovative water-quality control.

Several factors present in the Tar-Pamlico Basin nutrient reduction program have contributed to its success:

1. The pollution problem was caused by nutrients being discharged by both point and nonpoint sources.
2. A partial baseline of information existed before implementation of the trading program, and a constraint on nutrient loads established as part of the regulatory strategy of the Department of Environmental Management would have been imposed had the association not come up with an alternative plan.
3. A significant difference in control costs existed between point and nonpoint sources: $50 to $100 million for point sources and $11.7 million for nonpoint sources.
4. The flexibility given the members of the association by state and federal regulators to reduce nutrient loadings created a discovery incentive that paid off in the early stages of putting the market structure into place.
5. Monitoring and enforcement were placed in the hands of those with a stake in achieving allowable pollutant load levels and

in answering to the public for the overall water quality in the basin.

6. A broker was hired to facilitate the free flow of information among all groups involved in the Tar-Pamlico trading program, with the goal of reducing transactions costs.

Conclusion

Ultimately, dealing with water pollution requires making judgments about what is the right amount of pollution. In a true market, this decision would be left to voluntary transactions between willing buyers and sellers of pollution rights. Before enactment of the 1972 CWA, common law came close to providing that solution as polluters were required to pay damages to people who bore the cost of pollution. Under the CWA, however, the EPA and state regulators took responsibility for determining the level of water quality and the method by which that quality would be achieved. Plagued by a lack of information and by the fickle winds of politics, governmental agencies cleaned up some of the nation's waters but at an extremely high cost. The limits of the CWA's regulatory approach bring into relief the strengths of the common law in providing a remedy for the damages caused by pollution and in deterring further pollution. While the common law has inadequacies, it is far superior in getting the incentives right. The deterrent effect of a few well-established cases can be effective in reducing pollution without dragging every polluter into court, and codification of generally accepted liability rules can lend orderliness and certainty to the common law process.

Between the common law and technologically based regulations under the CWA are markets for tradable discharge permits. TDPs do use governmental control to establish the acceptable level of pollution, but they provide flexibility in achieving that level. At least this gets the incentives right on the pollution control side of the equation. Establishing markets in pollution rights, however, depends on possessing accurate data about the true state of polluted or pure water bodies and about the value of improving water quality. Apart from such information, it is difficult or impossible to measure success or failure in restoring and maintaining water quality. Data on water quality also allow us to focus control efforts on lakes and streams that are polluted rather than on those whose natural state has not been significantly altered by human activities. When the

CWA was passed in 1972, reliable water quality data simply did not exist, and no one knew how big the gap was between existing water quality and the goal of rendering the nation's waters fishable and swimmable (Meiners and Yandle 1994b, 2). We know more now, but the data are by no means comprehensive, uniform, and accessible.

The goal of all environmental policy should be to get the incentives right by clarifying the rights to pollute and to be free from pollution. With such rights well-defined, enforced, and tradable, individuals have an interest in monitoring their rights and in finding ways to get additional environmental quality at minimum cost. Using incentives embedded in property rights and common law principles will take us further, more quickly, and more cost-effectively toward improving water quality than coercion has under the CWA.

Notes

1. The Clean Water Act § 502(14), 33 U.S.C. § 1362(14), defines point sources of pollution as any discernible, confined, and discrete conveyance from which pollutants are or may be discharged, including any pipe, ditch, channel, or conduit. Typical point sources include factories, sewage plants, and other water treatment facilities, and power plants. In contrast, nonpoint source pollution is defined as any source of water pollution not associated with a discrete conveyance (Rodgers 1994, 292). It essentially consists of polluted runoff from a variety of sources including irrigated lands, overflowing sewage systems, and storm water.

2. *Federal Water Pollution Control Act*, 33 U.S.C. §§ 1251–1387.

3. See *Pennington v. Brinsop Hall Coal*, 5 Ch. D. 769 (1877), in which an upstream mining company was enjoined from pumping contaminated water from its mines into Borsdane Brook, near Wigan, England, because it damaged a downstream cotton mill that had been in operation for 40 years. The injunction was granted in spite of the mining company's urging the court to limit the plaintiff's remedy to damages, explaining an injunction would throw 500 employees out of work (Brubaker 1995, 268).

4. In *Strobel et al. v. Kerr Salt Company*, 164 N.Y. 303, 320, 58 N.E. 142, 147 (1900), the court stated the parameters of the reasonable use doctrine as follows:

> A riparian owner is entitled to a reasonable use of the water flowing by his premises in a natural stream . . . and to have it transmitted to him *without sensible alteration in quality* or unreasonable diminution in quantity. . . . As all other owners upon the same stream have the same right, the right of no one is absolute, but is qualified by the right of the others to have the stream *substantially* preserved in its natural size, flow, and purity, and to the protection against *material* diversion or pollution (Brubaker 1995, 272) (emphasis added).

5. Clean Water Act § 101(a), 33 U.S.C. § 1251(a) (1988). The CWA addresses surface water only. Ground water is not covered.

6. Clean Water Act § 101(a)(1) and (2), 33 U.S.C. § 1251(a)(1) and (2) (1988).

7. Technology-based effluent limitations were adopted in the CWA because they were easier to implement and enforce than water quality standards, which would require working backward from a polluted body of water to determine which point sources were responsible and how much each must be abated. The CWA also did require the states or the EPA to establish water quality standards, but states have been slow in doing so both prior to and after adoption of the act (Bonine and McGarity 1984, 426).

Performance-based regulatory standards, such as water quality standards, stand in contrast with technology-based standards. Performance-based standards set a goal to be achieved and allow polluters to find the most effective ways of achieving the goal. The outcome is what counts. With technology-based standards, the process, rather than the outcome, is what matters (Meiners and Yandle 1994b, 10).

8. In this sense, water quality standards can be technology-forcing, because polluters are forced to develop the technology necessary to comply with the standards.

9. 33 U.S.C. § 1319(b).

10. 1 F.3d 1523 (9th Cir. 1993).

11. *Water Quality Act of 1987*, 33 U.S.C. § 1329.

12. Under the CWA, states are authorized to administer their own discharge permit programs subject to the EPA's approval of each state's program. The CWA also authorizes states to issue water quality standards so long as they are consistent with the act. Management of water quality on a watershed basis would shake up this established system of state authority by removing it from the states and giving it to local and regional basin authorities subject to the EPA.

13. Apart from grant money, the states see CSO controls as unfunded mandates (Hanson 1994, 38).

14. For a discussion of how agricultural subsidies encourage wetland drainage, see Gardner (1995).

15. *Clean Water Act* § 404, 33 U.S.C. § 1344.

16. Much of the following material is drawn from the work of Meiners and Yandle (1994a and 1994b).

17. Historically, trespass plaintiffs were required only to prove the invasion itself. Intent was irrelevant, and proof of damages was not required.

18. *Maddox v. International Paper Co.*, 47 F. Supp. 829 (W.D. Louisiana 1942).

19. 34 Misc. 459, 70 N.Y.S. 284, aff'd 74 N.Y.S. 1145, 175 N.Y. 346, 67 N.E. 622 (1903).

20. *State of New Jersey v. Ventron Corporation*, 94 N.J. 473, 468 A. 2d 150 (1983). The corporations were also found liable for violation of New Jersey's Spill Compensation and Control Act. However, the polluting activities occurred before passage of the 1972 CWA and imposition of its permit requirements.

21. 200 U.S. 496 (1906).

22. Significantly, the Court stated in its opinion that although the evidence as presented was insufficient to support Missouri's allegations, what the future might show it could not tell. In other words, the Court acknowledged that improved science might enable Missouri to prove its case. *Missouri v. Illinois*, 200 U.S. at 526, 26 S.Ct. at 272.

23. In *Milwaukee v. Illinois*, 451 U.S. 304, 325, 101 S.Ct. 1784, 1796–97 (1981), discussed below, Chief Justice Rehnquist stated:

> The invocation of federal common law by the District Court and the Court of Appeals in the face of congressional legislation [(the

CWA)] supplanting it is peculiarly inappropriate in areas as complex as water pollution control. . . . Not only are the technical problems difficult . . . but the general area is particularly unsuited to the approach inevitable under a regime of federal common law. Congress criticized past approaches to water pollution control as being "sporadic" and "ad hoc," apt characterizations of any judicial approach applying federal common law.

Note, however, that in *Milwaukee* the Chief Justice addressed only federal, as opposed to state, common law. Federal common law is created by federal courts in cases where no clear federal statutory or constitutional rule applies, and where the federal courts are not required to apply state law. It is a limited area of law when compared with state common law, which is often well developed but not always clear.

24. For centuries, nuisance law was a body of strict rules that protected landowners' rights to be free from interference with the use and enjoyment of their property. But those rules were loosened in the 19th century (Lewin 1990) to accommodate the development that accompanied the industrial revolution. As of the 1960s, courts had forsaken strict protection of property rights from pollution in favor of balancing the benefit of polluters' conduct to society with individuals' right to be free from unhindered enjoyment of their property. When the polluter was a factory that provided jobs to hundreds of workers and the complaining neighbor was a small farmer whose crops or livestock were being harmed by the pollution, many courts allowed polluters to continue their operations. Although courts often required polluters to pay damages, they did not enjoin the pollution. Not only was pollution allowed, this court balancing plunged nuisance law into a state of relativity and confusion, leading scholars to describe it as an "impenetrable jungle." (See Prosser and Keeton 1984, 616).

25. *International Paper Co. v. Ouellette*, 479 U.S. 481, 107 S.Ct. 805 (1987). Although under *Ouellette* state common law survived preemption by the Clean Water Act at least in part, its viability is limited. First, state common law will survive preemption only if it does not stand as an obstacle to the full implementation of the CWA. Second, as a practical matter, proving that a discharger should be liable for damages under the common law when it is complying with a federal water pollution law can be a challenge.

26. Clean Water Act § 505(a), 33 U.S.C. § 1365(a). The citizen suit provision applies only to point source dischargers because effluent limitations and permits are not applicable to nonpoint sources.

27. In fact, permit holders have successfully raised what has become known as the "permit as a shield" defense, which entails using their permits as a defense against liability for discharging a pollutant not covered by the permit. On December 14, 1994, "the Second Circuit Court of Appeals held that as long as a discharger complies with effluent limits established for the specifically listed pollutants in its permit, then it is shielded from enforcement actions for discharging any pollutant among the universe of pollutants not regulated in the permit" (*U.S. Water News* 1994c, 1). Not all federal courts agree with the Second Circuit's decision, however. The permit as a shield defense is debated within the federal court system and among government and private environmental attorneys.

28. *Gwaltney of Smithfield, Ltd. v. Chesapeake Bay Foundation*, 484 U.S. 49 (1987).

29. Order dated 8 February 1995, in *Knee Deep Cattle Co., et al. v. Bindana Investments Co., et al.*, Civil No. 94-6156-TC, U.S. District Court, District of Oregon. Much of the

following information came from a personal telephone conversation with David Moon, attorney for the Stevensons, 17 May 1995.

30. Findings and Recommendation of the U.S. Magistrate Judge in *Knee Deep Cattle Co. v. Bindana Investments Co.*, p. 13 (citing *Saboe v. Oregon*, 819 F. Supp. 914 [D. Ore. 1993]).

31. The difference in control costs between point and nonpoint sources stems in large part from the differences in the very nature of the two types of dischargers. These differences give rise to the need for a trading ratio between point and nonpoint sources, which is discussed below.

32. It is important to note that most discussions of water pollution markets focus on one pollutant at a time or closely related pollutants such as nitrogen and phosphorus, which are both nutrients, as opposed to addressing all pollutants that enter a water body. The pollution problems suffered by many basins generally result from excessive amounts of either nonconservative (degradable) or conservative pollutants. Because they decay over time, control of nonconservative pollutants such as biochemical oxygen demand (BOD) requires staggering discharges by time and location so that pollution levels do not violate water quality standards. A major source of BOD is publicly owned sewage treatment works. In contrast, conservative pollutants cause trouble when they accumulate and tend to be a problem in water bodies that are not regularly flushed out. Concentrations of conservative materials do not change as water moves downstream because such materials do not degrade or decay. According to Letson, trading programs are simpler and more appealing when they involve conservative pollutants such as nutrients, as opposed to nonconservative pollutants, which are uncertain and politically charged (Letson 1992, 226; Bartfeld 1993, 63).

33. Within these units, allocation of discharge rights would be governed by the preferences of member landowners and other discharging entities and the organizations' charters. See Bartfeld (1993).

34. The task of directly monitoring individual dischargers would become virtually impossible if nonpoint sources were added to the regulatory burden of states and the EPA under the Clean Water Act.

35. Although the structure for the Dillon Reservoir TDP market was incorporated into state law, the market was never implemented because, in the process of allocating phosphorus loads for point sources, the loads were overestimated and point sources were able to reduce their loads far below their limits. In addition, anticipated growth within the basin did not occur. As a result, trading between point and nonpoint sources became unnecessary (Zander 1991; Bartfeld 1993, 83–85).

36. The following material was drawn largely from Hall and Howett (1994) and Riggs (1993).

37. "On the technological end, the nature of nonpoint source pollution makes it difficult to detect, monitor, and enforce (against) nutrient discharge—by definition, nonpoint source pollution is discharge from *diffuse* sources. The science of nutrient impact and removal is much more precise for point source discharge. On the political end, much of the nonpoint nutrient source is from agriculture. Farmers do not look kindly when outsiders interfere in their operations and impose controls and management practices" (Riggs 1993, ii).

38. Personal communication with Diane Brooks, North Carolina Division of Soil and Water Conservation, 29 August 1995.

8. Ground-Water Deeds

As with so many of our natural resources, concern is growing that ground-water supplies are being depleted by rapidly increasing demands. Kenski (1990, 6) typifies the concern:

> [T]he famous Ogallala Aquifer . . . stretches 800 miles (1300 km) and underlies parts of eight Great Plains states. It may be the largest underwater [sic] reserve of fresh water on Earth, but it is rapidly being depleted by the so-called ground water "mining," in which states continue to withdraw more rapidly than nature can renew. . . .
>
> In extreme cases in Texas, exhaustion of this aquifer has already resulted in land going back to sagebrush. . . . Land across the United States bears the scars of ground water depletion, and considerable sinking has occurred between Tucson and Phoenix, and around Houston, California's San Joaquin Valley, and parts of Texas, Louisiana, South Carolina, and Virginia. . . . If ground water withdrawals continue to exceed replenishment rates, some aquifers may run dry someday.

The Ogallala Aquifer, which underlies 174,000 square miles of the High Plains from South Dakota to Texas, provides 18 million acre-feet of water to 14 million acres of crops each year. This constitutes 30 percent of all irrigation water pumped in the United States and 20 percent of the nation's irrigated acreage. Declines in the aquifer's water table have averaged 11 feet since 1940 and exceeded 100 feet in some parts of the Plains states. The declines have led to projections that portions of the Ogallala will be totally exhausted by the turn of the century and that more than five million irrigated acres of land will revert to dry land farming or rangeland by the year 2020 (Dugan and Cox 1994, 1; Kromm and White, 1992, 15; Gregory 1992, 232).

The increased use of ground water, however, is not confined to the Ogallala. In 1970, 19 percent of the water used in the United States came from ground-water sources. By 1985, ground water accounted for a fourth of all fresh water used and provided drinking water for more than half the population (Guldin 1989, 13). About 95 percent of the rural population in the United States depends on ground water for domestic consumption (Pye and Kelly 1988, 206).

Irrigation is by far the largest consumer of ground water. Nationwide, 64 percent of all ground water withdrawn is used in irrigation. In the West, the figure jumps to 80 percent. Sprinkler irrigation caused a threefold increase in ground-water withdrawals between 1950 and 1975 in the West, and by 1990, ground water accounted for 37 percent of all irrigation water used in the United States (Solley, Pierce, and Perlman 1993, 37).

The increase in ground-water use might not be so worrisome if withdrawals from ground-water basins did not exceed recharge, but Kenneth Frederick estimated that withdrawals exceed recharge in western aquifers by more than 22 million acre-feet each year (Frederick 1981, 21). Such mining has been particularly severe in the Ogallala Aquifer. In northern Texas and southwestern Oklahoma, withdrawals exceed recharge by 22 percent in normal years and 161 percent in dry years. For the North and South Platte Basin, the percentages are 40 and 60, respectively (Beattie 1981, 291; Todd 1992, 235–36). To date, withdrawals constitute a small percentage of the total water stored in the Ogallala Aquifer; but ground-water use is growing rapidly, and severe overdraft is the result.

Aquifers are overdrawn in many parts of California. Statewide, average annual ground-water extractions exceed average annual replenishment by 2 to 2.5 million acre-feet per year. The state has identified 11 critically overdrafted ground-water basins and 42 more basins where overdraft has occurred but is not considered severe (Weber 1994, 660).

Both saltwater intrusion and land subsidence can result when ground-water tables are drawn down. Pumping from the Floridan aquifer has drawn saltwater inward from the seaward edge of the aquifer in several areas along the coasts of South Carolina, Georgia, and Florida. Pumping from numerous wells in the Kingsville, Texas, area has dropped the water level in the Evangeline aquifer 219 feet, causing saltwater intrusion. Overdraft in the Houston-Galveston region has caused subsidence up to 8.5 feet in a 4,700-square-mile area. Heavy ground-water pumping in the San Joaquin Valley in California has caused an area the size of Connecticut to subside by as much as 30 feet in some places. In parts of Arizona, the land has subsided as much as 12 feet and earth fissures have caused property damage (Anderson and Snyder 1996; Todd 1992, 236–38; Guldin 1989, 15).

Stream flows are also affected by ground-water pumping, especially from aquifers on the eastern seaboard of the United States:

> In addition to saltwater intrusion, heavy pumping in these coastal plain aquifers results in a reduction in instream flows. Both the limestone formations beneath the Southeastern Coastal Plain and the unconsolidated sands and gravels beneath the Atlantic Coastal Plain have many intersections with streambeds. Part of the reason that recharge is excellent for these aquifers is due to the ease with which stream flow can be diverted into the rock, sands, and gravels. Because heavy pumping induces a recharge response from all directions, intensive development of these coastal aquifers draws saline water from the oceans and drains freshwater from streams. (Guldin 1989, 15)

The traditional response of the federal government to ground-water overdraft has been to increase water supplies. In 1976, Congress passed Public Law 94-587 (Sec. 193), authorizing $6 million

> to study the depletion of natural resources of those regions of the States of Colorado, Kansas, New Mexico, Oklahoma, Texas, and Nebraska presently utilizing the declining water resources of the Ogallala Aquifer, and to develop plans to increase water supplies in the area and report thereon to Congress, together with any recommendations for further Congressional action.

Because of that legislation, farmers received funds to install dikes and dams to catch runoff and to experiment with other methods of increasing the supply of ground water.

In contrast with the federal government, states and localities have responded to increasing ground-water depletion with controls such as well-spacing requirements, limits on ground-water pumping, and closure of basins to new wells (Murphy 1988, 80). Several western states have passed legislation designating critical ground-water areas where existing pumping may be restricted and new pumping may be prohibited to preserve an acceptable amount of ground water. Under its Ground Water Management Act, passed in 1980,

Arizona implemented a comprehensive surface and subsurface water management plan that includes mandatory conservation, and Californians have been implementing various rationing plans (Gregory 1992, 248). Indiana, New Jersey, and several southeastern states require large capacity pumpers to reduce consumption during emergency shortages (Malone 1990, 14).

As with surface water, ground-water crises are related to the institutional and legal frameworks governing the resource. Currently, ground-water institutions are a combination of vague property rights and central, bureaucratic agencies. Because those institutions distort information and incentives, users are not likely to use ground-water supplies efficiently. When ground water is abundant, the nature of the institutions makes little difference; but growing demand places claims on ground water in direct competition with one another. Problems with drawdown, land subsidence, saltwater intrusion, rising pumping costs, and pollution suggest the need for institutional reform that pays attention to the structure of property rights.

A Primer on Hydrogeology

For the most part, ground water does not flow in streams beneath the Earth's surface nor do ground-water basins resemble lakes. Ground water is found in areas where porous materials, such as sand, clay, or rock, underlie the surface. Water percolates downward from the Earth's surface into the materials until it reaches an impermeable layer. The geological formations in which ground water is stored are known as aquifers. An aquifer can be thought of as a bowl filled with sand. Water poured onto the sand percolates downward to the bottom of the bowl, eventually saturating the sand and forming a pool. The top of the saturated sand is known as the water table.

Aquifers differ in shape, size, and storage capacity. The differences depend on a multitude of hydrological factors. For example, the rate at which water moves through an aquifer depends on the permeability or hydraulic conductivity of the rock, and the storage capacity depends on porosity.[1] The combination of permeability and porosity determines whether aquifers are capable of storing and supplying recoverable quantities of water (Heath 1988, 76–77). Discharge from an aquifer consists of seepage into surface streams and evapotranspi-ration through plants whose roots extend into the water table. Recharge occurs via seepage from streams and land areas where rainfall and runoff percolate through the ground into the aquifer.

"Under natural conditions, prior to the development of wells, a ground water system exists in a state of approximate equilibrium" (Glennon and Maddock 1994, 577), meaning discharge and recharge are in balance. When pumping begins, the equilibrium is disrupted and two things happen. First, the water initially pumped comes from water stored in the aquifer. Second, pumping can eventually draw additional recharge from any connected surface water or from nearby aquifers. The transition from storage to increased recharge may vary from days to millennia, depending on the characteristics of the aquifer. Where the transition is slow or connected supplies are absent, pumping will decrease the amount of water stored in the aquifer. Where the transition from ground-water storage to increased recharge is fast, surface-water supplies will decline in response to ground-water development (Balleau 1988). Either way, if ground-water withdrawals exceed natural and induced recharge, overdraft will result, and the aquifer's water level will drop.

The amount of water stored in an aquifer, known as ground-water stocks, serves two important purposes. First, stocks determine pumping lift costs, and second, they provide a source of insurance against changes in surface-water availability. Hence, ground-water stocks can be drawn down or augmented depending on expectations of recharge.

If there is open access to pumping from an aquifer, a race to the pump house, where ground water is pumped early and fast, results for three reasons. First, the classic "tragedy of the commons" occurs because of the rule of capture. In that setting, ground water not pumped will be used by others. Hence there is little incentive to conserve for the future. Second, not only is conserved water unlikely to be available in the future, it will cost more to pump if the water table declines as a result of overdraft. To avoid higher pumping costs, again users have an incentive to pump now rather than later. Finally, where the aquifer is permeable and lateral movement of water is rapid, pumping at one location can have a direct impact on the water table and water pressure at nearby locations. This happens because pumping creates a cone-shaped depression in the water table around the pump that literally sucks water from the surrounding aquifer and even can cause other wells to run dry.

Various aquifer characteristics and ground-water use either aggravate or mitigate well interference among pumpers. An impervious aquifer, for example, limits the transmission of ground water from one location to another, limiting the possibility of well interference.[2] Also, if ground water is costly to pump and transport, its use may be limited to lands overlying the aquifer. Hence diminishing returns from applying ground water to a fixed land base can constrain pumping. An expanding agricultural land base or increasing municipal and industrial uses, however, can offset diminishing returns and increase withdrawals. Other aquifer characteristics such as depth, purity, rate of recharge, pressure at which the water is stored, and connection to other aquifers and surface waters will affect well location, pumping costs, well interference, and amounts and timing of pumping.

In short, geohydrology makes the problem of defining and enforcing private ground-water rights more complicated than for other resources. Water stored underground is more difficult to measure, hydrological connections between surface and ground water are not always obvious, and third-party impacts associated with drawdown can be significant.

On the other hand, the science of ground-water hydrology has become more precise in recent years, making the definition and enforcement of rights to ground water easier. Moreover, as pumping from ground-water basins increases, additional data become available to help determine recharge, discharge, and permeability (transmissivity), making it easier to specify ground-water rights. As with any property rights, institutional evolution occurs as ground water becomes more scarce and inefficient allocation becomes more costly.

The Evolution of Ground-Water Rights

The evolution of ground-water rights has followed a pattern similar to that of surface-water rights. As long as ground water was plentiful, it made little sense for the early American settlers to devote much effort to devising institutions to govern its allocation. English common law rules were the simplest to adopt, so the English rule of *absolute ownership* was the first used in the United States to establish property rights in ground water. That rule gave the overlying land-owner complete freedom to extract ground water from under his land and use it on or off his property without liability. Precedent for the rule was established in the English case of *Acton v. Blundell*[3] in 1843, where Lord Chief Justice Tindal gave the following opinion:

> [I]n the case of a well sunk by a propriator in his own land, the water which feeds it from a neighboring soil does not flow openly in the sight of the neighboring proprietor, but through the veins of the earth beneath its surface; no man can tell what changes these underground sources have undergone in the progress of time. It may well be, that it is only yesterday's data, that they first took the course and direction which enabled them to supply the well: again, no propriator knows what portion of water is taken from beneath his own soil: how much he gives originally, or how much he transmits only, or how much he receives. . . .[4]

Because the hydrology of ground water was unknown and unknowable to early English courts, they avoided the issue by classifying ground water as property with the same status as rocks or minerals on or under the land. As Frank Trelease has pointed out, "It was in the light of this scientific and judicial ignorance that the overlying landowner was given total dominion over his 'property,' that is, a free hand to do as he pleased with water he found within his land, without accountability for damage" (Trelease 1976b, 272). This form of property rights worked well as long as third-party injuries were rare; that is, as long as ground water was not scarce.

As the demand for water grew in the United States and individuals began to compete for water and land use, the English rule of absolute ownership had to be modified. United States courts softened the English rule with the American *reasonable use* rule, under which overlying landowners are accorded coequal rights to the ground water subject to "reasonable" use on overlying land. As with the riparian doctrine applied to surface waters in eastern states (see Chapter 4), the standard for what constitutes a reasonable use has been developed by case law. In general, any application of ground water to a beneficial use in an amount reasonable in relation to adjacent landowners is deemed reasonable.

Because the determination of reasonableness is subjective and can change in response to economic and social conditions, however, the

167

American rule of reasonable use can create uncertainty in the nature and extent of ground water rights. This uncertainty increases as water becomes more scarce, causing new users to challenge existing uses as unreasonable. Challenges have produced varying answers on

> whether it is reasonable to (a) sell water, (b) use it on nonoverlying land, or (c) use it outside the natural drainage basin.
>
> Answers may differ to those questions, depending on whether "reasonable use" focuses on reasonable use of land or of water, and whether the case involves the basin to which water would return if it were used on overlying land.
>
> More troublesome is a tendency to deny that it is reasonable to sell water. This relates to what may be thought of as the water mystique, that water is a God-given resource inappropriate to be bought and sold. Or to a notion that one may do, in his own nonpecuniary interest and at his neighbor's expense, what he may not do by way of commercial exploitation. (Corker 1971, 105)

The Restatement (Second) of Torts Section 858 (1979)[5] injects even more uncertainty into ground-water rights by allowing courts to balance the reasonableness of a withdrawal against the nature and extent of the harm caused to other ground-water users. In calling for courts to balance the equities and hardships between competing ground-water users, the Restatement encourages courts to examine the total circumstances of the case (Malone 1990, 11; Matthews 1986). This mandate essentially gives courts carte blanche to examine the relative wealth of the parties and to determine who is better able to bear the burden of the harm, if any, caused by the withdrawal. The goal is an overall determination of "fairness" in each case. Fortunately, only a minority of states has adopted the Restatement approach.

In the western states, conflict over ground-water use could not be avoided as population grew, leading to the repudiation of the riparian-based reasonable use rule and the allocation of rights to ground water under the prior appropriation doctrine. Rather than tying water rights to land ownership, appropriative ground-water rights (like surface-water rights) were, and still are, acquired by application of the water to a beneficial use on a first-in-time, first-in-right basis. In times of shortage, junior rights holders may be prevented from pumping until senior rights are satisfied. Most western states now require a permit to withdraw ground water, but the standards for granting the permits are equivalent to those for appropriative rights in surface water (Sax and Abrams 1986, 794). As with surface-water rights under the prior appropriation doctrine, ground-water rights are not limited to use on overlying lands.

California adopted a combination of the reasonable use rule and the prior appropriation doctrine, known as the *correlative rights doctrine*. Under the correlative rights doctrine, landowners overlying an aquifer share the ground water subject to the reasonable use rule. Any surplus ground water may be claimed by nonoverlying landowners under the prior appropriation doctrine. In times of shortage, the overlying users must reduce their use on a pro rata basis and the nonoverlying users are cut off entirely because no surplus exists.

Current ground-water doctrines, like surface-water doctrines, have evolved as a result of changes in the benefits and costs of defining and enforcing property rights. The arid western states follow the prior appropriation doctrine, with California using the correlative rights doctrine. The more humid eastern states allocate ground water according to the principle of reasonableness. A few states, including Texas, still adhere to the absolute ownership rule. The differences between the East and West can be traced to the greater abundance of water relative to demand in the East. Hence, there has been little incentive to modify the original doctrines of absolute ownership and reasonable use. However, as some eastern states have experienced ground-water overdraft, they have begun to modify their laws to conform more closely to those adopted in the West.

Unfortunately, a majority of state water law systems ignore the physical connection that exists between most ground water and surface water. Instead, states operate separate institutional systems for surface-water rights and ground-water rights. Although several states include in their surface water rights systems any ground water located directly beneath the cut bank of a stream, this distinction makes little sense hydrologically because it fails to take into account the fact that ground water outside the cut bank of a stream may also be connected to the stream. The difficulty of determining the connection between ground water and surface water has caused states to ignore this fundamental characteristic of water resources in their allocation and management schemes. As water scarcity becomes more widespread, however, recognition of conjunctive use of surface water and ground water will become indispensable to any efficient allocation scheme.[6]

While increasing incidents of ground-water scarcity have brought pressure to change ground-water institutions, the result has not necessarily been better defined and enforced property rights and markets that encourage efficient use. Current institutions are deficient in both the tenure certainty and the transferability of ground-water rights. The relative and subjective nature of ground-water rights under the reasonable use rule is a primary cause of inefficiency in ground-water use because it renders ground water a commons subject to the rule of capture. Limits on the transferability of ground-water rights also discourage efficiency by not allowing the water to be allocated to higher valued uses. In reasonable use jurisdictions such as Georgia, ground-water rights must be used on overlying land and are generally not severable from the lands to which they originally attached. Ground-water transfers as such are rare, and when they are allowed they are subject to administrative or judicial review.

In California, to correct for problems inherent in application of both the correlative rights and prior appropriation doctrines to ground water, the state supreme court in *City of Pasadena v. Alhambra*[7] created yet a third doctrine, the mutual prescription doctrine. The Pasadena case involved the adjudication[8] of the Raymond Basin that had been overdrafted for years by both overlying correlative rights holders and nonoverlying prior appropriators. Rather than shutting down the nonoverlying prior appropriators and reducing the correlative rights on a pro rata basis, the court held that the prior appropriators had acquired prescriptive rights[9] equal to the correlative rights in the basin. In applying the mutual prescription doctrine, the court treated all correlative and appropriative rights equally. After determining the basin's safe yield,[10] the court reduced all pumping on a pro rata basis based on amounts pumped by each right holder in the five years before initiation of the case. By quantifying both the correlative and appropriative rights in the basin, the court partially eliminated the common pool problem, reduced uncertainty among ground-water rights, and allowed for their transferability (Garner, Ouellette, and Sharff 1994, 1025–29).[11]

In the 1975 court case, *City of Los Angeles v. City of San Fernando*,[12] however, the California Supreme Court partially undermined the mutual prescription doctrine. The *San Fernando* court rejected the claims of several parties to prescriptive water rights as against rights held by the city of Los Angeles. The court based its ruling on section 1007 of the California Water Code, which grants municipalities and water utilities immunity against prescription of their ground-water rights. Following *San Fernando*, the confusing interplay of the correlative rights and prior appropriation doctrines, as well as the mutual prescription doctrine and section 1007 of the Water Code, left California ground-water rights in a state of uncertainty.

In sum, as long as rights to ground water are not well defined, enforced, and transferable, ground water will not be conserved and used efficiently. Although the reasonable use rule may work in eastern states when supplies are plentiful, it becomes difficult to apply in the face of increasing ground-water scarcity. Likewise, the use-it-or-lose-it rule associated with the prior appropriation doctrine discourages conservation. Growing scarcity is forcing states to consider alternative institutions including markets.

Privatizing Ground-Water Basins

The big hurdle in the evolution of ground-water rights is resistance to changing status quo use and control. Individuals who are now pumping from an aquifer are not likely to voluntarily reduce their rate of extraction. Nor are bureaucratic agencies likely to give up power they may have over allocation. Getting all parties to agree to privatization requires demonstrating how market forces can enlarge the pie through improved allocation and determining which government institutions are necessary to facilitate this improvement.

Privatizing ground-water basins can give pumpers an incentive to optimize extraction. If a basin were owned by a single individual, that person would extract at a rate that would maximize the basin's net present value, taking into account the current and future value of the ground-water stocks and any interconnections between pumps. For the individual owner, the immediate value of stocks will be mainly a function of the value of water in production or consumption. The future value will be a function of the extent to which stocks reduce pumping costs, expand the surface area of the aquifer, and insure against annual variations in other water supplies.

As the water table declines, pumping costs rise, less water is available for future use, and the aquifer's overlying surface area decreases. Wells on the old perimeter go dry, making it necessary to transport water to formerly overlying lands.

Defining Ground-Water Rights

Though a single owner might take all these values into account, multiple pumpers acting independently will do so only if rights to the ground-water stocks and flows are well defined and enforced and if third-party effects are minimized. Vernon Smith (1977) proposed a way of doing this. Smith's scheme would issue a property deed for a share of ground water from a particular basin to each individual ground-water user i, $i = 1, 2 \ldots n$, for n users in total. Each deed would have two components, one allowing a claim to a percentage of the annual recharge or flow into the basin, and the other to a percentage of the basin's storage or stocks. The property rights would be allocated to individuals in proportion to their pumping rates during a specific base time period.

To illustrate how the stock and flow rights would work, Smith used the Tucson Basin and 1975 as the base period. Based on that year's extraction of 224,600 acre-feet, each individual's proportion of stocks and flows, P_i, would be $x_i / 224,600$, where x_i is the amount of water used by the individual in 1975. Based on that proportion, P_i, each pumper would receive two rights: (1) the flow right would be based on a fraction of a long-run average of the net annual recharge to the basin, which for the Tucson Basin was estimated to be 74.6 thousand acre-feet. Therefore, the property right of individual i to the annual recharge would be 74.6 P_i thousand acre-feet in perpetuity; and (2) the second property deed would convey a right to a share of the basin's stock, which for the Tucson Basin was approximately 30 million acre-feet in 1975. The share of this stock granted to individual i would also be P_i (Smith 1977, 7–10).

The initial allocation of water rights can promote waste,[13] especially if it induces a race to the pumphouse. For example, if policymakers were considering the idea of privatizing a ground-water basin based on average use during the five years prior to privatization, a race to the pumphouse could ensue among pumpers wanting to increase their share of rights. To avoid this race to increase individual rights, water deeds could be based on use over a longer period of time, or they could be assigned to landowners in proportion to ownership of land overlying the aquifer.

Tracking Ground-Water Use in a Privatized Basin

Given some initial allocation of rights to stocks and flows such as that proposed by Smith, enforcement of rights requires an operational accounting system. Pumps would be metered, and each owner of a right would begin the accounting period with an initial stock. At the end of the period, an adjustment would be made to the user's stock account by subtracting the amount pumped and adding the appropriate share of aggregate recharge. Because recharge is random, a running five-year average could be used and updated annually. If return flows from irrigation were of consequence, they could be added to an individual's stock or recharge account. In either case, return flows should be tracked and attributed to individual users to maintain an incentive to reduce consumptive use of each share of the ground-water asset. Maintaining meter integrity would be no different than for electricity and water meters. Violations for pumping water in excess of the amount owned could be handled with fines or deducted with a penalty from the pumper's share of subsequent years' recharge.

This type of accounting system has been in place since 1978 in the Genevois Basin, which underlies the border area between France and Switzerland. A treaty signed by the Canton of Geneva and the Prefecture of Haute-Savoie created a commission to supervise ground-water use.

> The commission keeps a complete inventory of public and private pumping installations in the two countries. Each installation has a metering device indicating the volume of water taken by each user. . . . France's contribution to defraying the recharge costs is assessed by reference to the amount of water taken by French users together with the contribution to the natural recharge of the aquifer made by French territory. . . . The commission has at its disposal a system of control which allows it to know with certainty the intensity of use of the aquifer and thus plan withdrawals rationally with the needs of users in mind. (Barberis 1991, 185)

Ground-Water Transfers

Allowing transfers among owners in a ground-water basin improves allocation in at least two ways. First, it moves water from

173

lower to higher valued uses. Second, transfers allow individuals to better deal with risk in relation to variations in water availability over time. Contracting among water owners offers an opportunity for the relatively more risk-averse parties to trade with the relatively less risk-averse parties. Those who are relatively risk-averse will want to hold more stocks as a contingency against water shortage associated with random fluctuations in recharge and demand. As a result of these market transactions, prices of ground-water rights will reflect different values of water and different risk preferences among the producers in the basin.[14]

Any system for privatizing ground water and allowing transfers between willing buyers and sellers must protect third parties. Market transactions encourage private decisionmakers to seek mutually beneficial trades, but if third parties are affected by the transactions, restrictions on transfers may be necessary. Consider the case in which an individual with a right to extract ground water from an aquifer sells his water to someone outside the basin or to someone who changes the use so that the return flow or recharge to the aquifer is reduced. Because third-party rights holders would be affected, ground-water transfers or changes of use should be restricted to only that water historically consumed, as with surface-water transactions (see Chapter 5). For example, if consumptive use were measured and determined to average 65 percent of each water right in an aquifer, as it was in the Tehachapi Basin in California, a person who wanted to transfer 130 acre-feet out of the basin would have to relinquish his right to 200 acre-feet. The remaining 70 acre-feet (35 percent) would be left in the basin to provide what would have been recharged.

While the exchange of consumptive rights to stocks and flows improves efficiency with respect to use and allows individuals to share risk, the property rights system does not completely solve the commonality problems associated with pumping costs and spatial distribution. An individual user may hold title to a certain stock of water, but the conditions under which he can obtain the water in the future are altered by the use rates of other pumpers in the basin. First, rapid pumping in the aggregate will increase the future cost of pumping for any individual. Second, an individual with a well near the perimeter of the aquifer who conserves his stocks could find his well dry if the aquifer is drawn down by other pumpers.

The stock rights could be sold, but the value would depreciate with a declining surface area of land overlying the aquifer.

To achieve efficiency, given positive pumping costs or the potential that some overlying lands might be left dry by basin drawdown, there must be a limited modification of Smith's property rights scheme. When initial stocks are allocated to private owners, some stocks could be withheld from allocation to ensure that the water level in the basin does not fall too low. The ideal or equilibrium level of stocks to be withheld, however, is difficult to determine because many of the hydrologic and economic variables are random and subjective. Improved information will be available after the initial appropriation of stocks for private property has been made, and, *ex post*, better estimates will evolve as pumping occurs. Unless there are significant economic or hydrologic surprises, the economic costs of error and the choice of stocks withheld should be relatively small.

Emel (1987) proposes a more elaborate scheme for defining rights to stocks and flows. To protect pumpers from pumping externalities, Emel would limit the allowable rate of decline of the basin's overall water table and set a maximum allowable cumulative interference rate among wells. The two limits could be appended to Smith's stock and flow rights along with the consumptive use limitation. Actual determination of each limitation in a specific basin would be made by an administrative agency or basin association and therefore might not coincide with economic efficiency. Quantification of the limits would provide certainty to ground-water rights, however, by defining objectively in advance the extent of allowable third-party impairment, the determination of which is a major hurdle to both ground-water and surface-water markets.

The Unitization Alternative

Unitization is an alternative means of achieving efficiency in the face of pumping costs and well interference. It is an approach used to develop oil and natural gas deposits that lie in subterranean reservoirs similar to ground water. It provides an opportunity to manage a basin as if it were owned by a single entity. When individual pumpers unitize a reservoir, they agree to develop the reservoir as a whole and divide the costs and profits proportionally. This arrangement enables them to obtain the most efficient production

175

from the field by carefully spacing wells and applying a reservoir-specific rate of extraction. By drilling the optimal number of wells in strategic locations over the reservoir, developers can optimize pumping costs and extraction rates. In addition, they can control and adjust extraction in response to market conditions. Monitoring and enforcement costs are reduced because the resource is recovered from a few, closely controlled wells. In short, "[c]ooperative unit production from a reservoir eliminates the perverse rush to drill, with its attendant excessive costs and reduction in eventual recovery" (Murray and Cross 1992, 1116).

Faced with inefficiencies caused by excessive pumping under the rule of capture, some oil and natural gas producing states have required unitization. As a result of a compulsory unitization statute for oil and gas reservoirs, Louisiana's oil and gas wells are, on average, one-third more productive than those in Texas, which does not require unitization (Murray and Cross 1992, 1150).

Unitization, coupled with quantified, transferable ground-water rights, could allow for efficient development of ground-water aquifers. Drilling and using an optimal number of wells could result in reduced pumping costs as well as monitoring and enforcement costs. Well interference problems could be minimized. Although the reduction in the number of wells would require transportation of pumped water to the land on which it is used, that cost must be weighed against the elimination of pumping externalities as well as increased opportunities for users on the periphery of the basin to use their rights in cases where reduction of the aquifer's perimeter would otherwise prohibit it. Moreover, transportation costs might be minimized by use of the existing surface-water infrastructure of irrigation districts, mutual ditch companies, and federal water projects.

Of course, the transaction costs of cooperative agreement for development of an aquifer may be so high as to outweigh the benefits of unitization in some basins, particularly if the number of existing pumpers is large. But as ground water becomes more scarce, the costs of inefficient allocation rise, thus increasing the incentive to overcome those transaction costs. Transaction costs could be reduced by taking advantage of existing user organizations such as municipalities, water districts, and other ground-water user associations.

In the final analysis, assigning private rights should induce less extraction because the ground water will have tangible value to individual users, which is not the case under the rule of capture. As producers compare water table declines under a private ownership regime with experiences of uncontrolled pumping, they are likely to observe a more conservative behavior. This should generate expectations that pumping costs will increase less rapidly in the future than they would in a commons setting. As long as pumpers adjust to this expectation, rates of withdrawal over time should approach optimality.

Because ground-water markets require definition and enforcement of rights to storage and recharge and because this definition and enforcement will not eliminate all externalities, many responsibilities remain for governmental agencies. A private property rights market regime would place allocation decisions in private hands, generate price information about values in different uses, and encourage mutually beneficial trades. But all of this would depend upon centralized recording of titles and protection of third parties. As with surface-water rights in prior appropriation states, state water agencies would have responsibility for determining levels of existing stocks, recharge rates, and consumptive use rates. To guard against pumping and spatial distribution externalities (in the absence of a private unitization agreement), at minimum agencies would have to provide a hearing process where third parties could challenge market transfers and at maximum would have to determine allowable pumping and interference rates.

Private Rights in Practice

Assigning private, transferable rights to ground water can potentially improve allocative efficiency, but do the potential gains justify the costs of establishing the rights? The answer is no as long as ground water is relatively abundant and the cost of defining and enforcing rights is high. But as ground-water scarcity threatens pumpers with increased costs and limited supplies, market-based allocation schemes become more attractive and even necessary, as the following examples illustrate.

Oklahoma

In 1973, Oklahoma enacted a law that provided for the assignment of transferable rights to ground water. Under that law, ground-water basins can be dewatered as long as the dewatering takes place over a period of no less than 20 years. Rights to water in the basins are transferable, except when transfers are challenged by affected third parties, in which case the challenge is resolved in an administrative process.

Before rights can be assigned, however, hydrologic studies must be completed to determine the amount of water in each basin and the basin's maximum annual yield. Such studies are costly and sometimes take years to complete. Nearly 20 years after passage of the legislation, only 12 of 150 basins in Oklahoma had been studied (Anderson 1990, 15). While Oklahoma has laid a market-based foundation for allocating its ground water, the cost of quantifying ground-water rights remains high in relation to the costs imposed by scarcity.

California

Better examples of how privatization can improve ground-water allocation exist in California, where scarcity has been a severe problem in several basins. In contrast with its vast and complicated institutional system for governing surface water, California does not have a comprehensive statewide ground-water management statute or program. As a result, local public entities serve as the primary ground-water managers. In the absence of state-controlled ground-water management, basins are governed by a combination of authorities. In basins in which ground-water rights have been adjudicated by a court, court-appointed watermasters are given management authority. In unadjudicated basins, a variety of public entities, including cities, counties, ground-water management districts, local water user agencies, and any combination thereof may have a hand in controlling ground-water pumping (Garner, Ouellette, and Sharff 1994; Weber 1994; Patrick and Archer 1994). Often, local efforts at governing ground-water resources consist of pumping controls and restrictions on exports to reduce overdraft. In adjudicated basins, however, rights are quantified, setting the stage for ground-water markets.

Tehachapi Basin. The Tehachapi Basin, located in Kern County, California, approximately 35 miles southwest of Bakersfield and 100 miles north of Los Angeles, is an example of an adjudicated basin. The 37-square-mile basin is the largest of three adjudicated basins in the area covered by the Tehachapi-Cummings County Water District.[15] Water in the basin has been used primarily in agriculture, but municipal and industrial uses have increased substantially in the past few decades. The only source of natural recharge to the basin is precipitation in the watershed.

Ground-water overdraft began in the Tehachapi Basin in the 1930s following a steady increase in irrigation. By 1960, withdrawals exceeded recharge by 60 percent. The water level in the overall basin dropped by an average of 70 feet per year between 1951 and 1961, while the level around the city of Tehachapi fell 110 feet. During that time, ground-water storage in the valley fell by more than 61,000 acre-feet. From 1961 to 1968, the water table continued to drop an average of three feet per year. Consequently, pumping costs increased dramatically and some wells ran dry. Fears that continued overdraft would seriously affect the agriculturally based economy brought about the formation of the Tehachapi-Cummings County Water District.

In 1965, a citizen advisory committee was formed to consider the options for managing the basin. The committee decided to import surface water from the California Aqueduct and to adjudicate ground-water rights in the basin. Because the basin is situated at an elevation of 4,000 feet, importing surface water required a pipeline to lift aqueduct water more than 3,400 feet. That made surface water far more costly than ground water, and that, in turn, made it unlikely that users would reduce ground-water use without some additional incentive.

Adjudication of the Tehachapi Basin offered the main hope for controlling overdraft. In 1966, the water district filed suit in Kern County Superior Court, asking the court to adjudicate ground-water rights in the basin. The judgment, handed down five years later, followed the mutual prescription doctrine and limited total extraction to safe yield. The court quantified each party's base ground-water right on the basis of the highest average annual extraction rate over five consecutive years during any period after overdraft began. The base rights totaled 8,250 acre-feet. Safe yield was estimated to be two-thirds of the base rights, or 5,500 acre-feet. The court thus allocated to each pumper two-thirds of his base right. The court also ruled that users pumping less than their allocated amount could stockpile part of the excess for up to two years, but the amount stockpiled was limited to 25 percent of the allowed allocation.[16] The costs of adjudication totaled $300,000 for 100 users, or less than $55 per acre-foot.

To encourage the use of imported surface water that became available in late 1973, an exchange pool was established. The pool allowed reimbursement of users located near the surface-water source for the difference between surface-water costs and average ground-water pumping costs. Suppose, for example, that surface water for agricultural use was priced at $100 per acre-foot and average ground-water pumping costs were $40 per acre-foot.[17] If an individual not adjacent to the surface-water source wanted to use more than his allocated share of ground water, the watermaster could allow him to pump ground water in excess of the adjudicated right at a charge of $60 per acre-foot. During the same period, a user adjoining the surface-water source would be required to substitute an equivalent amount of surface water for ground water. That user would be reimbursed for the $60 per acre-foot difference between the price of surface water and the average cost of pumping ground water.

There are, however, two restrictions on the exchange of ground-water rights in the Tehachapi Basin. First, the Kern County Assessor has ruled that water rights severed from the land are subject to the same taxes as mineral rights. Because those taxes are high, the exchange of ground water has occurred only by sale of the overlying land or short-term leases. Second, to guard against third-party impairment, the watermaster must approve extraction at a location other than where the water right was developed.

Three lessons can be learned from the adjudication of the Tehachapi Basin. First, rights to ground water can be defined and enforced. While the Tehachapi adjudication involved only rights to recharge, the fact that water can be stockpiled suggests that definition and enforcement of rights to the ground-water stocks are also feasible. Second, major externalities in the Tehachapi Basin have been eliminated through adjudication. Water levels are no longer declining, eliminating the upward pressure on pumping costs, and wells in the basin have recovered by 50 feet. The importation of surface water has provided incidental recharge that has raised the water table in some areas. The city of Tehachapi no longer rations water as it did during some periods before adjudication, and rising water tables have brought previously marginal wells back into production.

Third, adjudication of transferable ground-water rights can facilitate reallocation of a scarce resource to new uses. Before adjudication, agriculture was the primary water user in the Tehachapi basin and the lion's share of ground-water rights adjudicated in the 1966 law-suit belonged to farmers. Those rights are now leased and sold locally, mostly to cities or community service districts who purchase both land and ground-water rights for increased development. While agriculture is slowly declining in the face of burgeoning population, farms located along the surface-water source are thriving. The resulting adjustments in ground-water use have been less acrimonious because of voluntary exchange.

Though limited privatization of rights to recharge has produced some improvements, further decentralization and privatization could increase efficiency. Remaining problems stem from (1) restrictions on stockpiling, (2) the absence of rights to the basin's storage, (3) subsidies that distort the true cost of imported surface water, and (4) constraints on the transfer of ground-water rights.

1. The 25 percent limit on stockpiling creates the incentive to "use it or lose it." It also removes water from the property rights system. Eliminating it would decentralize decisions and move the system toward a long-run equilibrium. For example, if a farmer is entitled to 100 acre-feet of ground water and uses only 60 acre-feet during the year, his allowable allocation for the next year would be 125 acre-feet. Rights to only 25 of the 40 acre-feet not used may be retained by the farmer. While the 15 acre-feet are not removed from the basin, the right to use the water is lost. Restrictions on carryover only make sense if the basin is severely overdrafted on the one hand, or at or near capacity on the other, in which case stockpiling could impair surface drainage. Neither is the case in the Tehachapi Basin.

2. A complete property rights system calls for assigning rights to ground-water stocks as well as recharge, but the Tehachapi adjudication included no such provision. While it is true that the safe-yield limitation eliminates externalities from draw-down, the absence of rights to the stocks means that valuable water will be locked up and left in the ground. Although spatial distribution of wells and environmental problems may dictate withholding some portion of the stocks for a time, it is difficult to justify locking up the entire storage of an aquifer. Just as a user is granted a perpetual right to a percentage of flow, that user could be given a right to a percentage of the stock as

181

proposed by Smith (1977). Because surface water for agriculture is much more expensive than ground water, efficiency could be improved by allowing the use of less valuable ground-water stocks.[18]

3. The efficiency gains implicit in the price differences between surface and ground water are understated to the extent that surface-water delivery is subsidized for agricultural users. Although today's cost of water from the state water project is approximately $120 per acre-foot, lifting the water 3,150 feet into the Tehachapi Basin adds over $65 to the cost per acre-foot. Furthermore, only municipal and industrial users without leases for state water are required to pay the full cost, giving a subsidy to agricultural users and inducing them to use too much surface water. Eliminating the subsidy would reduce the overall demand for water, because ground-water users would be less inclined to supplement their ground-water rights with imported surface water if forced to pay the true cost of the surface water.

4. Finally, restrictions on the transfer of water rights have reduced the efficiency of the system. For example, the Monolith Portland Cement Company held about 1,200 acre-feet of rights in 1980. In recent years, it has lost large quantities of water due to the carryover limitation. In addition, because the company's rights are on the east end of the basin and agricultural demands are on the west end, watermaster approval is necessary to effect transfers. Approval of cross-basin transfers is not routinely granted because it is believed that large-scale transfers to one location could create cones of depression and increase pumping lifts. Though this potential externality cannot be ignored, it is worth asking whether potentially higher pumping costs are greater than the value of water being forgone because of restrictions on transfers. Such a restriction on transfers may be an expensive solution to a small problem. A better solution would be to objectively establish allowable well interference rates in advance as suggested by Emel (1987). Doing so would reduce transaction costs by providing willing buyers and willing sellers with the information they need to determine potential gains from trade.

Mojave Basin. The Mojave Basin, located 100 miles east of the Tehachapi Basin, provides a more recent example of adjudication.[19]

When development in the basin threatened ground-water supplies in 1990, the city of Barstow filed suit to stop further development. A year later, the Mojave Water Agency requested complete adjudication of all water rights in the watershed. It is estimated that overdraft in the basin began in the 1950s and currently stands at between 70,000 and 90,000 acre-feet annually. Agriculture is the largest consumer of ground water, but rapid urbanization in the last 20 years has greatly increased municipal use.

The court's judgment, entered in September 1995, divided the basin into five subareas and granted all pumpers ground-water rights based on their highest annual amount pumped in the five-year period from 1986–90. To discourage excessive pumping and raise funds to buy imported surface water, the judgment allowed the agency to impose a pumping tax on increasing increments of each water right. The increments were set at 5 percent and, after the first year, are scheduled to be phased in at a rate of one increment each year for four years, for a total of 20 percent. Thus, after five years, all pumpers will be able to pump 80 percent of their right free from the pumping tax, with the remaining 20 percent assessed the tax. Thereafter, the increments may be either increased beyond the 20 percent or decreased, depending on overdraft in each subarea.

As in the Tehachapi Basin, supplemental surface water from the state water project has played a role in the Mojave Basin. The court's judgment was based upon the availability of 50,800 acre-feet of imported surface water under a contract between the Mojave Water Agency and the state water project. Before the adjudication, the agency used ad valorem tax assessments to buy contract water, which currently costs $107 per acre-foot. As a result of the adjudication, however, at least four assessments, including the pump tax described above, may be levied against ground water pumped in the basin. Some of the money raised will be used by the agency to purchase imported surface water. A biological resource assessment will be used to fund a trust for purchasing water to maintain natural resource amenities in the basin.

Transfers of the adjudicated ground-water rights within and between uses and within and between sub-basins are permitted to encourage efficiency. Agricultural users may transfer their entire right to urban or other types of uses, but the transferred right will be adjusted to consumptive use only. If a transfer occurs within

183

one of the five subareas, the parties need only give notice to the watermaster. Transfers between subareas, however, require watermaster approval to guard against third-party impairment. Though temporary transfers (leases) occurred while the adjudication was pending, the uncertainty created by the absence of a final court judgment has steered users away from long-term and permanent transfers.

The Mojave Basin adjudication took only five years to complete because most of the parties stipulated to the plan outlined above. Like the Tehachapi Basin, which also took only five years to judgment, the urgency of the overdraft situation motivated ground-water users to find a workable solution. Significantly, the solution in each basin included quantifying ground-water rights and allowing their transfer. However, in the Mojave Basin, as in the Tehachapi Basin, limiting rights to recharge but not stocks, and limiting transfers, have impeded efficiency.

Texas

A final example of the potential for private ground-water rights comes from the Edwards Aquifer in Texas, one of the few states that still adheres to the absolute ownership rule under which pumpers own any ground water they can "capture" from beneath their land, so long as they do not waste it. Unfortunately, this absolute ownership rule has taken its toll on the Edwards Aquifer. In recent years, drought and overpumping have dropped water levels in the aquifer, threatening to dry up several large springs flowing from its eastern edge. Discharges from the two largest, Comal Springs in New Braunfels and San Marcos Springs in San Marcos, provide environmentally unique amenities attractive to recreationists and wildlife, including several endangered species.

Annual recharge of the Edwards Aquifer averages 635,500 acre-feet but varies dramatically from as low as 43,700 up to as high as 2,003,600 acre-feet. Some 4,000 wells pump 588,000 acre-feet of water from the Edwards each year, and flows from the aquifer's springs average 340,000 acre-feet. Of the withdrawals, municipal and military uses constitute 62 percent, irrigation 17 percent, industry 9 percent, and other uses 12 percent (Griffin and Boadu 1992; Vaughan and Emerson 1996).

Because of its high porosity and transmissivity, the Edwards Aquifer transmits water quickly. But heavy pumping has resulted in highly variable water levels and flows from the aquifer's springs. In 1989, after several wet years, the water level at one indicator well was 699 feet above sea level. Two years later it had dropped to 627 feet, and by 1990 it had dropped to 623 feet. In addition, annual declines between January 1 and the yearly low are now three times greater than in the 1960s. Recurrence of serious drought would dry up Comal Springs and reduce the flow from San Marcos Springs by half. The flow of the Guadalupe River, a third of which comes from the Edwards, could be cut by 90 percent. Continued overuse of the aquifer will dry up the aquifer's springs, lower water tables, and cause saline water intrusion from the aquifer's southern and eastern edges (Griffin and Boudu 1992, 283; Vaughan and Emerson 1996, 11).

In 1990, the Texas legislature considered, but did not pass, the Edwards Aquifer Administration Act that would have established marketable ground-water rights for the region (Griffin and Boadu 1992, 285) and thereby reduced overdraft. The Sierra Club filed suit against the Department of Interior and the Fish and Wildlife Service in 1991, invoking the Endangered Species Act to require the Fish and Wildlife Service to protect the endangered species living in and near the Edwards Aquifer and its springs (Vaughan and Emerson 1996, 13–15). The court ordered a former Texas water official to prepare an emergency withdrawal reduction plan for the aquifer. As submitted, the plan required irrigators and the city of San Antonio, which relies exclusively on Edwards Aquifer water, to reduce withdrawals by as much as 40 percent in dry years. Not surprisingly, the judge subsequently created a five-member panel to develop an alternative to the reduction plan (*U.S. Water News* 1995a).

Responding to the Sierra Club litigation, the Texas legislature passed a bill in 1993 calling for adjudication of ground-water rights in the Edwards Aquifer and allowing for their transfer. The method chosen for quantifying the rights would have resulted in claims far exceeding the basin's capacity but would have been accompanied by pro rata reductions. Though the legislation took a few steps in the right direction, it would have limited transfers to leases and made 50 percent of each right appurtenant to the land. Therefore, it had very little hope of improving efficiency and was not much of a loss when it was invalidated for violating the federal Voting Rights Act.

A better proposal for addressing the needs of Edwards Aquifer ground-water users has been developed by two Environmental

185

Defense Fund economists, Benjamin Vaughan and Peter Emerson. Recognizing the commons problem created by the current allocation scheme, Vaughan and Emerson call for privatizing the Edwards Aquifer by adjudicating and quantifying ground-water rights based on average use over a relatively long time period, such as 20 years.[20] Rights would not encompass an actual amount of water, but rather a proportion of the Edwards's annual safe yield. The annual yield is measurable because of the tight relationship between the aquifer's stock and flows at its springs. Given seasonal rainfall, recharge, and pumping patterns, the U.S. Geological Survey can predict the Edwards's minimum safe yield before spring planting each year. Markets could then allocate the water rights among competing uses.

Vaughan and Emerson also propose an alternative, prior appropriation system under which ground-water rights would be adjudicated. Under that scheme, rights would be divided into broad classes according to their priority date, that is, the date pumping began. For example, all rights with a priority date between 1930–40 would be in one class, 1950–60 another class, and so on. As with the proportional rights, the yield would be announced annually. In dry years, the most junior users would be prohibited from pumping until the senior rights were met. Alternatively, all junior users in the affected class could be reduced on a pro rata basis.

Under either proposal, Vaughan and Emerson predict that markets in short-term transfers and dry-year options would emerge and would tend to be more pervasive than outright sales. As such, years with normal rainfall would bring less trading, and agriculture would proceed as before. Even if large-scale, long-term transfers did occur to meet the demands of San Antonio or other municipalities, agriculture could continue with different cropping patterns and irrigation technologies.

Conclusion

Approaches to ground-water allocation have traditionally begun with central management because policy analysts have assumed that the definition and enforcement of ground-water rights are infeasible. As the value of water rises, however, additional efforts will be devoted to capturing the value of the ground water. Will these efforts be devoted to influencing bureaucratic managers or courts, or will they be devoted to defining and enforcing rights that can be traded in a market? The evidence from the Tehachapi and Mojave Basins in California suggests that privatization has improved allocation at reasonable costs. Yet bureaucratic restrictions on pumping from stocks and on transfers continue to thwart further efficiency gains. The basic proposal put forth by Smith (1977) for establishing both stock and flow rights remains a model for ground-water privatization. Where geohydrology results in third-party impairment, some restrictions on transfers may be necessary. Experiments with unitization of ground-water basins could go beyond the Smith approach to internalize all pumping interconnections and optimize extraction. The fact that environmental groups are proposing a property rights approach to ground-water management suggests that the time is ripe for institutional reform that will facilitate ground-water markets.

Notes

1. According to Heath (1988, 76–77), permeability, or hydraulic conductivity, is a function of *pore size* and determines the water-transmitting capacity of the rock. Porosity is a function of the *number of pores* in the rock and determines its storage capacity.

2. Well interference may also be nonexistent in highly transmissive aquifers, such as the Edwards Aquifer in Texas, where water moves quickly through the aquifer to replace water that is withdrawn. In such aquifers, pumping results in an aquifer-wide drop in the water table.

3. 12 M. and W. 349, 152 Eng. Rep. 1223 (Exch. 1843).

4. 12 M. and W. at 349, 152 Eng. Rep. at 1223.

5. Section 858 states:

> (1) A proprietor of land or his grantee who withdraws ground water from the land and uses it for a beneficial purpose is not subject to liability for interference with the use of the water by another, unless
>
> (a) the withdrawal of ground water unreasonably causes harm to a proprietor of neighboring land through lowering the water table or reducing artesian pressure,
>
> (b) the withdrawal of ground water exceeds the proprietor's reasonable share of the annual supply or total store of ground water, or
>
> (c) the withdrawal of ground water has a direct and substantial effect upon a watercourse or lake and unreasonably causes harm to a person entitled to the use of its water.
>
> (2) The determination of liability under clauses (a), (b) and (c) of Subsection (1) is governed by the principles stated in sections 850 to 857 [which set forth the Restatement rules governing riparian water rights, *i.e.*, reasonable use].

Restatement (Second) Section 850A states:

The determination of the reasonableness of a use of water depends upon a consideration of the interests of the riparian proprietor making the use, of any riparian proprietor harmed by it and of society as a whole. . . .

6. Abrams has suggested unifying both surface- and ground-water rights under the prior appropriation system and not attaching the rights to either surface or ground water. Rather, users would fill their rights from either source depending on the overall supply status of the basin involved (Sax and Abrams 1986, 850–55).

7. 33 Cal.2d 908, 207 P.2d 17 (1949).

8. In many states, adjudication does not occur until overdraft causes harm to ground-water users, motivating them to file suit against each other. In adjudicating an aquifer under the correlative rights doctrine, the court quantifies ground-water rights not only in relation to each other, but also in relation to the capacity of the basin. When there is not enough water in a basin, each user is limited to a proportionate share of the total amount available based on reasonable and beneficial use (Garner, Ouellette, and Sharff 1994, 1028). In prior appropriation jurisdictions, rights are determined and the doctrine is applied to meet senior rights and possibly cut off junior rights in times of scarcity. In eastern states, ground-water rights are generally not quantified until a lawsuit is filed by one ground-water user alleging harm from the unreasonable use of another pumper. Adjudication of reasonable use rights is limited to the disputing parties only, however, and therefore is of limited utility. Many jurisdictions now require ground-water users to obtain a permit to pump a specified amount of ground water, but these amounts are often based on the claims of the applicant and a general agency decision that water is available, not on specific information about the actual capacity of an aquifer as is obtained in an adjudication.

9. Prescriptive rights are property rights acquired by use over a long period of time, similar to adverse possession.

10. The term "safe yield" is subject to some controversy, but has generally been defined as the amount of water that can be withdrawn from an aquifer without adverse effect, and is linked to the amount of annual recharge. For a more detailed discussion of safe yield, see Weber (1994).

11. Unfortunately, the case also created a race to the pumphouse incentive for both prior appropriators and overlying landowners in other ground-water basins in California. In ordering a pro rata reduction of all pumpers, the court encouraged ground-water users to establish as large a present use as possible so that any pro rata reduction will be figured in relation to a larger initial quantity of water (Sax and Abrams 1986, 830).

12. 14 Cal. 3d 199, 537 P.2d 1250, 123 Cal. Rptr. 1 (1975).

13. See Anderson and Hill (1981).

14. For a more complete discussion of risk preferences, see Provencher and Burt (1993).

15. This analysis is drawn largely from Tehachapi Soil Conservation District (1969), Gates (1969) and Lipson (1978), as well as conversations with John Otto, Assistant Manager, Tehachapi-Cummings County Water District, Tehachapi, California. For a more detailed discussion, see Anderson, Burt, and Fractor (1983).

16. Justifications for this rule were that excessive stockpiling might cause the aquifer to fill up, thus impairing surface drainage; and if too many stockpiled rights were

exercised at one time, there might not be enough water to satisfy all demands because of cones of depression.

17. The average pumping costs for ground water are determined by the watermaster and applied to all participants in the exchange pool regardless of their actual pumping costs.

18. It would be efficient to use ground water instead of surface water as long as the cost of surface water is greater than the sum of ground-water pumping costs and user costs, which is the imputed value of a unit change in the ground-water stock.

19. Much of the following discussion of the Mojave basin is drawn from Garner, Ouellette, and Sharff (1994), personal communication with Eric L. Garner of Best, Best and Krieger, Riverside, California, 28 November 1995, and Judgment After Trial in *City of Barstow et al. v. City of Adelanto et al.*, case no. 208568 in the Superior Court of the State of California, Riverside County.

20. As such, the rights would be flow rights only. The Environmental Defense Fund economists deliberately preclude allocation of the stock of the Edwards Aquifer in their privatization proposals because they believe that the value placed by society on Comal and San Marcos Springs is too high to allow water levels in the aquifer to drop and threaten the springs. Their proposals would purportedly protect the springs by reserving the stocks.

9. We've Come a Long Way, Baby

Since the 1980s, when economists and policy analysts began to recognize that water markets could help allocate water, we have come a long way. Trades between agricultural users and cities are more commonplace: witness the trade between the Imperial Irrigation District and the Municipal Water District of Southern California. Environmentalists are searching for ways to lease agricultural water for instream uses such as salmon and steelhead spawning habitat in Oregon. And the EPA is experimenting with devolving pollution control to local authorities where polluters can bargain to find the cheapest way to improve water quality as in North Carolina's Tar-Pamlico Sound. Instead of protracted court battles, Indian tribes are negotiating water settlements that "can provide them with water rights, financial capital, fewer restrictions on water use and marketing, and the political support of non-Indians for necessary federal legislation" (Smith 1992, 189–91). The result is that tribes such as the Shoshone-Bannock in Idaho and the Ute in Utah that have settled water rights disputes are leasing their water for handsome returns.

Even at the Bureau of Reclamation, home of massive water projects that subsidize water use, a task force was established in 1995 to explore the possibilities of privatizing bureau projects. Discussions center on making a profit or cutting losses. What would determine the sale price of a project? Who would honor long-term contracts between the bureau and the water users? Would existing agricultural users have the right to sell their water to nonagricultural users? It is hard to believe that these are the questions resonating from meeting rooms at the bureau.

And this market revolution has not been confined to the United States. Led by South Australia in 1983 and followed by New South Wales in 1989 and Victoria in 1991, Australian states have begun allowing permanent transfers of water entitlements through markets. Transferable water rights were a response to increasing scarcity. As is often the case, informal structures were evolving before the

191

government responded with legislation throughout the 1980s that codified water trading. Before the legal changes, for example, farmers transferred water entitlements through "duality of ownership" or "licence stacking" whereby they purchased two landholdings and transferred the water entitlement from one to the other. Their willingness to undertake higher transaction costs associated with such transfers suggests the gains that were available from water trades. Sturgess and Wright (1993, 23–4) report the increase in farm income for water transfers along the Murray-Darling River Basin stretching 2,530 kilometers from the Snowy Mountains of eastern Australia to its mouth in South Australia.

> In 1988/89 it was estimated that transfers of irrigation-water entitlements increased rural income by $5.6 million. This comprised 280 transfers of 85 000 megalitres in total. . . . In 1990/91 the addition to rural income as a consequence of water transfers had nearly doubled to some $10 million. This comprised 437 transfers of a total of some 120 000 megalitres. However, even more interesting was the drought year of 1987/88 in which 687 transfers occurred, amounting to 340 000 megalitres. These transfers lifted rural income for that year by an incredible $17 million. If benefits of this scale can be obtained by a system of water transfers circumscribed by regional barriers, the benefits that would flow from the redefinition of water property rights to allow the free transfer of water between regions . . . would be greater still.

As markets continue to operate, transaction costs fall, arbitrage increases, brokers enter to connect willing buyers and willing sellers, and even futures markets develop. With all of this, New South Wales and her sister states are leading the way for water marketing in Australia.

Chile, known for its application of market solutions to a variety of social problems, implemented a market-oriented water policy in 1974. The Constitution of Chile, passed in 1980 and modified in 1988, reversed the expropriation of water rights by the state begun in 1966 and established secure, transferable water rights. The Constitution states, "The rights to private individuals, or enterprises, over water, recognized or established by law, grant their holders the property over them."[1] With these permanent water rights, individuals and organizations can buy or lease water quite readily. The achievements from Chile's market-oriented system are summarized by Schleyer (1994, 76).

> [T]he dramatic increase in agricultural production and employment has been accomplished without the need for new hydraulic infrastructure. The increase has been achieved mostly by shifting land from cultivation of grain, corn, oil-seeds, and cattle-raising to the more water-intensive fruit production. The freedom to buy and sell or "rent" water has given farmers greater flexibility to shift crops according to market demand.
>
> Efficiency in urban water and sewage services has been greatly increased with no impact on prices. . . . One of the greatest achievements of Chile's water policy is allowing cities to buy water without having to buy land or expropriate water. As a matter of fact, growing cities now buy rights from many farmers, in some cases buying a small portion of each farmer's total rights. There has [sic] been no negative effects in the agricultural zones surrounding water-demanding urban areas.

Water marketing in Chile demonstrates that reallocation can take place without all of the acrimony that so often dominates water issues.

European countries are not as far along with water trading, but they are experimenting with higher water fees as a way of reducing consumption and pollution. For example, in Germany taxes and water charges are being used effectively to induce users to switch from ground-water to surface-water supplies. Kraemer (1995, 231) notes that "The successful application of taxes and charges as incentives to reduce water abstraction from the natural water cycle or to change patterns of consumption is one of Germany's best-kept secrets." In France's Artois-Picardie River basin, the use of water charges reduced withdrawals by 15 percent and industrial abstractions by 55 percent between 1970 and 1989. Charges also significantly reduced water pollution levels. Tuddenham (1995, 213) concludes that "One of the major merits of this system is that the concept of water having an economic value has now become generally accepted." These systems should not be confused with actual water markets where willing buyers and willing sellers exchange water rights, but they indicate a recognition that prices matter.

Most of the increased use of markets in the United States has been limited to transfers within local areas and among traditional extractive uses. As discussed in Chapter 6, for several years only the Montana Department of Fish, Wildlife, and Parks was authorized to lease water in Montana under very strict regulations. It was not until 1995 that new legislation allowed anyone to acquire water rights for instream flows. Acquisitions, however, are limited to leases as opposed to sales. In the case of endangered salmon species in the Columbia River Basin of the Pacific Northwest, water marketing is beginning to take hold as a policy solution. Despite this headway, water trading between states and between basins remains almost unheard of. Moving water marketing to the next level will require innovative thinking about nontraditional uses and about cross-border and interbasin transfers. This is the challenge for the next generation of water marketing.

Interstate and International Transfers

A major obstacle to water marketing occurs with international water basins that encompass 47 percent of the world's land mass. Currently these basins generate envy, anger, and conflict between nations with differential water availability. The director of the United Nations Environment Programme, Mostafa Tolba, concluded that "national and global security are at stake. Shortages of fresh water worsen economic and political differences among countries and contribute to increasingly unstable perceptions of national security" (quoted in Clarke 1993, 92). This is especially the case in the Middle East, but water exports between countries such as the United States and Canada and between states within a country also generate controversy. Fortunately signs of hope are emerging to suggest that transborder market transfers can reduce the potential conflict.

Regional water trading in Australia's Murray-Darling Basin is indicative.[2] Fed by three large feeder rivers, the Goulburn, the Lachlan, and the Darling, the Murray-Darling Basin covers 1,058,800 square kilometers and drains parts of four states, New South Wales, Victoria, South Australia, and Queensland. The region incorporates half of Australia's cropland, half of its sheep population, more than half of its orchards, a quarter of its cattle (beef and dairy), and three-quarters of its irrigated crops and pastures. Like transboundary rivers in the United States such as the Colorado, Missouri, and

Mississippi, the Murray-Darling has all the potential for conflicting claims.

For many years drawing rights in the Murray-Darling Basin were unlimited and conflict was inevitable. In the 1970s, state governments introduced water licenses for those drawing water from streams and rivers in the basin. Water trading that arose in response to scarcity in the 1980s occurred largely within the borders of a single basin or state. But demands for water began to cross borders in the early 1990s. In 1992, the first interbasin water transfer involved a five-year lease of 7,982 acre-feet from a property on the Murrumbidgee River in New South Wales to a cotton farm on the Lower Darling River in South Australia. Local farmers opposed a permanent transfer, fearing it would harm the local economy. But a lease was less threatening and was permitted because it would increase the flow on the Murray River between the two locations and increase net wealth by as much as $2 million (Sturgess 1996, 135).

Since then, temporary interbasin transfers have expanded considerably. From July 1, 1994, to June 30, 1995, a net 87,000 acre-feet of water was traded out of the Murrumbidgee, 15,904 acre-feet to the Lower Darling, 75,829 acre-feet to the Murray, and 4,789 acre-feet back into the Murrumbidgee from the Murray (Sturgess 1996, 135). Sturgess (1996, 137) describes the evolution of this interbasin market:

> These water markets were not the outcome of careful forethought or deliberate design; they developed incrementally in response to demands from irrigators. Water rights have not been defined fully and consistently, with the result that entrepreneurs have been able to capture unregulated water, to the disadvantage of the environment and other irrigators. . . . It is widely acknowledged by state water managers that insufficient consideration has been given to environmental end-use and in-stream requirements and considerable effort is now being invested in the definition of these needs.

The Murray-Darling Basin Commission, originally formed in 1917 to build dams and other physical infrastructure on the river and to regulate river traffic, is now managing water trades and serving as a regional federation of the states in the basin. In the process, the commission is moving to correct these imperfectly defined rights, establish environmental water rights, and translate varying types of state water rights into a common currency tradable within the region.

Hence the commission increasingly is being seen as an "honest broker" and facilitator of improved efficiency. According to Sturgess (1996, 144), "All of the available evidence would suggest that this intergovernmental agreement will continue to formalize into a regional federation concerned with basin management operating a common market between the states. . . ." Such a federation provides a model for interbasin trading in and between other countries where rivers defy political boundaries.

The evolution of transborder trading in the Murray-Darling Basin is the type of "North American water marketing federation" Huffman (1994a, 158) calls for to deal with water issues between the United States and Canada and the United States and Mexico. As he describes it,

> Effective transboundary water markets are dependent upon the development of unified systems of rights. This will be accomplished best by a careful relinquishment of national or state sovereignty sufficient to create rights enforcement institutions which are free from the distorting influence of nationalism, provincialism and political competition. The federal principle, understood as a division of sovereignty rather than a unification of states, merits consideration.

The North American Free Trade Agreement might have promoted such a federation, but unfortunately, free trade in water is discouraged by federal and provincial governments in Canada. Fritz and McKinney (1994, 89) conclude:

> Because of public resistance and governmental opposition to large continental water transfers, it is unlikely that the neighboring countries will gain from water trading opportunities that may be available under the North American Free Trade Agreement. Canadians appear willing to forego [sic] possible benefits of such trades in order to ensure the continuing integrity of the current water resource regime of their country.

The resistance to cross-border transfers between Canada and the United States has little to do with real markets and much to do with governmental intervention. When water transfers are proposed, they are usually for massive projects to deliver water from remote northern regions of Canada to populated areas in the United States. For example, the infamous North American Water and Power Alliance would have diverted as much as 250 million acre-feet of water from northern Canada to southern Canada, the southern United States, and Mexico. In 1964 the construction cost alone of the North American Water and Power Alliance was estimated to be between $80 billion and $100 billion ($300 billion to $380 billion in 1990 dollars). Similarly, the Great Recycling and Northern Development Canal project would have pumped water from James Bay south to the Great Lakes at an estimated cost in 1984 dollars of $100 billion. Such grandiose schemes capture the public's attention and create incorrect perceptions of what water transactions would be like under a free trade agreement that included water.

A fundamental problem with most proposals for international water transfers is that the people who would benefit would not have to pay the enormous costs of the projects. On the demand side, the "buying" country has an insatiable thirst because the real cost of water consumption is hidden in subsidies, taxes, or other fiscal illusions. On the supply side, the citizens of the "selling" country gain little or nothing as individuals if exports are allowed. If the resistance to transborder trading is to change, it will be because increasing water scarcity drives up the potential gains from trade and because trades will "develop incrementally in response to demands" as they did between the Australian states.

Pressure for interstate trades in the United States is beginning to emerge on the Colorado River where California and Nevada face shortages and high costs for alternative supplies and where Arizona is awash in subsidized water from the Central Arizona Project.[3] Despite its desert environment, Arizona has more water than it can currently use, and this despite the fact that water prices are heavily subsidized. Politicians have always played on the notion that the arid West requires government reclamation projects, the most recent of which is the Central Arizona Project. The project, begun in 1968 and declared substantially complete in 1993, includes dams, pumps, and a 336-mile aqueduct system capable of delivering water from the Colorado River to Tucson, nearly 3,000 feet above the source. The project delivers water to agricultural users in a three-tiered pricing scheme with prices of $17, $27, and $41 per acre-foot, well below the actual cost of the water but above the cost of alternative sources, chiefly ground water. Though the pricing scheme has

197

increased the demand for Central Arizona Project water, the system still is not being used to capacity. In 1994, the Central Arizona Project delivered 809,117 acre-feet of water to Arizona users, less than 55 percent of the 1.5 million acre-feet that are available to the state from the Colorado River Compact. Moreover, the project operates at a net loss of more than $24 million per year.

While Arizona is awash in water, California and Nevada use all of their allocation under the Colorado River Compact and then some. They currently benefit from Arizona's underuse because water left in the river is free for the taking. However, that source is not secure because any increase in use by Arizona necessarily reduces Colorado River water available to California and Nevada. Not surprisingly, those two states are continually searching for more secure supplies to meet growing population demands.

Fiscal losses from the Central Arizona Project and water scarcity in California and Nevada are bringing pressure to allow interstate marketing. A price of $140 per acre-foot would enable the Central Arizona Project to cover its losses. That price is substantially below the $150 per acre-foot being paid in California and Nevada for water from irrigation districts and the $1,600 per acre-foot for desalination (see Fuller 1996). The gains from trade inherent in such price differentials have led the Arizona Department of Water Resources to issue a report specifically addressing the concept of short-term leasing to California or Nevada of a portion of Arizona's Colorado River entitlement (see Fuller 1996). The Arizona report contends that a court decree regarding apportionment of Colorado River water among the states allows a state not fully using its share of the Colorado to enter into agreements to deliver that unused water to other states.

At a speech to the 50th annual meeting of the Colorado River Water Users Association, Interior Secretary Bruce Babbitt noted that "we are on the threshold of a new period in which the three lower division states together will regularly be using that full apportionment." He believes this will necessitate "encouraging conservation in use, facilitating voluntary transfers of water, and managing our storage and delivery systems so that we can meet the growing demands that the new century will bring."[4] The future of transborder water trading may be here.

Expanding Markets for Instream Flows

Incrementally we are moving in the direction of using markets to enhance the quantity and quality of stream flows. As discussed in earlier chapters, environmental groups such as the Environmental Defense Fund, The Nature Conservancy, and the Oregon Water Trust are brokering water deals for instream purposes. But most of the arrangements have been limited to small quantities on small streams.

The challenge is to expand the market approach to a larger scale. For example, consider the disruption to salmon spawning in the Pacific Northwest caused by dams on the main stem and tributaries of the Columbia River. As is so often the case with water projects, the governmental planning process did not account for the impact of dams on salmon. Initially there were not even fish ladders to allow anadromous fish migrating upstream a passage around the massive concrete barriers, let alone concern for how the smolt would find their way back to the ocean without assistance from a stream current. Those considerations were of little consequence because the eight federal dams on the Columbia were designed to deliver water to farmers trying to subsist in a desert and to produce cheap hydroelectric power to industries that would bring economic growth to the region.

Now it is widely recognized that salmon and steelhead stocks using the Columbia are threatened or endangered because the smolt are trapped in the pools of relatively warm water stored behind eight major federal dams. Finding a solution to the problem at this point, however, is expensive or controversial or both. One solution, for example, is to barge returning salmon through or truck them around the reservoirs, but there is disagreement among biologists over how much that actually reduces mortality, and either alternative is expensive. Another proposal is to draw down reservoirs by spilling water over dams to reduce the size of pools through which the returning smolt must negotiate in their return to saltwater. Because the drawdown reduces recreation, wastes water that could be used for hydroelectric production at other times, and raises pumping costs for irrigators, annual costs for this approach are estimated at approximately $125 million. Based on a high-end estimate of 280,000 fish saved by drawdown, the costs amount to $440 per fish per year. Accounting for the fact that many of the salmon would then die in the ocean, the estimated cost for each fish actually caught is $950! Either estimate shows that the cost of saving salmon on the Columbia is outrageous.[5]

Flow augmentation is another way to help smolt get through the reservoirs. But increasing flows requires that upstream users curtail consumption, not something they are likely to do without an incentive. Enter Zach Willey of the Environmental Defense Fund. He is negotiating willing seller-willing buyer water contracts that will enhance stream flows. His approach is to use revenues from increased hydroelectric production to pay irrigators to reduce their consumptive use and return water to the system. Estimates of how much more valuable water would be if left instream instead of diverted for agriculture range from a low of 2 times (Hamilton and Whittlesey 1992) to a high of 10 times (Hamilton and Wanderschneider 1989). In either case, gains from trade from water marketing are waiting to be realized.

Building on his experience with water marketing in California, Willey worked with the Bonneville Power Administration, the federal power market agency in the Pacific Northwest, to consummate a deal that will provide between 25,000 and 50,000 acre-feet of additional instream flows on the Snake River. This is the single largest water transfer from out-of-stream to instream flows in the region. The flows result from a three-year lease between the BPA and Skyline Farm of Malheur County, Oregon. Skyline Farms, with water rights to divert substantial flows from the Snake and Malheur Rivers, was willing to relinquish its diversion rights in return for payments from electricity producers. Power companies and the BPA will hold the water behind dams for release when it is needed by the salmon and when it can produce valuable electricity. According to Randy Hardy, BPA administrator,

> The Skyline pilot effort, negotiated between a willing seller and buyer, can demonstrate the energy, environmental, and economic benefits associated with transfers from out-of-stream to instream flows in the Columbia Basin. We're hopeful that the long-term power generation benefits will help us provide more cost-effective fish flow augmentation. To BPA, that makes good economic and environmental sense. The pilot project will also provide an opportunity to work with the local community to mitigate any impact associated with the water transfer. (EDF 1994)

200

This water deal lays the groundwork for similar trades throughout the Pacific Northwest. Willey and his colleague, Adam Diamant, have proposed a water leasing program for the Yakima River that could enhance stream flows for anadromous fish by providing financial incentives for farmers to fallow land or convert irrigated acres to dryland farming. In exchange for the conserved water, irrigators would be paid for the option to lease water when needed as well as for the water actually leased. Willey and Diamant estimate that increasing flows by 600 to 1,500 cubic feet per second on the Yakima River would cost between $500,000 and $2 million per year. Funding for their proposal would come from a variety of sources including state and federal agencies, user fees, and hydroelectric generation. Costly as this might seem, it is a far cry from the costs of the other proposals cited above.

Where to Next?

Postel, Daily, and Ehrlich (1996) contend that we are running up against the Earth's water-carrying capacity. They base the contention on estimates of global water availability compared with water consumption. On the availability side, they adjust global runoff downward to obtain a measure of the water that is available to humans. Comparing that to human consumption that has been growing exponentially, Postel, Daily, and Ehrlich (1996, 787) conclude that humans are consuming 54 percent of accessible runoff and that "If average per capita water demand remains the same in 2025 as at present (which is conservative, because withdrawals per capita increased nearly 50 percent between 1950 and 1990), global water demand ca. 2025 would total ~6400 km^3/year." This would amount to more than 70 percent of estimated accessible runoff.

Typical of their "gloom and doom" predictions for other resources, their estimates of water shortages ignore the role of prices. Despite continued assertions that the "sky is falling," famine, pestilence, droughts, pollution, and resource shortages have not occurred.[6] In each of those cases market forces have worked on both the supply and demand sides. Higher prices induce suppliers to find new sources of raw materials, including nonrenewable energy, and to find alternative raw materials when scarcity appears to be binding. Witness the impact of higher copper prices on the switch to silicone for fiber optics and satellite technology to eliminate communications via wires. On the demand side, higher resource prices induce conservation and a search for substitutes as with energy in the 1970s when growing scarcity seemed inevitable.

The big question for water is whether Adam Smith's invisible hand will be unshackled. If governments insist on sending the wrong signals to suppliers and demanders by subsidizing water storage and delivery, exponential growth in consumption will inevitably run into environmental and fiscal constraints. On the other hand, if the progress toward increased reliance on markets described in this book continues, supplies of water will increase as users trade with one another, and consumption will be tamed by higher prices.

One reason markets are likely to play a larger role in future water use is that conservationists and fiscal conservatives are forming coalitions that can limit the political subsidies that encourage increased water consumption. Thomas J. Graff, general counsel for the Environmental Defense Fund in California, raised a prophetic question after the 1982 defeat of an environmentally and fiscally unsound proposal to divert water from northern to southern California when he asked, "Has all future water-project development been choked off by the new conservationist-conservative alliance . . . ?" He went on to say that "The moral premises of conservationists, as they joined liberals and conservatives to sink Proposition 9 [the Peripheral Canal Project], were not inconsistent with the new conservative doctrine. Conservationists believe that the water-development sector can shrink without harming anyone, weak or powerful, and that more efficiency would benefit the environment as well" (Graff 1982, V-2).

Part of this efficiency comes from eliminating subsidized water projects that put a drain on the treasury and a strain on the environment including aesthetic damage, siltation, pollution, and, most recently, disruption of salmon spawning. Another source of efficiency is gains from trade available from reallocating water from lower valued diversion uses to higher valued instream uses. The work of the Environmental Defense Fund, led by Tom Graff and Zach Willey, to promote water markets in California was instrumental (see Chapter 5). The Nature Conservancy has branched off from its efforts to protect land through private ownership and conservation easements to establish easements for instream flows (see Chapter 6). And most recently, the efforts of the Oregon Water Trust to lease water from agricultural users to increase stream flows for spawning salmon and steelhead mark a milestone in the use of water markets to enhance environmental amenities (see Chapter 6).

At the same time that environmentalists have been recognizing subsidized destruction of the environment as the Achilles heel of federal water policy, fiscal constraints have been forcing Washington politicians and bureaucrats to change their ways. Beginning with President Carter's hit list in the late 1970s and continuing today with talks of privatizing Bureau of Reclamation projects, the rhetoric inside Washington's beltway has changed. The Omnibus Water Act passed in 1992 gave water marketing a toehold in California's massive federal storage and distribution system by upping the price of federal project water and allowing transfers. Concrete and steel solutions such as the Central Arizona Project, hopefully the last of the federal dam follies, survive only in the dreams of the eager-beaver dam builders in the Bureau of Reclamation or the Corps of Engineers. Though these projects were supposed to pay for themselves, they have left the general taxpayer picking up the tab. Hence we can thank the federal deficit for creating pressure to change the way we allocate water.

As the gains from trade grow, it will be hard to keep a good water market down. When water from a federal project such as the Central Utah Project is delivered to farmers at $8 per acre-foot to produce crops where its value added, at most, is $30 per acre-foot at a cost to the taxpayer of $400 per acre-foot (Utah Foundation 1994, 298), it is obvious something is wrong. When Santa Barbara, California, is building a desalination plant to produce potable water at a cost of $1,600 per acre-foot while farmers are using water to irrigate crops where it is worth less than $100 per acre-foot, the potential for mutually beneficial trades cannot be ignored. With an order of magnitude difference in value, both sides of a water market transaction can gain substantially. When environmental groups realize that the transaction costs associated with using the regulatory process are so high that amenity values are lost while lobbyists and politicians play games, water markets in which environmental consumers pay other users to reduce consumption become expedient. Trades induced by such pressures will make it difficult to retreat from the water market path.

Lest we get too complacent about the success of water markets, we should realize that history is on the side of political control. The

United States has experienced nearly a century of federal dominance in water policy centered around massive projects to control flooding and navigation in the East and to "make the desert bloom like a rose" in the West. First-world nations from Australia to Norway depend on governments for storage and delivery systems rationalized on the basis of economic development with almost no consideration given to fiscal or environmental impacts. Private individuals who have captured the benefits of water subsidies will not simply push themselves away from the trough, and politicians and bureaucrats who have enjoyed the power that accompanies command-and-control will not readily relinquish that power. Moreover, proponents of governmental support for dams and ditches undoubtedly will find support among the citizens of less developed countries who feel they deserve the same feast at the governmental trough that has been enjoyed by their rich neighbors. Therefore, when the World Bank or some other development agency proposes to dam the Zambezi River or to subsidize irrigation projects in the Middle East, fiscal and environmental arguments are unlikely to carry the day for market approaches. In short, where there is political power to subsidize water, political support will follow.

Dire predictions by Postel, Daily, and Ehrlich (1996) that the blue planet will face global water shortages may unfold if we cannot supplant water politics with water markets. Growing demands for consumption, pollution dilution, and environmental amenities will put pressure on limited water resources. But those pressures need not create water crises if individuals are allowed to respond through market processes. Perhaps more than with other natural resources, water allocation has been distorted by politics under the notion that "water is different." Some would say that water cannot be entrusted to markets because it is a necessity of life. To the contrary, because it is a necessity of life, it is so precious that it must be entrusted to the discipline of markets that encourage conservation and innovation. Unless distortions created by governmental intervention are corrected, water shortages will become more acute and crises will be inevitable. When this happens, it will be difficult to suppress market forces. It would be better, however, if we could get political and legal impediments out of the way of markets before necessity becomes the mother of invention.

Notes

1. Constitución Política de la República de Chile, Chapter III, Article 24, final paragraph: *"Los derechos de los particulares sobre las aguas, reconocidos o constituidos en conformidad a la ley, otorgarán a sus titulares la propiedad sobre ellos."*

2. For a thorough discussion, see Sturgess (1996).

3. For a complete discussion, see Fuller (1996).

4. Quoted in *Water Intelligence Monthly* (1996, 2).

5. For a discussion of the options being considered and their costs, see Herr (1994).

6. For critiques of this approach, see Simon (1995).

References

Ackerman, Bruce A., and Richard B. Stewart. 1988. "Reforming Environmental Law: The Democratic Case for Market Incentives." *Columbia Journal of Environmental Law* 13: 171–99.

Allston, Richard Moss. 1978. *Commercial Irrigation Enterprise, the Fear of Water Monopoly, and the Genesis of Market Distortion in the Nineteenth Century American West.* New York: Arno Press.

Anderson, Robert H. 1990. "Oklahoma's 1973 Groundwater Law: A Short History." *Oklahoma Law Review* 43 (spring): 1–25.

Anderson, Terry L. 1995a. *Sovereign Nations or Reservations: An Economic History of American Indians.* San Francisco: Pacific Research Institute.

———1995b. "Water Options for the Blue Planet." In *The True State of the Planet,* ed. by Ronald Bailey, 267–94. New York: Free Press.

Anderson, Terry L., Oscar R. Burt, and David T. Fractor, 1983. "Privatizing Groundwater Basins: A Model and Its Application." In *Water Rights: Scarce Resource Allocation, Bureaucracy, & the Environment,* ed. by Terry L. Anderson. San Francisco: Pacific Institute for Public Policy Research.

Anderson, Terry L., and Peter J. Hill. 1975. "The Evolution of Property Rights: A Study of the American West." *Journal of Law and Economics* 18 (April): 163–79.

———1979. "An American Experiment in Anarcho-Capitalism: The *Not* So Wild, Wild West." *Journal of Libertarian Studies* 3: 9–30.

———1980. *The Birth of a Transfer Society.* Stanford, Calif.: Hoover Institution Press.

———1981. "Establishing Property Rights in Energy: Efficient v. Inefficient Processes." *Cato Journal* 1 (spring): 87–105.

———1990. "The Race for Property Rights." *Journal of Law and Economics* 33 (April): 177–97.

Anderson, Terry L., and Ronald N. Johnson. 1986. "The Problem of Instream Flows." *Economic Inquiry* 24 (4): 535–54.

Anderson, Terry L., and Donald R. Leal. 1988. "Going with the Flow: Marketing Instream Flows and Groundwater." *Columbia Journal of Environmental Law* 13: 317–24.

———1991. *Free Market Environmentalism.* Boulder, Colo.: Westview Press.

Anderson, Terry L., and Pamela S. Snyder. 1996. "A Free Market Solution to Groundwater Allocation in Georgia." *Issue Analysis.* Atlanta, Ga.: Georgia Public Policy Foundation.

Anderson, Terry L., and Peter J. Hill, eds. 1995. *Wildlife in the Marketplace.* Lanham, Md.: Rowman and Littlefield Publishers.

Baden, John, and Rodney Fort. 1980. "Natural Resources and Bureaucratic Predators." *Policy Review* 11 (winter): 69–82.

Bailey, Ronald, ed. 1995. *The True State of the Planet.* New York: Free Press.

Baker, Donald M., and Harold Conkling. 1930. *Water Supply and Utilization.* New York: John Wiley and Sons.

Balleau, W. P. 1988. "Water Appropriation and Transfer in a General Hydrogeologic System." *Natural Resources Journal* 28 (spring): 269–91.

Barberis, Julio. 1991. "The Development of International Law of Transboundary Groundwater." *Natural Resources Journal* 31 (winter): 167–86.

REFERENCES

Bartfeld, Esther. 1993. "Point-Nonpoint Source Trading: Looking Beyond Potential Cost Savings." *Environmental Law* 23: 43–106.
Bate, Roger. 1994. "Water Pollution Prevention: A Nuisance Approach." *Economic Affairs* 14 (3): 13–14.
Bates, Sarah F. et al. 1993. *Searching Out the Headwaters: Change and Rediscovery in Western Water Policy.* Washington: Island Press.
Battle, Jackson B., and Maxine I. Lipeles. 1993. *Environmental Law.* Vol. 2, 2d ed. Cincinnati, Ohio: Anderson Publishing Co.
Baughman, John F. 1992. "Balancing Commerce, History, and Geography: Defining the Navigable Waters of the United States." *Michigan Law Review* 90 (March): 1028–61.
Beadle, J. H. 1882. *Western Wilds and the Men Who Redeem Them.* Cincinnati, Ohio: Jones Brothers.
Beattie, Bruce R. 1981. "Irrigated Agriculture and the Great Plains: Problems and Policy Alternatives." *Western Journal of Agricultural Economics* 6 (December): 289–99.
Beattie, Bruce R., and H. S. Foster Jr. 1980. "Can Prices Tame the Inflationary Tiger?" *Journal of the American Water Works Association* 72 (August): 441–45.
Beck, Robert E., and C. Peter Goplerud III. 1988. *Water Rights.* Charlottesville, Va.: Michie Co.
Beeman, Josephine P. 1993. "Instream Flows in Idaho." In *Instream Flow Protection in the West,* ed. by Lawrence J. MacDonnell and Teresa A. Rice. Boulder, Colo.: Natural Resources Law Center, University of Colorado School of Law, Chapter 13.
Bianucci, Larry R., and Rew R. Goodenow. 1991. "The Impact of Section 404 of the Clean Water Act on Agricultural Land Use." *Journal of Environmental Law* 10: 41–65.
Black, Henry Campbell. 1983. *Black's Law Dictionary.* St. Paul, Minn.: West Publishing Co.
Bonine, John E., and Thomas O. McGarity. 1984. *The Law of Environmental Protection.* St. Paul, Minn.: West Publishing Co.
Brooks, Tad. 1991. "Need Your Own Pond or Stream?" *Great Falls Tribune.* October 17: D1.
Brown, Gardner M., and Ralph W. Johnson. 1984. "Pollution Control by Effluent Charges: It Works in the Federal Republic of Germany, Why Not in the U.S.?" *Natural Resources Journal* 24 (October): 929–66.
Brubaker, Elizabeth. 1995. *Property Rights in the Defence of Nature.* London: Earthscan Publications Ltd.
Buchele, Thomas C. 1986. "State Common Law Actions and Federal Pollution Control Statutes: Can They Work Together?" *University of Illinois Law Review* 609–44.
Bureau of Reclamation. 1989. *Voluntary Water Transactions: Criteria and Guidance.* Washington: U.S. Government Printing Office, March 18.
Burling, James S. 1994. *Protecting Property Rights in Aquatic Resources After Lucas.* Sacramento, Calif.: Pacific Legal Foundation.
Burness, H. Stuart, and James P. Quirk. 1980. "Water Laws, Water Transfers, and Economic Efficiency: The Colorado River." *Journal of Law and Economics* 23 (April): 111–134.
Business Week. 1991. "Death Valley Days in California." February 11: 30.
Carlson, Gerald A., David Zilberman, and John A. Miranowski. 1993. *Agricultural and Environmental Resource Economics.* New York: Oxford University Press.
Chandler, A. E. 1913. *Elements of Western Water Law.* San Francisco: Technical Publishing Co.

References

Clark, Robert E., Robert E. Beck, and Edward W. Clyde. 1972. *Waters and Water Rights*. Vol. 5. Indianapolis: The Allen Smith Company.

Clarke, Brian. 1979. "The Nymph in Still Water." In *The Masters of Nymph*, ed. by J. M. Migel and L. M. Wright. New York: Nick Lyons Books.

Clarke, Robin. 1993. *Water: The International Crisis*. Cambridge, Mass.: MIT Press.

Clayberg, John B. 1902. "The Genesis and Development of the Law of Waters in the Far West." *Michigan Law Review* 1 (November): 91–101.

Clifton, Gregory J., and Paul J. Zilis. 1993. "Recent Developments in Appropriations for Instream Uses." *Colorado Lawyer* 22 (May): 987–90.

Clyde, Steven E. 1989. "Adapting to the Changing Demand for Water Use Through Continued Refinement of the Prior Appropriation Doctrine: An Alternative Approach to Wholesale Reallocation." *Natural Resources Journal* 29 (spring): 435–55.

Coase, Ronald H. 1974. "The Lighthouse in Economics." *Journal of Law and Economics* 17 (October): 257–76.

Cockle, Richard. 1994. "Trust Will Buy Rights, Leave the Water for Fish." *Oregonian*. December 7.

Cohn-Lee, Richard G. 1994. "*Mens Rea* and Permit Interpretation Under the Clean Water Act: *United States v. Weitzenhoff*." *Environmental Law* 24: 1351–70.

Colby, Bonnie G. 1988. "Economic Impacts of Water Law—State Law and Water Market Development in the Southwest." *Natural Resources Journal* 28 (fall): 721–49.

———1990. "Transactions Costs and Efficiency in Western Water Allocation." *American Journal of Agricultural Economics* (December): 1184–92.

Colby, Bonnie, Mark A. McGinnis, and Ken Rait. 1989. "Procedural Aspects of State Water Law: Transferring Water Rights in the Western States." *Arizona Law Review* 31: 697–720.

Conservation Foundation. 1987. *State of the Environment: A View Toward the Nineties*. Washington: Conservation Foundation.

Corker, Charles E. 1957. "Water Rights and Federalism: The Western Water Rights Settlement Bill of 1957." *California Law Review* 45: 604–37.

———1971. *Groundwater Law, Management, and Administration*. Legal Study No. 6. Washington: National Water Commission, October 21.

Council on Environmental Quality. 1980. *The Global 2000 Report to the President*, vol. 1. Washington: U.S. Government Printing Office.

CQ Almanac. 1992. "West Is Focus of New Water Policy." Vol. 48: 264–72.

Cuzan, Alfred G. 1983. "Appropriators vs. Expropriators: The Political Economy of Water in the West." In *Water Rights: Scarce Resource Allocation, Bureaucracy, and the Environment*, ed. by Terry L. Anderson, 1–43. San Francisco: Pacific Institute for Public Policy Research.

Davidson, John H. 1989. "Commentary: Using Special Water Districts to Control Nonpoint Sources of Water Pollution." *Chicago-Kent Law Review* 65: 503–18.

Davis, Peter N. 1993. "Law and Fact Patterns in Common Law Water Pollution Cases." *Missouri Environmental Law and Policy Review* 1 (summer): 3–16.

Dean, Howard. 1994. "Amending the Clean Water Act: View from the States." *EPA Journal* (summer): 34–5.

Dempsey, Candace. 1991. "In the Swim." *Horizon Air Magazine*. September 19.

Demsetz, Harold. 1967. "Toward a Theory of Property Rights." *American Economic Review* 57 (May): 347–79.

Dinar, Ariel, and David Zilberman. 1991. *Farm Level Irrigation and Drainage*. Norwell, Mass.: Kluwer Academic Publishers.

REFERENCES

Dugan, Jack T., and Dale A. Cox. 1994. *Water-Level Changes in the High Plains Aquifer—Predevelopment to 1993.* Water-Resources Investigations Report 94–4157. Lincoln, Nebr.: U.S. Geological Survey.

Dunbar, Robert G. 1983. *Forging New Rights in Western Waters.* Lincoln, Nebr.: University of Nebraska Press.

Dunn, Sandra K. 1994. "Endangered Species Act versus Water Resources Development: The California Experience." *Pacific Law Journal* 25: 1107–29.

Economist. 1992a. "The First Commodity." March 28: 11–12.

———1992b. "Wrong Place: Water in California." February 22: 24.

———1994. "California's Water: Want Some More?" October 8: 30–31.

Ellis, William S. 1993. "The Mississippi: River Under Siege." *National Geographic.* Special Edition. November: 90–105.

Ember, Lois R. 1992. "Clean Water Act Is Sailing a Choppy Course to Renewal." *Chemical and Engineering News* 70 (February 17): 18–22.

Emel, Jacque L. 1987. "Groundwater Rights: Definition and Transfer." *Natural Resources Journal* 27 (summer): 653–73.

Environmental Defense Fund (EDF). 1994. EDF, Federal Energy Agency Announce Water Project: Water Lease for Salmon Protection, Energy Savings Signed in Oregon. News Release, Washington.

Environmental Protection Agency (EPA). 1992. *1990 National Water Quality Inventory.* EPA No. 503/9-92/006. Washington: U.S. Government Printing Office.

Fenichell, Stephen. 1986. "The Dry Season." *Northwest Orient.* August: 13–19.

Foran, Jeffery A., Peter Butler, Lisa B. Cleckner, and Jonathan W. Bulkley. 1991. "Regulating Nonpoint Source Pollution in Surface Waters: A Proposal." *Water Resources Bulletin* 27 (3): 479–83.

Frederick, Kenneth D. 1981. "The Future Role of Western Irrigation." *Southwestern Review of Management and Economics* 1 (spring): 19–33.

Fritz, Gary, and Matthew J. McKinney. 1994. "Canadian Water Export Policy and Continental Water Marketing." In *Continental Water Marketing,* ed. by Terry L. Anderson, 71–92. San Francisco: Pacific Research Institute.

Fuller, Jeffrey R. 1996. "Interstate Marketing of Central Arizona Project Water: Law, Economics, and Politics." In *Water Marketing: The Next Generation,* ed. by Terry L. Anderson and Peter J. Hill, 101–25. Lanham, Md.: Rowman and Littlefield Publishers.

Gardner, B. Delworth. 1983. "Water Pricing and Rent Seeking in California Agriculture." In *Water Rights: Scarce Resource Allocation, Bureaucracy, and the Environment,* ed. by Terry L. Anderson, 83–116. San Francisco: Pacific Institute for Public Policy Research.

———1995. *Plowing Ground in Washington: The Political Economy of U.S. Agriculture.* San Francisco: Pacific Research Institute.

Gardner, B. Delworth, and John E. Warner. 1994. "Two Steps Forward—One Step Back." *Choices.* First Quarter: 5–9.

Garner, Eric L., Michelle Ouellette, and Richard L. Sharff Jr. 1994. Institutional Reforms in California Groundwater Law. *Pacific Law Journal* 25: 1021–52.

Gates, John M. 1969. "Repayment and Pricing in Water Policy: A Regional Economic Analysis with Particular Reference to the Tehachapi-Cummings County Water District." Ph.D. diss., Department of Agricultural Economics, University of California, Berkeley.

Getches, David. 1984. *Water Law in a Nutshell.* St. Paul, Minn.: West Publishing Co.

———1993. "Water Resources: A Wider World." In *Natural Resources Policy and Law: Trends and Directions*, ed. by Lawrence J. MacDonnell and Sarah F Bates, 124–47. Washington: Island Press.

Glennon, Robert, and Thomas Maddock III. 1994. "In Search of Sublow: Arizona's Futile Effort to Separate Groundwater from Surface Water." *Arizona Law Review* 36: 567–610.

Golze, Alfred R. 1961. *Reclamation in the United States*. Caldwell, Ida.: The Caxton Printers.

Goplerud, C. Peter III. 1995. "Water Pollution Law: Milestones from the ˙st and Anticipation of the Future." *Natural Resources and Environment* 10 (fall): ˙2.

Gould, George A. 1988. "Water Rights Transfers and Third-Party Effects." ˙nd and *Water Law Review* 23: 1–41.

———1989. "Transfer of Water Rights." *Natural Resources Journal* 29 (sprin ˙57–77.

Graff, Thomas J. 1982. "Future Water Plans Need a Trickle-Up Econom˙g." *Los Angeles Times*, June 14: V–2.

Gray, Brian E. 1993. "A Reconsideration of Instream Appropriative Wights in California." In *Instream Flow Protection in the West*, revised edition, ed˙wrence J. MacDonnell and Teresa A. Rice. Boulder, Colo.: Natural Resource Center, University of Colorado School of Law, Chapter 11.

———1994. "The Market and the Community: Lessons from Calif˙Drought Water Bank." *West-Northwest Journal of Environmental Law, Polic˙hought* 1 (spring): 17–47.

Gray, Brian E., Bruce C. Driver, and Richard W. Wahl. 1991. "Eco˙centives for Environmental Protection." *Environmental Law* 21: 911–61.

Greenwalt, Lynn A. 1976. "Natural Resource Perspectives." In ˙gs of the *Symposium and Specialty Conference on Instream Flow Needs*, vol. 2,˙.Orsborn and C. H. Allman. Bethesda, Md.: American Fisheries Society˙

Gregory, Alison Mylander. 1992. "Groundwater and Its Future:˙ Interests and Burgeoning Markets." *Stanford Environmental Law Journ˙*8.

Griffin, Ronald C., and Fred O. Boadu. 1992. "Water Marketing˙pportuni- ties for Reform." *Natural Resources Journal* 32 (spring): 265–˙

Guldin, Richard W. 1989. *An Analysis of the Water Situatio˙ited States: 1989–2040*. USDA Forest Service General Technical Repor˙ashington: U.S. Government Printing Office.

Hall, John, and Ciannat Howett. 1994. "Albemarle-Pamlico:˙n Pollutant Trading." *EPA Journal* (summer): 27–29.

Hall, Robert E., and Robert S. Pindyck. 1981. "What to Do˙ Prices Rise Again." *The Public Interest* 65 (fall): 59–70.

Hamilton, Joel, and Phillip Wanderschneider. 1989. "Insti˙ility of Con- tingent Water Marketing to Increase Migratory Flow˙n the Upper Snake River." *Natural Resources Journal* 33 (summer):˙ts for Salmon

Hamilton, Joel, and Norman Whittlesey. 1992. "Conting˙ington, D.C. Recovery." Working Paper. Natural Resources Defe˙s Debatable,

Hanson, David J. 1994. "Reauthorization of Clean W˙ Raises Objections." *National Journal* March 19: 37–3˙ (December):

Hardin, Garrett. 1968. "The Tragedy of the Comm˙ *Efficiency and* 1243–48.

Hartman, L. M., and Don Seastone. 1970. *Water* ˙ress. *Alternative Institutions*. Baltimore, Md: Johns Ho˙

REFERENCES

Haveman, Robert. 1973. "Efficiency and Equity in Natural Resource and Environmental Policy." *American Journal of Agricultural Economics* 55 (5): 868–78.

Hayek, Friedrich A. 1945. "The Use of Knowledge in Society." *American Economic Review* 35 (4): 519–30.

Hayward, Steven. 1991. "Muddy Waters." *Reason* (July): 46–47.

Heath, Ralph C. 1988. "Groundwater." In *Perspectives on Water: Uses and Abuses*, ed. by David H. Speidel, Lon C. Ruedisili, and Allen F. Agnew, 73–89. New York: Oxford University Press.

Hedges, Trimble R. 1977. *Water Supplies and Costs in Relation to Farm Resource Decisions and Profits on Sacramento Valley Farms*. Report 322. Berkeley, Calif.: Gianinni Foundation.

Herr, Andrew. 1994. "Saving the Snake River Salmon: Are We Solving the Right Problem?" Working Paper 94–15. Political Economy Research Center, Bozeman, M

Hibbard, Benjamin H. 1939. *A History of the Public Land Policies*. Madison: University of Wisconsin Press.

Hirshleifer, Jack, James C. DeHaven, and Jerome W. Milliman. 1960. *Water Supply: Economics, Technology, Policy*. Chicago: University of Chicago Press.

Howe, Charles W., Paul K. Alexander, and Raphael J. Moses. 1982. "The Performance of Appropriative Water Systems in the Western United States During Drought." *Natural Resources Journal* 22 (April): 379–89.

Huffman, James L. 1983. "Instream Water Use: Public and Private Alternatives." In *Water Rights: Scarce Resource Allocation, Bureaucracy, and the Environment*, ed. by Terry L. Anderson, 249–82. San Francisco: Pacific Institute for Public Policy Research.

———. "A North American Water Marketing Federation." In *Continental Water Marketing*, ed. by Terry L. Anderson, 145–59. San Francisco: Pacific Research Institute.

———. Markets, Regulation, and Environmental Protection." *Montana Law Review* (summer): 425–35.

Huffman, Roy E. 1953. *Irrigation Development and Public Water Policy*. New York: The Ronald Co.

Ingram, and Cy R. Oggins. 1992. "The Public Trust Doctrine and Community Values in ter." *Natural Resources Journal* 32 (summer): 515–37.

Jaunitt. 1994. "The Environment, The Free Market, and Property Rights: Post-Privatization of the Public Trust." *Public Land Law Review* 15: 167–97.

Johnson, R., Micha Gisser, and Michael Werner. 1981. "The Definition of a Surface Water Right and Transferability." *Journal of Law and Economics* 14 (October):

Kaufman, 1992. "An Analysis of Developing Instream Water Rights in Oregon." *te Law Review* 28: 285–332.

Kenski. 1990. *Saving the Hidden Treasure: The Evolution of Ground Water Policy*. State University Press.

Kinney. Law of Irrigation and Water Rights and Arid Region Doctrine of Appropriation. Vol. 1. San Francisco: Bender-Moss.

Knees, Economic Related Problems in Contemporary Water Resource Management. *ral Resources Journal* 5: 236–58.

Kraemer. 1995. "Water Resource Taxes in Germany." In *Green Budget Reform: ial Casebook of Leading Practices*, ed. by Robert Gale, Stephan Barg, Gillies, 231–41. London: Earthscan Publications Ltd.

212

Krautkraemer, John, and Zach Willey. 1991. "Learning from California's Five-Year Drought." *EDF Letter* (June): 4.

Kromm, David E., and Stephen E. White. 1992. "The High Plains Ogallala Region." In *Groundwater Exploitation in the High Plains*, ed. by David E. Kromm and Stephen E. White, 1–27. Lawrence: University Press of Kansas.

Laatz, Joan. 1994. "Rancher Leases Water Rights to Keep Stream Full for Salmon." *Oregonian* (June 19).

Lasky, Moses. 1929. "From Prior Appropriation to Economic Distribution of Water by the State—Via Irrigation Administration." *Rocky Mountain Law Review* 1 (April): 161–216.

Leopold, Aldo. 1949. *A Sand County Almanac*. New York: Oxford University Press.

Letson, David. 1992. "Point/Nonpoint Source Pollution Reduction Trading: An Interpretive Survey." *Natural Resources Journal* 32 (spring): 219–32.

Lewin, Jeff L. 1990. "*Boomer* and the American Law of Nuisance: Past, Present, and Future." *Albany Law Review* 54: 189–300.

Lilley, William III, and Lewis L. Gould. 1966. "The Western Irrigation Movement, 1878–1902: A Reappraisal." In *The American West: A Reorientation*, ed. by Gene Gressley, 57–74. Laramie: University of Wyoming Press.

Lipson, Albert J. 1978. *Efficient Water Use in California: The Evolution of Groundwater Management in Southern California*, 4-2387/2-CSA/RF. Washington: Rand Corporation, November.

MacDonnell, Lawrence J. 1989. "Changing Uses of Water in Colorado: Law and Policy." *Arizona Law Review* 31: 783–816.

Malik, Arun S., David Letson, and Stephen R. Crutchfield. 1993. "Point/Nonpoint Source Trading of Pollution Abatement: Choosing the Right Trading Ratio." *American Journal of Agricultural Economics* 75 (November): 959–67.

Malone, Linda A. 1990. "The Necessary Interrelationship Between Land Use and Preservation of Groundwater Resources." *UCLA Journal of Environmental Law and Policy* 9: 1–72.

Marston, Ed. 1994. "On Friday, the Fish Took Some of It Back." *High Country News* (October 31): 15.

Matthews, Juliane R. Bourquin. 1986. "A Modern Approach to Groundwater Allocation Disputes: *Cline v. American Aggregates Corporation*." *Journal of Energy Law and Policy* 7: 361–76.

Matthews, Olen Paul. 1994. "Changing the Appropriation Doctrine Under the Model State Water Code." *Water Resources Bulletin* 30 (2): 189–96.

Mayhew, Stewart, and B. Delworth Gardner. 1994. "The Political Economy of Early Federal Reclamation in the West." In *The Political Economy of the American West*, ed. by Terry L. Anderson and Peter J. Hill, 69–94. Lanham, Md.: Rowman and Littlefield Publishers.

McCurdy, Charles W. 1976. "Stephen J. Field and Public Land Law Development in California, 1850–1866: A Case Study of Judicial Resource Allocation in Nineteenth-Century America." *Law and Society Review* 10 (1): 235–66.

McDevitt, Edward. 1994. "The Evolution of Irrigation Institutions in California: The Rise of the Irrigation District, 1910–1930." Ph.D. diss., Department of Economics, University of California, Los Angeles.

McElyea, Russ. 1989. "The Case for Private Instream Appropriations in Colorado." *University of Colorado Law Review* 60: 1087–1111.

213

REFERENCES

McKinney, Matthew J. 1993. "Instream Flow Policy in Montana: A History and Blueprint for the Future." In *Instream Flow Protection in the West*, ed. by Lawrence J. MacDonnell and Teresa A. Rice. Boulder, Colo.: Natural Resources Law Center, University of Colorado School of Law, Chapter 15.

Mead, Elwood. 1903. *Irrigation Institutions*. New York: Macmillan Co.

Meadows, Donella H. et al. 1972. *The Limits to Growth*. New York: Potomac Association.

Meiners, Roger E., and Bruce Yandle. 1994a. "Clean Water Legislation: Reauthorize or Repeal?" In *Taking the Environment Seriously*, ed. by Roger Meiners and Bruce Yandle, 73–101. Lanham, Md.: Rowman and Littlefield Publishers.

————1994b. *Reforming the Clean Water Act*. Washington: Manufacturers' Alliance for Productivity and Innovation.

Meyers, Charles J., and Richard A. Posner. 1971. *Market Transfers of Water Rights*. Legal Study 4. Washington: National Water Commission.

Milliman, Jerome W. 1982. "Can Water Pollution Policy Be Efficient?" *Cato Journal* 2 (spring): 165–96.

Mitchell, William, and Randy T. Simmons. 1995. *Beyond Politics*. Boulder, Colo.: Westview Press.

Murphy, Earl F. 1988. "Some Legal Solutions for Contemporary Problems Concerning Groundwater and Aquifers." *Journal of Mineral Law and Policy* 4: 49–117.

Murray, Paula C., and Frank B. Cross. 1992. "The Case for a Texas Compulsory Unitization Statute." *Saint Mary's Law Journal* 23: 1099–1154.

National Research Council. 1992. *Water Transfers in the West: Efficiency, Equity, and the Environment*. Washington: National Academy Press.

New York Times. 1981. "Depletion of Underground Water Formation Imperils Vast Farming Region." April 11: B4.

Newsweek. 1981. "The Browning of America." February 23: 26–7.

Parfit, Michael. 1993. "Troubled Water Runs Deep." *National Geographic*. Special Edition. November: 78–88.

Patrick, Kevin L., and Kelly E. Archer. 1994. "A Comparison of State Groundwater Laws." *Tulsa Law Journal* 30: 123–56.

Penick, James Jr. 1974. "The Progressives and the Environment: Three Themes from the First Conservation Movement." In *The Progressive Era*, ed. by Lewis L. Gould, 115–31. Syracuse, N.Y.: Syracuse University Press.

Pisani, Donald J. 1992. *To Reclaim a Divided West: Water, Law, and Public Policy, 1848–1902*. Albuquerque: University of New Mexico Press.

Postel, Sandra. 1992. *Last Oasis: Facing Water Scarcity*. New York: W.W. Norton and Company.

Postel, Sandra L., Gretchen C. Daily, and Paul R. Ehrlich. 1996. "Human Appropriation of Renewable Fresh Water." *Science* 271 (February 9): 785–88.

Powell, John Wesley. 1879. *Report on the Lands of the Arid Region of the United States*. Washington: U.S. Government Printing Office.

Prosser, W., and W. Keeton. 1984. *Prosser and Keeton on Law of Torts*. 5th ed. St. Paul, Minn.: West Publishing Co.

Provencher, Bill, and Oscar Burt. 1993. The Externalities Associated with the Common Property Exploitation of Groundwater. *Journal of Environmental Economics and Management* 24: 139–58.

Pye, Veronica I., and Jocelyn Kelly. 1988. "Ground Water Contamination in the United States." In *Perspectives on Water: Uses and Abuses*, ed. by David H. Speidel, Lon C. Ruedisili, and Allen F. Agnew, 205–13. New York: Oxford University Press.

214

Randall, Alan. 1981. *Resource Economics: An Economic Approach to Natural Resource and Environmental Policy*. Columbus, Ohio: Grid Publishing.

Reisner, Mark, and Sarah Bates. 1993. *Overtapped Oasis: Reform or Revolution for Western Water*. Washington: Island Press.

Riggs, David W. 1993. "Market Incentives for Water Quality: A Case Study of the Tar-Pamlico River Basin, North Carolina." Center for Public Policy Studies, Clemson University, Clemson, S.C.

Robinson, Michael C. 1979. *Water for the West: The Bureau of Reclamation 1902–1977*. Chicago: Public Works Historical Society.

Rodgers, William H. Jr. 1994. *Environmental Law*. St. Paul, Minn.: West Publishing Co.

Rogers, Peter. 1993. *America's Water: Federal Roles and Responsibilities*. Cambridge, Mass.: MIT Press.

Rubin, Debra K. et al. 1993. "A Whole Lot of Planning Going On." *ENR* 231 (September): 38–44.

Rucker, Randall R., and Price V. Fishback. 1983. "The Federal Reclamation Program: An Analysis of Rent-Seeking Behavior." In *Water Rights: Scarce Resource Allocation, Bureaucracy, and the Environment*, ed. by Terry L. Anderson, 45–81. San Francisco, Calif.: Pacific Institute for Public Policy Research.

Sax, Joseph L., and Robert H. Abrams. 1986. *Legal Control of Water Resources: Cases and Materials*. St. Paul, Minn.: West Publishing Company.

Schaefer, Elizabeth. 1991. "Water Shortage Pits Man Against Nature." *Nature* March 21: 180–81.

Schleyer, Renato Gazmuri. 1994. "Chile's Market-Oriented Water Policy: Institutional Aspects and Achievements." In *Water Policy and Water Markets*, ed. by Guy Le Moigne et al., 65–78. World Bank Technical Paper 249. Washington: World Bank.

Shaw, Jane S., and Richard L. Stroup. 1988. "Gone Fishin'." *Reason* August/September: 34–37.

Shupe, Steven J. 1988. "The Legal Evolution of Colorado's Instream Flow Program." *Colorado Lawyer* 17 (May): 861–64.

Shupe, Steven J., Gary D. Weatherford, and Elizabeth Checchio. 1989. "Western Water Rights: The Era of Reallocation." *Natural Resources Journal* 29 (spring): 413–34.

Simmons, Randy T. 1994. "The Progressive Ideal and the Columbia Basin Project." In *The Political Economy of the American West*, ed. by Terry L. Anderson and Peter J. Hill, 95–111. Lanham, Md.: Rowman and Littlefield Publishers.

Simon, Julian, L., ed. 1995. *The State of Humanity*. Cambridge, Mass.: Blackwell Publishers.

Sims, Steven O. 1993. "Colorado's Instream Flow Program: Integrating Instream Flow Protection into a Prior Appropriation System." In *Instream Flow Protection in the West*, ed. by Lawrence J. MacDonnell and Teresa A. Rice. Boulder, Colo.: Natural Resources Law Center, University of Colorado School of Law, Chapter 12.

Slattery, Kenneth O. and Barwin, Robert F. 1993. "Protecting Instream Resources in Washington State." In *Instream Flow Protection in the West*, ed. by Lawrence J. MacDonnell and Teresa A. Rice. Boulder, Colo.: Natural Resources Law Center, University of Colorado School of Law, Chapter 20.

Smith, Rodney T. 1983. "The Economic Determinants and Consequences of Private and Public Ownership of Local Irrigation Facilities." In *Water Rights: Scarce Resource Allocation, Bureaucracy, and the Environment*, ed. by Terry L. Anderson, 167–217. San Francisco: Pacific Institute for Public Policy Research.

REFERENCES

————1984. *Troubled Waters: Financing Water in the West.* Washington: Council of State Planning Agencies.

————1992. "Water Rights Claims in Indian Country: From Legal Theory to Economic Reality." In *Property Rights and Indian Economies*, ed. by Terry L. Anderson, 167–194. Lanham, Md.: Rowman and Littlefield Publishers.

Smith, Rodney T., and Roger Vaughan. 1991. "Interior's Policy of Voluntary Water Transactions: The Two-Year Record." *Water Strategist* 4 (January): 1–13.

Smith, Vernon L. 1977. "Water Deeds: A Proposed Solution to the Water Valuation Problem." *Arizona Review* 26 (January): 7–10.

Solley, Wayne B., Robert R. Pierce, and Howard A. Perlman. 1993. *Estimated Use of Water in the United States in 1990.* U.S. Geological Survey Circular 1081. Washington: U.S. Government Printing Office.

Southerland, Douglas. 1968. *The Landowner.* London: Anthony Bond.

Sowell, Thomas. 1987. *A Conflict of Visions.* New York: William Morrow and Company.

Spencer, Leslie. 1992. "Water: The West's Most Misallocated Resource." *Forbes* April 27: 68–74.

Sprankling, John G. 1994. "An Environmental Critique of Adverse Possession." *Cornell Law Review* 79 (4): 816–84.

Steinhart, Peter. 1990. "The Water Profiteers." *Audubon* March: 38–51.

Stroup, Richard, and John Baden. 1983. *Natural Resources: Bureaucratic Myths and Environmental Management.* Cambridge, Mass.: Ballinger Press.

Sturgess, Gary L. 1996. "Transborder Water Trading Among the Australian States." In *Water Marketing: The Next Generation*, ed. by Terry L. Anderson and Peter J. Hill, 127–45. Lanham, Md.: Rowman and Littlefield Publishers.

Sturgess, Gary L., and Michael Wright. 1993. *Water Rights in Rural New South Wales: The Evolution of a Property Rights System.* Sydney: Center for Independent Studies.

Tehachapi Soil Conservation District. 1969. *Tehachapi Project Report.* March 31. Techachapi, Calif.

Thompson, Barton H. Jr. 1993. "Institutional Perspectives on Water Policy and Markets." *California Law Review* 18 (3): 673–764.

Todd, David. 1992. "Common Resources, Private Rights and Liabilities: A Case Study on Texas Groundwater Law." *Natural Resources Journal* 32 (spring): 233–63.

Toft, Dennis M. 1994. "EPA and Affected States to Step Up Enforcement of the Clean Water Act." *National Law Journal* June 20: C6–11.

Tregarthen, Timothy D. 1976. "The Market for Property Rights in Water." In Water Needs for the Future: Legal, Political, Economic, and Technological Issues in National and International Perspectives: *Denver Journal of International Law & Policy* 6 (Special Issue): 363–75.

Trelease, Frank J. 1955. "Preferences to the Use of Utility." *Rocky Mountain Law Review* 27: 133–60.

————1957. "A Model State Water Code for River Basin Development." *Law and Contemporary Problems* 22 (2): 301–22.

————1976a. "Developments on Groundwater Law." In *Advances in Groundwater "Mining" in the Southwestern States*, ed. by Z. A. Saleem, 271–78 . Minneapolis: American Water Resources Association.

————1976b. "Alternatives to Appropriation Law." In Water Needs for the Future: Legal, Political, Economic, and Technological Issues in National and International Perspectives: *Denver Journal of International Law & Policy* 6 (Special Issue): 283–305.

Tucson Water Department. 1996. "Tucson Water General Statistical Profile." Tucson, Ariz.

Tuddenham, Mark. 1995. "The System of Water Charges in France." In *Green Budget Reform: An International Casebook of Leading Practices*, ed. by Robert Gale, Stephan Barg, and Alexander Gillies, 200–19. London: Earthscan Publications Ltd.

Ulrich, Rudolph. 1953. "Relative Costs and Benefits of Land Reclamation in the Humid Southeast and the Semi-Arid West." *Journal of Farm Economics* 30: 62–73.

Umbeck, John. 1977. "The California Gold Rush: A Study of Emerging Property Rights." *Explorations in Economic History* 14 (1977): 197–226.

USA Today. 1993. "Facing a Future of Water Scarcity." September: 68–71.

U.S. Department of Agriculture. 1971. *Irrigation Water Requirements*. Washington: U.S. Government Printing Office.

U.S. Geological Survey. 1990. *National Water Summary 1987—Water Supply and Use.* Washington: U.S. Government Printing Office.

U.S. Geological Survey. 1991. *National Water Summary 1988–89—Hydrologic Events and Floods and Droughts.* Washington: U.S. Government Printing Office.

U.S. Water News. 1994a. "Drought Returns to the West." August: 1, 4.

———1994b. "Farmers Sowing More 'Green Stripes.' " July: 4.

———1994c. "Permits Can Shield Pollution Liability." May: 1, 2.

———1995a. "Limiting Well Usage Is Like Peeling Onion." July: 7.

———1995b. "Litigation Threat to Force Clean Water Act Renewal." April: 1, 7.

U.S. Water Resources Council. 1978. *The Nation's Water Resources, 1975–2000.* Washington: U.S. Government Printing Office.

Utah Foundation. 1994. "The Central Utah Project." Utah Foundation Research Report 572. Salt lake City, Utah.

Vaughan, Ben F. IV, and Peter M. Emerson. 1996. "Protecting the Edwards Aquifer: An Efficient and Ecological Alternative." In *Water Marketing: The Next Generation*, ed. by Terry L. Anderson and Peter J. Hill, 167–89. Lanham, Md.: Rowman and Littlefield Publishers.

Wahl, Richard W. 1989. *Markets for Federal Water: Subsidies, Property Rights, and the Bureau of Reclamation.* Washington: Resources for the Future.

———1994. "Market Transfers of Water in California." *West-Northwest Journal of Environmental Law, Policy and Thought* 1 (spring): 49–69.

Washburn, Edgar B. 1986. "The Implications of the Public Trust Doctrine for Land and Water Titles." In *Western Resources in Transition: The Public Trust Doctrine and Property Rights.* Conference Proceedings, Political Economy Research Center, Bozeman, Mont., May 17.

Water Efficiency Working Group. 1987. *Water Efficiency: Opportunities for Action: Report to the Western Governors.* Denver, Colo.: Western Governors' Association.

Water Intelligence Monthly. 1996. "Babbitt Endorses Water Markets and Places High Premium on Political Consensus." January: 2–3.

Webb, Walter Prescott. 1931. *The Great Plains.* New York: Grosset and Dunlap.

Weber, Gregory S. 1994. "Twenty Years of Local Groundwater Export Legislation in California: Lessons from a Patchwork Quilt." *Natural Resources Journal* 34 (summer): 657–749.

Weinberg, Marca, and Zach Willey. 1991. "Creating Economic Solutions to the Environmental Problems of Irrigation and Drainage." In *The Economics and Management of Water and Drainage in Agriculture*, ed. by Ariel Dinar and David Zilberman, 531–56. Norwell, Mass.: Kluwer Academic Publishers.

REFERENCES

Willey, Zach. 1990. "Environmental Quality and Agricultural Irrigation: Reconcilia-
tion through Economic Incentives." In *Agricultural Salinity Assessment and Management*, ed. by Kenneth K. Tanjii, 391–425. New York: American Society of Civil
Engineers.
———1992. "Behind Schedule and Over Budget: The Case of Markets, Water, and
Environment." *Harvard Journal of Law and Public Policy* 15: 391–425.
World Bank. 1992. *World Development Report 1992.* New York: Oxford University Press.
World Resources Institute. 1990. *World Resources 1990–91.* New York: Oxford Univer-
sity Press.
———1992. *The 1992 Information Please Environmental Almanac.* Boston: Houghton-
Mifflin Company.
———1993. *The 1993 Information Please Environmental Almanac.* Boston: Houghton-
Mifflin Company.
Worster, Donald. 1985. *Rivers of Empire: Water, Aridity and the Growth of the American
West.* New York: Pantheon Books.
Yandle, Bruce. 1994. "Community Markets to Control Agricultural Nonpoint Source
Pollution." In *Taking the Environment Seriously*, ed. by Roger E. Meiners and Bruce
Yandle, 185–207. Lanham, Md.: Rowman and Littlefield Publishers.
Zahner, Don. 1980. "The Man Who Kept a River." *Fly Fisherman* 12 (1): 16–17.
Zander, Bruce. 1991. "Nutrient Trading—In the Wings." *EPA Journal* 17
(Nov–Dec): 47–50.
Zern, Ed. 1981. "By Yon Bonny Banks." *Field and Stream* (September): 120–23.
———1982a. "Fishing Insurance: A Group Policy." *Field and Stream* (January): 12,
22–23.
———1982b. "Rx for Ailing Waters." *Field and Stream* (November): 87–89.

Index

Index

reclamation projects, 41
solution to public good problems,
113–14
Property rights
absolute ownership rule, 166–67
correlative rights doctrine in
California, 169–71
defining ground-water rights,
172–73
mutual prescription doctrine in
California, 170–71
prior appropriation doctrine,
33–34
protection under rules for water
pollution control, 141–43
reasonable use rule, 167–68
riparian water rights, 32–34
U.S. western frontier, 44
value of, 152
to water, 23
in water allocation, 13–14
See also Prior appropriation
doctrine; Riparian water rights;
Water rights
Protected Rivers Act (1988),
Idaho, 117
Public choice theory, 25–28
Public goods
characteristics of, 112–13
private resources to provide, 113–14
Public interest
argument related to rent seeking,
86–87
government decision making based
on, 21–28
as justification for beneficial use
concept, 81–82
public trust doctrine as argument
for, 86–87
regulation related to, 86–87
See also Interest groups; Rent seeking
Public sector
development of irrigation districts,
61–63
incentives in water policy decisions,
21–22
reclamation projects, 61–71
See also Government intervention
Public trust doctrine, 58–59, 86–87, 98
Pye, Veronica I., 162

Quirk, James P., 106

Rait, Ken, 84, 102
Randall, Alan, 29

Rationing
of ground water, 164
of water, 7–8, 18
Reasonable use rule, 167–69
Reclamation
federal control of federal project
water, 89–92
movement in United States, 44
private projects, 41–44, 61
public funding, 61–71
See also Irrigation
Reclamation Act (1902)
government role in water
reclamation, 63–65
provisions for development using
irrigation, 43, 64–65
Reclamation Project Act (1939), 66
Reclamation Projects Authorization and
Adjustment Act (1992), 12
Reisner, Mark, 84
Rents
in context of water, 48
under federal reclamation legislation,
63–71
as force for resource allocation, 47–48
government–induced redistribution,
48–49
Rent seeking
barriers to, 49
circumstances for occurrences of,
25–26
conditions for, 90–91
effect of, 49, 60
federal reclamation project water,
89–92
incentives in public reclamation
projects, 62–71
in public choice theory, 25–26
public interest as tool for, 86
user influence, 59–61
using government powers to control
water rights, 53
Report on the Lands of the Arid Region
(Powell), 61
Riggs, David W., 137, 148, 149, 150, 151
Riparian water rights
abrogation and retention, 43–44
in common law, 32–34, 134
dilution of interpretation, 54–56
Robinson, Michael C., 36, 37, 64
Rogers, Peter, 9t
Rubin, Debra K., 138
Rucker, Randall R., 70t

Salt River Valley Water Users
Association, 40

225

About the Authors

Terry L. Anderson has been a professor of agricultural economics and economics at Montana State University since 1972 and is executive director of PERC, the Political Economy Research Center. He holds M.A. and Ph.D. degrees in economics from the University of Washington and a bachelor's degree from the University of Montana. Anderson has traveled and lectured extensively on six continents and been a visiting professor at universities such as Stanford and Oxford. In addition to his teaching skills, which have won him several teaching awards, he is author or editor of 14 books, including *Free Market Environmentalism*, which has been translated into three languages. He also has published numerous articles in professional journals and popular publications as diverse as the *Wall Street Journal* and *Fly Fisherman*. He is an avid outdoorsman who enjoys climbing frozen waterfalls and hunting with bow and arrow in Africa.

Pamela Snyder is a research associate at PERC, where she specializes in water policy. She was raised in Rapid City, South Dakota, and received her B.S. in political science/public management from Liberty University, Lynchburg, Virginia. She received her J.D. from the University of Oregon, where she was associate editor of the *Journal of Environmental Law and Litigation* and served as an officer of the law school's Federalist Society chapter. Snyder practiced law in Bozeman for two years before joining PERC in January 1994.

Cato Institute

Founded in 1977, the Cato Institute is a public policy research foundation dedicated to broadening the parameters of policy debate to allow consideration of more options that are consistent with the traditional American principles of limited government, individual liberty, and peace. To that end, the Institute strives to achieve greater involvement of the intelligent, concerned lay public in questions of policy and the proper role of government.

The Institute is named for *Cato's Letters,* libertarian pamphlets that were widely read in the American Colonies in the early 18th century and played a major role in laying the philosophical foundation for the American Revolution.

Despite the achievement of the nation's Founders, today virtually no aspect of life is free from government encroachment. A pervasive intolerance for individual rights is shown by government's arbitrary intrusions into private economic transactions and its disregard for civil liberties.

To counter that trend, the Cato Institute undertakes an extensive publications program that addresses the complete spectrum of policy issues. Books, monographs, and shorter studies are commissioned to examine the federal budget, Social Security, regulation, military spending, international trade, and myriad other issues. Major policy conferences are held throughout the year, from which papers are published thrice yearly in the *Cato Journal.* The Institute also publishes the quarterly magazine *Regulation.*

In order to maintain its independence, the Cato Institute accepts no government funding. Contributions are received from foundations, corporations, and individuals, and other revenue is generated from the sale of publications. The Institute is a nonprofit, tax-exempt, educational foundation under Section 501(c)3 of the Internal Revenue Code.

CATO INSTITUTE
1000 Massachusetts Ave., N.W.
Washington, D.C. 20001